DATE DUE

DEMCO 38-296

CRITICAL PERSPECTIVES ON YUSUF IDRIS

R

CRITICAL PERSPECTIVES ON YUSUF IDRIS

Edited by Roger Allen

An Original by Three Continents Press

A Three Continents Book

Published in the United States of America by
Lynne Rienner Publishers, Inc.
1800 30th Street, Boulder, Colorado 80301

Library of Congress Cataloging-in-Publication Data
Critical perspectives on Yusuf Idris / edited by Roger Allen. — 1st ed.
    p. cm. — (critical perspectives ; 43)
    "An Original by Three Continents Press."
    Includes bibliographical references.
    ISBN 0-89410-671-6 : $25.00. — ISBN 0-89410-672-4 (pbk.) : $15.00
    1. Idris, Yusuf — Criticism and interpretation.   I. Allen, Roger M.A.   II.
    Series.
PJ7838.D7Z63   1992
892'.736—dc20

                                                            92-35320
                                                            CIP
                                                            AC

Essays by Contributors are gratefully acknowledged at the end of essay concerned. In a few cases we have been unable to contact authors and/or publishers
concerned: we shall appreciate information from parties concerning their possible rights.

Contents

Preface

Yusuf Idris was one of the most illustrious litterateurs in the Arab World in recent times. So prolific and varied was his output — especially during the 1950s and '60s — it is hardly surprising that the compiler of a volume of critical studies such as this finds himself confronted with an *embarras de richesses*. Several volumes of a size equal to the present one could have been compiled, each filled with excellent and varied critical studies of his work at different periods in his career. This volume is an anthology; in other words, a work that through the process of selection has made critical judgments of its own.

As the contents page that precedes makes clear, the arrangement of this collection is essentially generic, with separate sections devoted to the short story — of which Idris was the acknowledged master — the novel, and the drama. In each section an attempt has been made to include some critical studies that adopt a more general perspective and others that focus on particular works or (in the case of the short story) collections of them. These sections devoted to particular genres are preceded by a short biographical section; the first segment gives a brief outline of the author's life; the second is somewhat unique: a piece written by Idris himself in English, sent to the editor of this volume, and published here for the first time, in which he describes in poignant detail the circumstances in which he grew up. The work finishes with a bibliography of works of and about Yusuf Idris written in English.

In selecting these "critical perspectives" I have tried not only to choose studies that analyze a representative set of Idris's output but also to strike a balance between studies originally written by critics in the Arab World and others written by Western specialists on modern Arabic fiction and drama. It is my hope that this juxtaposition of works by Arab and Western critics devoted to one of Egypt's most distinguished litterateurs may be an appropriate symbol of the ever increasing links between practitioners of literature studies in the two regions that have characterized recent decades. Idris himself, a participant in several literary conferences and seminars in the West, served as a personification of such contacts and aspirations. In what was to be his final telephone conversation with me, he expressed his delight that an increasing number of Western readers were being made aware through translations of the thriving short story tradition in the Arab World, particularly in view of the problematic status of the genre in the West. With that thought in mind, may I conclude by expressing the hope that this collection of essays may stimulate more readers of English to explore the many fascinating and disturbing worlds that Idris's fictions create.

ROGER ALLEN
Philadelphia
April 1992

EDITORIAL NOTE

No attempt has been made to reconcile the differences in (or absence of) transliteration system used in the selections that follow. However, the bibliography, including a listing of Idris's works, does adhere to the Library of Congress sytem. For the general reader it may be useful to know that, under that system, the author's name appears as Yusuf Idris. For those interested in the pronunciation of the name, the closest approximation might be represented by "Yoosef" (with emphasis on the "yoo" syllable) Idress (with emphasis on the "drees" syllable and with the "s" pronounced as "s" and not as "z"). Where footnotes in the original versions of the studies included here do not contribute to the particular context of this anthology, they have been omitted.

A Biographical Sketch

Yusuf Idris was born in May 1927 in the village of Al-Bayrum in the Nile Delta of Egypt. His early childhood and schooldays seem to have been one of the unhappiest periods in his life, as he himself outlines in the next segment of this collection. In 1945 Idris moved to Cairo to begin the study of medicine at Cairo University. Alongside his academic studies, he participated vigorously in the student movement which was an integral part of the political turmoil during that much troubled period in modern Egyptian history leading up to the Revolution of 1952; these activities led Idris to be jailed for brief periods in 1949 and 1951. In this latter year Idris graduated, and the completion of his medical training and internship at Qasr el-Aini Hospital coincided with the transforming events of the Egyptian Revolution. He opened a medical clinic in Cairo and for a time served as medical inspector for some of the poorest districts of the capital city, a function that provided him with a wealth of information for his short stories. In fact, he was to maintain his connection with medicine until 1967 when he finally quit medical practice.

Idris's career as a writer was divided between creative writing — in the genres of the short story, novel, and play—and journalism. Beginning to write short stories as a student, he was encouraged by several literary figures, not least among whom was the famous poet, Ibrahim Naji (d. 1953), to publish his early efforts in newspapers in the early 1950s. His first collection, *Arkhas Layali*, was published in 1954 and was an instant success. It was followed over the next five years or so by a positive flood of creativity: several short story collections, two novels, and three plays. The realism, the instinctive artistry, and the creative use of language in these works, all aroused considerable critical interest in Egypt and beyond.

During the 1960s there is a detectable shift in Idris's approach towards a more symbolic and surrealistic mode, a trend which allowed him creatively to explore some of the more disturbing philosophical and societal issues that were preoccupying his mind, but which also, as he himself acknowledged with characteristic frankness, provided the vehicle for the expression of unpalatable truths within a society in which writers who transcended certain boundaries of political expression would find themselves penalized. The 1960s also witness the performance of Idris's most famous play, *Al-Farafir* (1964), written in the wake of a series of articles published in the monthly magazine, *Al-Katib*, in which he challenges the

1

received history of drama in the Arab World and advocates the search for indigenous dramatic genres. The play was a tremendous critical success as a performed play, but the nihilist implications of its content—at least insofar as they reflected on the course of the Egyptian Revolution—were sufficiently troubling for performances to be stopped.

While it is hardly surprising that Idris was unable to maintain the creative pace established in the 1950s, it is during the 1960s that one becomes aware of some of the factors that contributed to the diminution in output that was to characterize the last two decades of his life. The fits of depression to which he was prone became more common and of longer duration. The effect of the June War of 1967 was as profound on Idris as it was on a host of other writers in the Arab World. In the 1970s he had severe heart problems that were partially resolved by a major operation in London in 1976. But, if his health often deprived him of the necessary time and concentration needed for the composition of creative fiction, it was his journalistic activity that consumed much of his energy. During the 1960s he wrote a series of articles under the title "Yawmiyyat" for the newspaper, *Al-Jumhuriyyah*, and in 1969 his name was added to the illustrious cadre of writers who produced columns for *Al-Ahram*, a list that already included Tawfiq al-Hakim, Najib Mahfuz, and Lewis 'Awad. Idris now became a regular contributor to the columns of Cairo's most famous newspaper, commenting on a wide variety of issues, local and international, personal reminiscences and more public harangues; collections of his articles penned over the years have appeared under such titles as *Bi-Sarahah Ghayr Mutlaqah* (1968) and *Shahid 'Asrihi* (1982?). The appearance of a piece of fiction by Idris now became a rare event, and the final decade of his life sees the publication of just three small collections of short stories: *Uqtulha* (1982?) , *Ana Sultan Qanun al-Wujud* (1983?) , and *Al-'Atb 'Ala al-Nazar* (1987).

For the final two decades of his life Idris continued to be dogged by poor health. It was clearly something that weighed on his mind as someone trained in medicine; it was, no doubt, a contributing factor to frequent bouts of severe depression. There can be little doubt that this state of affairs caused him considerable frustration in his professional and personal life, some of which is reflected in his own account that follows. It may perhaps also help to explain, at least partially, the outburst of rancor with which he greeted the announcement of Najib Mahfuz's winning the Nobel Prize in Literature in 1988. Idris was not the only Arab author to comment negatively on Mahfuz's "worthiness" to receive such international recognition, but the intemperate nature of Idris's comments gave more than a hint of a personality that was partially reflecting its own inner conflicts through a bitter attack on the work of another great Egyptian writer of fiction whose personality, training, career, and societal focus were so utterly different from that of his own. The award in 1988 of the Saddam Husayn Prize in Literature to Yusuf Idris (shared with the Palestinian novelist, Jabra Ibrahim Jabra) can hardly have served as sufficient recompense in the quest for that international recognition that he believed his works to deserve.

Idris died on August 1st, 1991 in a London hospital while being treated for a brain haemorrhage. With his death, modern Arabic literature lost one of its most creative and controversial figures. In the realm of the short story in particular his contributions show an innate gift for capturing within the compact and allusive world created by that genre a wealth of human experience and emotion, one that is quintessentially Egyptian and yet, at the same time, of universal significance and appeal.

Yusuf Idris on Yusuf Idris

EDITOR'S NOTE: In 1982 I was contacted by the editors of World Literature Today *(University of Oklahoma). They asked whether I thought Yusuf Idris would be willing to serve on the Jury for the Neustadt Prize in Literature awarded by the journal each year. I suggested that they write to him in Cairo and provided his address at the Al-Ahram Building on Al-Galaa Street. Nothing was heard for several months, but, in the hope that he would be able to attend the conference at which the prize was to be awarded, the editors went ahead with the publication of the article that I had agreed to write on Idris for the journal (see* WLT *Vol. 55 no. 1 [Wint. 1981]: 43-47). Idris eventually sent a letter apologizing for his tardy reply and regretting that he would not be able to come.*

Several months later (a gap that is explained by Idris himself below) the journal and I received a copy of a statement in English that the editors of the journal had requested that he send as a preliminary to his arrival. The text of that statement [dated 15//11/1983], revised by the editor, is the text that now follows. It was composed and typed in English, and, as Idris notes in an accompanying letter, he resorted to his "second language" because he felt "it was a 'must' to enable me to feel perhaps that I am writing about somebody else." I trust that readers of this anthology will share my feeling that, while this volume is intended as a collection of critical articles about Yusuf Idris's writings, this document written by Idris himself is an appropriate, indeed poignant, introduction to the articles that follow, and is of considerable value not only because it is a unique piece of the author's writing but also because it affords some valuable insights into his background and motivations.

With regard to the editing process that I have followed, I can only refer to the text of Idris's letter:

> If you find the language awful, the style strange, and in my view not literary at all, pardon me. It was the best I can do. That is why I give you full authority not to publish it or to use another writer-editor to shape it into good English or even to publish it as it is, with such an explanation including the contents of this letter.

Those readers of this collection who are familiar with Yusuf Idris's style and narrative techniques may notice, I hope, that I have made every effort to preserve

as much as possible of the intrinsic "Idrisian" features of his original English
text (which is by no means as "strange" as his letter might seem to imply) and
indeed to retain some of those colorful phrases that are so much a part of his
style.

I did not get the sensation all that often, but, when I did, I really felt that I had
to be the most miserable child on earth. I had left my original family—my father,
mother, and sisters, a family I scarcely even knew—and went to my grandmother's
house (my mother's mother, that is, whom they call "Sitti" in Arabic) in order to
start going to school. I was six years old at the time, a very thin, pale little boy who
rarely smiled, so much so that I cannot recall anything that made me laugh at this
stage of my childhood. Never did I have that euphoric feeling that comes with
being alive, a young, fresh human being living on this earth.

At that time my father was working as a specialist in the cultivation of arid
land. Such lands would originally have been part of a series of lakes in the extreme
north of the Nile Delta. Every year after the summer flood the Nile water would
deposit its rich supply of silt on the soil; lakes would then dry out and be irrigated
and re-irrigated until they were ready for cultivation. Since this kind of work
requires huge numbers of workers and large amounts of funding, only big foreign
companies or the government were able to take it on. The government would only
employ civil servants for the job, but companies used experts like my father. He
had originally been a student at the Al-Azhar Mosque-University [in Cairo], but
had quit in order to spend some time as an apprentice before becoming a self-
made technocrat typical of that particular period in Egyptian life. Having gained
a high reputation in his job he became a "Ma'mour," a senior official who would
direct, inspect, and govern a huge area of land along with its sizeable population.

I grew up as the Ma'mour's son, in other words, more or less the crown prince
in a petty kingdom. I remained far removed from modern civilization, living in
a huge house that was surrounded by a large garden. There were plenty of
servants, and those huge-breasted teenage peasant-girls were more than willing
to "play" with me and even offered to reveal to me their most intimate female
secrets. For, even though I was extremely young, it seemed they found satisfaction in having sex with the one and only real "prince" they knew. This little prince
was able to lord it over a people consisting of children, both young and old,
bossing them about, chasing them, doing whatever he liked with them; no one
would have dared to raise a finger or even an eyebrow in protest. Quite the
contrary, they would regard my acts of aggression as a sign of favor, a honorable
gesture to be cherished.

But this status that I enjoyed never spoiled me. In fact, I felt a great deal of pity
towards them; it was as though human beings are originally created without any
sense of class distinctions, something that only comes later as part of the "cultural
environment." When I compared my life with theirs—and I was always comparing, I used to sympathize with their plight. These folk were the poorest stratum
in Egyptian society: peasants from the very lowest echelons of the peasantry, with
no original village to serve as home, no family, no name, nothing; just the residue

of broken tribes and families, homeless vagabonds, yet heads of households; anything but respectable citizens.

I have spent the whole of my life harking back to those few months in my childhood. I can still recall spending time with my own family, the house, the way of life, my father as I used to see him at that time emerging from the distant horizon like a sudden vision, to the accompaniment of the far-off braying of the "Rokouba." This was the name given to the large donkey my father used to ride; it's a type that is only used for riding because no other kind of animal can do the job; even horses are totally unsuitable in this kind of area which is full of ditches, small canals, and very tiny bridges. My father would come home, sweating profusely from the onslaught of the summer sun. The fact that he wore European dress did not help, of course; it made him look just like a foreigner, albeit a sunburned one. I used to throw myself at him immediately and try to put my tiny arms around his waist, inhaling deeply the smell of his sweating body as it blended with the odor from his clothes and the Eau de Cologne that he insisted on using throughout his life. I gazed at him with almost the same degree of reverence as the poor peasants and workers. My love for him was so great that I used to burst into tears whenever I remembered him. Even though he was large and sunburned and his wrinkled face always wore a serious expression, he was the kindest and most loving man I have even known.

By contrast my mother was much younger. She was much more beautiful than he; in fact, at the time of their marriage she was by far the most beautiful girl in our village. Her family was much poorer than his, and that accounts for his marrying her in spite of the difference in their ages and the fact that he had been married twice before. Young, beautiful, and healthy, she was and perhaps still is one of the most aggressive characters I have ever known. As a Middle-Eastern man, my father was anxious to have a son. The other two wives were unable to do the job for him, and so he selected a virile [sic] young girl, hoping that she could provide him with the son he so desperately wanted. That she did. One month after the marriage she was pregnant and later gave birth to a boy. What a day that was for her poor family and also for my father's family who had been opposed to such an incompatible marriage from the outset, not least because my father's other two wives were relatives of theirs. However, the happiness was to last no longer than two months. The child died from "summer diarrhoea," a dehydrating illness that is responsible for almost ninety percent of infant mortality in Egypt. There was a huge quarrel over who was responsible for this unhappy ending to such a happy story. The result was a divorce.

This was an event that made my father blame himself for the next four years. As far as my mother was concerned, it was even worse; she held him responsible until the very last moment of their life together. The problem was that my father seems to have discovered too late that he had divorced a woman with whom he had fallen deeply in love, perhaps for the first time in his life. For four whole years he kept trying to negotiate for a remarriage, a process which led my father to write his entire estate over to his wife's name.

After their remarriage, my mother was pregnant again in less than a month. This time it was me. The household effects, clothes, perfumes, and jewelry that she demanded from either Cairo or Paris, they were all brought to her by a husband who absolutely adored her and who was now virtually humiliating himself in the process. Eventually I was born. Every single person, in her family, his family, the whole village, in fact the entire estate where my father served as director, everyone was concerned about the fate of this newborn child, a child who happened to have green-colored eyes and the fair complexion of the children of "khawagat," the name given to foreigners in Egypt. Two months after my birth, the crisis began. I refused to nurse. My mother had an abscess on her breast which made her unable to feed me. Artificial milk had hardly been heard of, and so wet nurses were brought in. I got severe attacks of summer diarrhoea and colic. They tell me that for three whole months, while my mother remained sick with her abscess, the pain made me cry day and night. I was handled by nearly every female relative, yelling and screaming all the time. Death hovered over me all the time. The stars of the night witnessed a strange sight, as my female relatives would remove the head-coverings that they wore in the Islamic fashion, leaving their heads exposed as they begged God to spare my life.

Unfortunately this summer diarrhoea is a kind of virus infection of children's bowels, and even now there is no specific treatment for it. My family resorted to all kinds of medicine in order to treat the condition, including such traditional Arabic cures as burning the central part of my scalp with a red-hot iron bar. The big scar is still up there, looking almost like a skullcap.

Till today, no one can say how I didn't come to die, just as nobody knows how I come still to be alive. In any case, I did not die. I survived, and my father could not have been happier. My mother was happy too. Not only did she have me, but went on to produce five other brothers and two sisters, all of whom lived. And with that progeny all my father's reservations regarding my mother disappeared. He surrendered to her whims unconditionally, giving her not only love, care, and attention, but everything she wanted, money, jewelry, even ready cash.

When I reached school age, a problem arose. My father's home and workplace was far from any school or town, and so I had to go and live with my mother's family in our original village. There was a primary school in the nearby town of Fakous in Sharqiyya Province, the one between the Suez Canal and the Eastern branch of the Nile in the Delta. I can still remember the trip from my family home to the village. It was only about 25 miles, but it still took a whole day from six in the morning till nighttime. The only way to travel was by donkey; there were no buses, railways, or anything else. It was not merely a long journey for me; it was a one-way trip. It took me away from my family for ever and deposited me in an entirely different community and atmosphere. From now on, I had to live as a stranger among strangers, an orphan whose parents were still living, yet totally out of reach. And from this point on, I remain for most of my life in a state of profound nostalgia, needing a family of my own, a father, a mother, a brother or a sister.

My grandmother's house, my "Sitti," was a wide, mud-brick peasant house in which no less than 25 grown-ups lived, ate, slept, and existed. My grandmother, grandfather, their sons and daughters, relatives near and distant, men and women working for this large family that depended for its livelihood on renting land from small landowners in order to cultivate crops and taking one third every year, this was the household in which I lived. I had come to one of the very poorest families in the village. Had I grown up since my childhood in such a family environment, I would not have noticed the dreadful difference between this life of poverty and the life of comfort I had enjoyed in my father's house. However, now it seemed to me that I had gone down the social scale, from the rank and family status of a crown prince to the level of the ordinary peasants and workers over whom I had been able to lord it in my previous home. This huge change was abundantly obvious all the time, added to which was the fact that I was alone, the only child in fact below the age of ten, living among a group of grown-ups the youngest of whom was at least twenty-five. Deprived of my father's and mother's presence and protection, I found myself compelled to live with the ugly reality of poverty. All of us thirty people used to sleep together in a single large room which they called the "oven" room since it contained the oven that was used for baking bread. Its hot top provided the only place for sleeping in winter and even during the heat of summer. For the first several weeks I couldn't sleep at all. The room was swarming with flies, cockroaches, and a variety of bugs and reptiles. There was a huge din of groans and snores, crying sometimes, and attempts at sexual congress. Everything repulsive and inhuman seemed to be gathered together in this small, totally dark room, unventilated except for a tiny hole somewhere in the ceiling. The top of the oven was actually so high up that, when lying on it, I could reach up and touch the palm branches that were split and laid side by side to form the roof, looking just like the ribs in a corpse's chest viewed from the inside.

Whether I was still asleep or not, I had to wake up by five o'clock in order to get ready for the awful trip to school. The water was usually freezing cold. I would shiver as I got dressed, then swallow some maize, bread, and Greek cheese made in the house (although without the slightest trace of cream in it), and then, still shivering, I would start my walk to school. That used to take me between one and a half and two hours. I would arrive in the very worst shape, only to face "inspection" by the school-masters and to be found to have dirty shoes or hair or nails. For that I would be punished with between ten and thirty strokes of the cane on the back of my hand from the angry school-master; I was always guilty of some crime or other. I was deprived of real parents who could understand what school was all about, and no one in my new large family had ever been to school. I was never given any money and so never managed to supply myself with books, notepads, or anything needed for school. For all these things I would always be punished. I was even punished for my clothing. My mother was always extremely mean with money. She wanted any penny or millieme to be saved and saved till it turned into a pound, then a hundred pounds. She would then be able to buy another acre of land in her village and rub the fact into the face of her landless and

impoverished family. All this had to be done by my father, of course, and it was
always in her name. As a result, when it came to buying books and clothes for
school, she usually chose the very cheapest things on the market: summer suits
for winter time, and winter suits for summer time. My well-dressed school-
masters would get very upset when they saw me wearing a white suit and white
Clarke summer shoes, completely plastered in winter mud. They would drag me
out of the morning line in order to demonstrate how untidy I was and how stupid
my parents were. They used to insult me and my parents in front of the entire
school. This was even more humiliating than being beaten. On the way home I
would take the same route, crying bitterly to myself and only pausing in order to look
up and shout to God: "Where are You?" Truth to tell, my shouts were primarily
addressed to the sunburned, wrinkled face of my father with its kindly expression.

If you are born and raised in poverty, you never really feel what it is to be poor.
But if you are dropped into a state of poverty from the social heights in which I
had grown up—and, in my case, without any help or warning, you find yourself
removed from a neat table around which you gather with your closest relatives,
father, mother, sisters and brothers, a happy gathering that eats separately but
clustered around a delicious, rich and cozy meal prepared by a mother. Instead
you find yourself in a place where there is just one large, round piece of wood
(laughingly called a "table") around which gather thirty, and sometimes more,
people to fight over the food with grimy fingers. And what "food" it actually was!
Soup made of grass from the fields and rice. Meat, and tiny pieces of it at that, was
only served on the major feasts of Ramadan and Kourban Bairam, and on other
religious occasions. Most of the time, I lost out on the battle to grasp a handful
of rice, mostly because I would indulge in daydreams about the table at my own
home and especially the kind of food we would eat there, sometimes specially
cooked for me by a caring mother.

*****

It may sound strange, but this is the way it really happened. I have been asked
to write a sketch about myself as a writer. For an entire year and without any
apparent reason I have been procrastinating. This year I decided to do it, still
postponing things even as I decided to start work. I started and found myself
returning to that area of my life that I have always tried to avoid remembering,
my earliest childhood. I wrote several pages and then stopped. I tried again, but
was obliged to stop again. This time, the cause was a severe migraine that attacked
me several times a day. I was examined by doctors who said that there was no
apparent reason. I tried to ignore it so as to fulfill my promise on schedule, but
the migraine got worse and worse. I had to stop again and to lie down in bed for
a while. I seemed to be physically sick. One month later now and apparently cured
of my illness I can think of no other cause for the onset of these migraines than
my sudden decision to face my childhood, something that lurked in my subconscious memory as a spot labeled "taboo"; almost as though it carried a sign saying
"Very painful memories; no trespassing."

Now that I have written about it, I have not found it as unbearably ghastly as I used to imagine it would be. Writing about it is far different from actually living through it. Writing in this case is merely the process of recalling the scars that have been left in one's memory from the large fire that used to blaze there. Scars can still cause pain even if they are only the vestiges of wounds, but it is not in any way like being freshly burned or wounded in the "here and now," especially if that "here and now" is actually childhood. As children we don't see things as they really are; they are either glorified, minimized, or enlarged to horrific dimensions. Childhood is the age of exaggerated responses to life, to being alive, to feelings, and even to dreams. That is precisely the feeling that I have had in recalling that period in my life. It seems like the sketch for a nightmare, as I have recalled the features of its particular narrative and the incidents involved in a completely different way from the process of living through its agonies, sensing as I did the sense of suffocation and the useless efforts to free myself from its clutches. I can still recall the day when I really "fled" from the cruel atmosphere. My grandmother, no less than her daughter my own mother, retained her toughness and utterly unfeminine nature, while my grandfather remained weak-voiced and asthmatic. They and their relatives were far more strangers to me that any passing stranger I may have met during my daily trip to and from school (even though my grandmother told me not to speak to anyone, whatever happened). Even that particular piece of advice was a humiliation; I felt that they were somehow afraid of my virginity, as though I were a girl. How painful words like these turned out to be, just like nails hammered into your sense of dignity! And, if words had that effect, then what about deeds, the humiliations you suffered day after day in class, in school, in the streets of the small town, and even on the streets of our village where the peasant boys treated the white-skinned, green-eyed "foreigner" as though he were somehow less masculine than they were!

I actually did run away. One day, I decided to leave, to keep walking, day and night, until I found my real father and mother. However I was caught by the nosey folk in the next village and sent back home. There I was given one of the worst beatings I ever got from either my grandmother or her daughter, my own mother.

In this vast ocean of nastiness and sheer misery I would have fallen prey to illness and even died if it had not been for two things. The first was the fact that I would daydream all the time. It wouldn't matter whether I was in class, walking those long miles to and from school alone, or trying to do my homework in the light of a very primitive gasoline lamp with an old chair as a desk, I used to dream of discovering and inventing things, becoming very rich, being as mighty as a king or as a Count of Monte Cristo, being a magician or musician. I never dreamed of becoming a writer, not only because at that age I had no idea of the importance of writers, but also because, even if I had realized it, it would never have become part of my daydreaming since writers are so uninfluential in a society such as ours. They can never become as mighty as kings, nor as rich as merchants or even thieves. Instead they remain just as helpless as I was then, failing to earn a decent living and devoting themselves to bookworm jobs and meaningless words.

The second of these things was the tales that my great-grandmother told. She was a very old, wrinkled creature, and, even though they told me she was ninety years old, she felt closer to me and my childhood world than any of the other occupants of the house. She loved sugar, but was forbidden to have any, even in coffee. For that reason I used to smuggle sugar for her and sometimes cigarettes. In return, she would let me sit in her tiny lap and tell me everything about life as it used to be seventy years ago, or about 120 years ago from now. She would recount how rich "our" family used to be, how she had married, how she was the queen of our tribe because in those days families were large and lived together in one long lane or even a whole street. They would grind the wheat for everyone, cook for the entire family, and do all the washing at once. She not only told me about every minute detail of family life and all the different personalities in the family group, both wicked and good, but also sang to me the old Egyptian folk songs. These included Bedouin and Coptic songs for the dead and for marriage ceremonies, songs for working in the fields and even songs to accompany circumcision rites for the male children in the family; songs, in fact, for every conceivable occasion. All these things had a profound effect on my imagination. As a writer, all I can hope is that one day I will be able to sit down and reconstruct that very colorful, beautiful, and marvellous phase of Egyptian and Arabic** life and customs.

As I said, I would probably have died were it not for these two avenues of escape. In fact, there were not really escapes, but rather the past or the future. The point is that, for me, they formed the only real present, my only truly living moments. They were the moments when I really existed and had the feelings of a happy child. The rest, life as it really was, was just one long escape from being, from the miseries of existence.

All this may explain why I was not surprised to discover that the mere notion of recalling my scattered childhood memories made me physically sick. My childhood can be regarded as the innermost nuclear oven of my existence. I have only made use of the energy that such a childhood has given me at the expense of depriving myself of it. I only use such energy in order to combat such memories and not to recall them. I use it because it goads me into writing, creating, and struggling in order that other people and especially children may not have to suffer the things that I still remember. I see no point in actually going through the furnace and reliving it all again. I will never write about my childhood; it is inhumanly painful to do so. In the meantime, I have to admit that without this childhood I would never have become a writer. And so, my thanks to it, but damn it for all time! You can take my career and prestige, even if I were to be the best writer in the entire history of humanity, and give me instead a moment, just one

[** IDRIS'S FOOTNOTE: Sharqiyya Province is the point of contact between the Eastern Arab world and the Egyptian Delta and its peasantry. In our province one finds a mixed cocktail of folkloric cultures derived from Arab, Egyptian, Coptic and Muslim civilizations. But that is another story.]

moment, of my lost childhood. I would accept it without the slightest hesitation. A happy childhood is something that can never be recaptured or relived whatever status you may gain later on and whatever happiness you give to others by creating paradises, whether true or false. What is the use of hell, even if its role is to create paradises? It still continues to burn, and the heat it gives off still causes intense pain.

*****

So there is a sketch of my life as a child. It's the same kind of sketch that might be written if you traced the life history of a criminal or a genius. I was lucky because I became a writer. But that's just a matter of luck. It was my good fortune that this childhood of mine gave me an unbelievable desire to be somebody, to change the world I had lived in as a child, if nothing else.

The longest journey in my life was the period from the ages of 16 to 21. After that, everything constituted a short cut. Being one of the hardest working students, I was accepted as a medical student. In medical school I was able to satisfy my earnest desire to study medicine and science. In the meantime I was also involved in supporting Egypt's national cause. Discovering that I was not the only one who had suffered, I determined to change the fate of Egypt and its future directions. Later on, when I discovered that other countries in the Arab World, and even other parts of the world as a whole, were suffering the very same problems, I devoted myself to the Nationalist movement against the British occupation of Egypt, thus joining hands with liberals throughout the world in their demands for freedom from poverty, tyranny, and misery. It was while I was writing leaflets and revolutionary pamphlets that I discovered early in my career as a medical student that I was born to be a writer, a writer of short-stories and plays in particular. So I left a career in medicine and devoted myself completely to writing. After thirty years of writing and after the publication of 33 books I can see no great difference between the world I struggled against and the world as it is now. There is however an enormous difference between the world I dreamed of and the world in which I now find myself living.

That may be why I am still writing. Or, to be honest with my innermost feelings, that is why I feel that I have not yet begun to write.

YUSUF IDRIS
15th November, 1983.

Yusuf Idris's Short Stories: Themes & Techniques

Roger Allen

The title story of Idris's first published collection of short stories, *Arkhas Layali (The Cheapest of Nights)* appeared in 1954, but its subject is as relevant today as it was over two decades ago.* A man has emerged from a mosque in a provincial village after the evening prayer; he has had a cup of tea which was especially strong, and his brain is racing. As he wades his way down an alley full of children, he mingles curses against the man who gave him such strong tea with nasty but realistic thoughts about the teeming mass of young humanity all around him, many of whom, as he notes, will die of starvation for sure. As he wanders around the village in search of companionship, he begins to feel both cold and lonely. With another curse on the man who gave him the tea, he turns round and heads for home. There he crawls over the bodies of his six children in order to find the warmth and consolation of his somnolent wife, whom he arouses. Nine months later, he is being congratulated on the birth of yet another child, while he wonders all the while where all these children could possibly come from!

The perennial problem of Egypt's increasing population and a doctor's concern with ignorance of birth control methods are here combined in a short story which amply demonstrates the qualities which made Idris's initial short story collections both popular and admired by critics. In the first place he is concerned to portray the poorer classes of Egyptian society as accurately as possible. Previous writers had also concerned themselves with such people, but frequently within the context of general philosophical discussions on such topics as the futility of life. Idris presents the poor people as he finds them and allows the bald facts and their implications to speak for themselves. In this he is helped considerably by his use of language which is uncomplicated and explicit. An inherent part of this process involves the use of the spoken language, the colloquial dialect of Cairo or the provinces, when his characters speak. This lends a special vividness to the curses and invocations found in this and many other of

---

*It is translated in the collection, *Arabic Writing Today: The Short Story*, ed. Mahmoud Manzalaoui, Cairo: Dar al-Ma'arif, 1968. p. 227.

Idris's stories. But, apart from the use of the colloquial, Idris displays in this collection the ability to create cameo-portraits with an economy in the use of language. His descriptions show the character living in his own surroundings; but there is no moral at the end, and indeed, few, if any, of the characters emerge any better off than they were at the beginning of the story.

This "cameo" aspect is well illustrated by the story "A Stare" ("Nazra"). A narrator describes in the first person a chance encounter with a little girl who is carrying a tray full of food on her head. The tray is about to slip, and she asks him to adjust it on her head for her. He watches anxiously as she crosses the street, deftly weaving her way through the traffic. She stops, and he imagines that the tray is about to fall off once again. Rushing across the street, he is almost knocked down himself. But all she is doing, he discovers, is watching some other children playing with a ball. Then, with a final wistful stare, she is "swallowed up" by the street. Here, in a few short paragraphs, we see some of the contrasts in Egyptian society expressed — perhaps unconsciously — through the emotions of the narrator. While the girl goes on her way regardless, the narrator becomes very anxious. One wonders whether he realizes that his advice to her to return to the oven, his surprise at her asking a complete stranger to help her, his comments on her appearance, all these things reflect on him. Is there not perhaps some hidden moral in the fact that she, a personification of the burdens of poverty in Egypt, crosses the street unscathed — no small achievement in Egypt — while the narrator, rushing over impetuously to help her, is almost knocked down? But she is not in any trouble; she is merely staring longingly at a group of children luckier than herself.

The collection, *The Cheapest of Nights*, is full of stories about Egyptians like this little girl, from the poorer classes. Some of them are portrayed at their work in the provinces, others confront the features of modern life during brief visits to Cairo, still others live in the slums of the big city itself. In "Incident" ("Al-Hadith") we follow some provincials on a visit to Cairo; they see the sights about which they have heard so much and we hear their comments, frequently not very complimentary, on the conduct of Cairenes. "A Quarter of a Jasmin Patch" ("Rub' Hawd") tells the story of Isma'il Bey, a landowner who suddenly decides one day to inspect his property. He scolds a peasant who is not hoeing his jasmin patch properly and demands a hoe to do it himself. He cannot even break up the hard ground with the implement he is given, and then suddenly his heart flutters. As he is carried back to the house, the sardonic peasant takes the hoe and breaks the ground apart with his first blow.

Idris's second collection appeared under the title *Farahat's Republic (Jumhuriyyat Farahat)* and contained three short stories and the novel, *Love Story (Qissat Hubb)*. "Farahat's Republic" is set in a Cairene Police Station where a Station Sergeant, Farahat, presides over all the chaotic goings-on with an iron hand and a loud voice.* Into this scene comes the narrator. He is obviously

*The short story version of this work (it has also been adapted by the author as a play) has been translated in *Modern Arabic Short Stories*, trans. Denys Johnson-Davies, Oxford: Oxford University Press, 1967.

from a higher class than most of Farahat's other customers or victims, but he too has been arrested on some charge or other. Farahat does not realize this and soon engages the narrator in conversation; in fact, he essentially becomes the narrator himself. While Farahat intersperses his narrative with staccato orders, insults and curses to all comers, he paints a picture of a dreamworld which he envisages. Inside the gruff and callous exterior of the man who metes out such instant and apparently indifferent justice there resides the heart of a dreamer. When at the end of the story Farahat discovers that the man with whom he has been sharing his dream is under arrest too, his whole mood changes and his dreams for the future vanish.

I am grateful to Trevor Le Gassick for the information that Idris originally entitled the story "Abd al-Baqi's Republic." It would not have been lost on the Egyptian reading public so used to reading between the lines of works of literature that the name "Abd al-Baqi" consists (as do several Muslim names) of the word *"abd"* (meaning "slave, servant") and one of the epithets used to describe God in the Qur'an (the so-called "beautiful names"); the name thus means literally servant of the One who remains." Exactly the same features are found in the name Abd al-Nasir (Nasser).The fact that the tale has the word "Republic" itself in its title and that the name of the chief character was changed before publication gives this work a particular significance; beyond the purely local social implications of the events which it reveals to the reader there lies a wider, political message.

This work gives us a convincing picture of a mercurial character dealing with his fellow human beings in an exasperated fashion. The grandiose dreams which he envisions disappear abruptly at the conclusion of the story. Other projects actually implemented by the government of Egypt during the revolutionary period may not vanish so quickly; the results of building that modern Pyramid, the High Dam at Aswan, are only now beginning to be realized....

The short story, "The Wallet" ("Al-Mahfaza"), treats in a very effective fashion one of Idris's most common themes, poverty and its effects on an Egyptian family. The availability of primary education to the younger generation in Nasser's Egypt means that Sami, the young boy in the story, is able to go to school. However, he is too ashamed to tell his colleagues who keep asking him to go to the cinema with him that he cannot accompany them because he has no money. His father and mother both refuse his requests for the necessary ten piasters; they claim that they have none to give him, but he cannot and does not believe them. The core of the story relates to Sami's attempt to get some money from his father, by theft from his wallet while the household is asleep. Sami's reactions are described as he steals into his parents' bedroom, and the tension is built up by switching of tenses from the narrative past to the vivid present. In attempting to take money from his father's wallet, Sami is regarding his father as the all-powerful figure who can do anything; he regards it as inconceivable that his father has no money to give him so that he can go to the cinema. When Sami discovers that his father's wallet is indeed empty, his first reaction is one of resentment. Where else could he keep his money? If there is none, where does it all go? But then, he sees his father lying asleep in his bed, his hair dishevelled and his mouth open. The feeling of resentment turns to one of pity. Sami feels that he himself should be aspiring to earn a living so that he can give his father some money, instead of vice versa. After replacing the wallet, he steals back to his own room. When his younger brother asks for the inevitable drink of water, he gets him one willingly instead of ignoring him as he has usually done before. An awareness of the real situation of his family and the sight of his sleeping father have aroused a sense of family responsibility in him. Yet again, Idris succeeds in this story in showing the plight of the poorer classes through the depiction of a single character who is endeavoring to change his lot on however small a scale; Sami emerges no better off at the end of the story, but he has learned a lesson.

The next short story collection by Idris to appear after *City Dregs (Qa' al-Madina)* was *An Affair of Honor (Hadithat Sharaf)* which was published in 1958. The title story (already available in translation as "Peace With Honor"*) is set in a provincial farm estate *(izba)*. Fatima, generally acknowledged as being the prettiest girl on the estate, is caught in a field with Gharib, a young man who can succeed in making any woman swoon just at the sight of him. Fatima has been warned all along to beware of the 'shame', and the whole community is convinced that it has now happened to her. The two most handsome inhabitants of this microcosm become the focus of the jealousies and instinctive suspicions of the community. While Gharib flees the estate, Fatima is subjected to the humiliation of an 'examination'. When she is found to be safe, everyone rejoices; the honor of the estate has not been sullied. For a while, Gharib abandons his rakish ways, but he cannot keep it up for long. Fatima on the other hand has lost some of her innocence and is even capable of a certain amount of defiance. At the end of the story, she is still unmarried, a forbidden fruit too luscious for any of the villagers to allow anyone else to marry. The question of societal attitudes and especially taboos on the individual is a theme to which Idris has frequently addressed himself, and especially in matters of sex. In an article in the periodical, *Mawaqif* (no. 9, 1970), Idris has the following to say on the subject:

> I choose woman as being the best expression of frankness in society. . . I can say that I write about sex as being part of life. Sex for me equals life. As far as I am concerned, any other significance is invalid . . . the relationship between men and women is in need of a revolution. They are not two different, separate and distant entities. They are very close to each other . . . a single entity, a single human being. . . Thus, sex does not imply men coming to women and vice versa, but

*It is translated in the collection, *Arabic Writing Today: The Short Story,* ed. Mahmoud Manzalaoui, Cairo: Dar al-Ma'arif, 1968, p. 227.

rather the desire of both to plunge deeper and deeper into life
and to embrace the continuity of mankind.

Idris's concern with attitudes to the subject of sex in Egyptian society emerges
in the story, "An Affair of Honor", and we shall see it as a central theme in some
of his more recent stories to be discussed below.

In the story, "The Big Hand" ("Al-Yad al-Kabira") from this same collection
we find another situation which Idris uses on several occasions in his short
stories, namely the implications of the presence or absence of a father-figure to
a particular family. Other examples are "The Seesaw" ("Al-Marjiha") from *The
Cheapest of Nights* and "House of Flesh" ("Bayt min Lahm") from the collection
of that name, to be discussed below. In "The Big Hand", the narrator describes
in the first person his reactions on returning to his village, the walk from the
railroad station to his house, the comments of the villagers whom he passes, but
above all the greetings from his father and mother. On one occasion however, he
returns to find the atmosphere very different. His father has just died; the house
is empty, and the rest of the family are at the cemetery. He himself goes to the
cemetery and communes with his dead father. After reminiscing for a while, the
narrator engages his father in a conversation, expressing the love which the whole
family feels toward him and the anguish which he himself feels because his father
has died while he was away. When the narrator returns home, the whole family
sits in silence. Then suddenly, everyone bursts into tears. They have all faced the
reality that the head of the household is now dead and gone forever.

*   *   *

The works which we have described thus far constitute a remarkable outpour-
ing of literary effort. In the years between 1954 and 1958, Idris published five
collections of stories and three plays, and all that by the age of thirty. These years
coincided with the first decade of the Egyptian Revolution, and the heady
experiences of the Czech arms deal, the withdrawal of European and Israeli forces
after the Tripartite Invasion of 1956, and the attempts at the unification of a
"United Arab Republic" with Syria. At the same time, tight control began to be
exercised on the publication media in Egypt, and writing was kept under strict
censorship. Apparently, the collection, *An Affair of Honor*, suffered as a result of
this process and was eventually published for the first time in Lebanon.

It is perhaps only after the advent to power of Anwar al-Sadat in 1970 and the
so-called "correctional revolution" *(thawra al-tashih)* that it has been fully
possible to discover quite how capricious was the observance of civil liberties in
Egypt during the period of the 1960s up till the fateful debacle with Israel in 1967.
Nagib Mahfuz has discussed this period with remarkable candor in his novel, *Al-
Karnak* (the name of a ficticious café), but both he and Yusuf Idris began to

* See *Arabic Writing Today: The Short Story*, ed. Mahmoud Manzalaoui, Cairo: The
American Research Center in Egypt and Dar al-Ma'arif, 1968.

address themselves to the problems of contemporary man and of the individual in society (often in unfavorable circumstances) during the 1960s. Both used symbolism and even surrealism to couch their thoughts in terms which could be understood by their readership and yet survive the attentions of the censor. In Idris's case, there continue to be stories which reflect the social concerns treated in his earlier collections, but these are juxtaposed with other stories which reflect the absurd and illogical aspects in the existence of contemporary man.

These points can best be demonstrated by describing the two stories from Idris's next collection, *The End of the World (Akhir al-Dunya*—1961). The first, "Playing House" ("La'bat al-Bayt"), takes us into the world of two children at play and into the mind of one of them, Samih, the little boy who loses his temper with Fatin, the girl with whom he is "playing house", wishes her good riddance, but then rapidly comes to hope that she will return. The portrayal of such childish petulance is well managed as we follow Samih's changes of mood from initial exasperation, through boredom, to regret and a desire for reconciliation. But, in spite of the charming children's environment within which the story is convincingly set, we may still note that such instant flashes of temper and almost immediate regret are not confined to the world of children.

With "The Omitted Letter" ("Alif al-Ahrar") we come to one of Idris's most effective expressions of the conditions of modern man; it is a veritable tragicomedy about his position in and response to the kind of existence governed by the demands of technology and administrative bureaucracy. There is much in this story which is amusing. It is a flea which keeps Ahmad Rashwan, the ultimate in punctilious civil servants, awake and thereby provokes the incredible and crucial question as to how he differs from his own typewriter. Everything about the company, from its fancy glass doors, to the posturings of Ahmad's boss and the upward and downward movement of the mouse-like figure of the Director-General as he swivels his chair, all these things are portrayed with a generous dose of sarcasm. And yet, the essential question is a real and critical one: is modern man being dominated by the machines which are supposed to help him; does he have any freedom of choice, can he exert any initiative? These are the issues which Ahmad resolves to settle for himself when he refuses to insert into a typed document a letter which he has deliberately left out as an assertion of his own individuality. Needless to say, the company bureaucracy, in the form of Abd al-Latif, his boss, is quick to inform Ahmad that he has no individuality. Abd al-Latif makes no concessions to Ahmad's feelings as he makes this fact brutally clear to him, but the Director-General tries a more gentle approach. Everyone has to obey orders, he tells Ahmad, even the Director-General himself. But by now, Ahmad has become obsessed by the notion of the dignity of mankind and his own superiority over his colleagues, and continues his defiance. After he is fired, he discovers that the typewriter key for the letter which he has deliberately left out is not working and rushes to tell his boss. As a final blow to Ahmad's crusade for individual rights, his boss tells him that machines can be repaired; we are left to infer that defiant employees who insist on asserting their individuality are fired.

Idris's output continued at the same rapid pace during the early part of the 1960s, and the year 1962 saw the appearance of not only the novel, *Shame (Al-Ayb)* but also a collection of lengthy short stories under the title *The Black Soldier (Al-Askari al-Aswad)*. This latter volume contains three long works: the title story, "Lady Vienna" ("Al-Sayyida Fianna") and "Men and Bulls" ("Rijal wa Thiran"). It has to be admitted that in all three works, the artistic dimension tends to take a back seat while the author indulges in some writing which shows clear journalistic tendencies. In "Lady Vienna" an Egyptian finds himself in Vienna and searches for a woman who will satisfy his needs; he encounters a woman who feels a similar need for an African man. One has only to read Yahya Haqqi's *The Lamp of Umm Hashim* (in translation, *The Saint's Lamp* tr. Mustafa Badawi, Leiden: Brill, 1973) or Al-Tayyib Salih's *Season of Migration to the North* (translated with the same title by Denys Johnson-Davies, London: Heinemann, 1970) to realize that the theme of cross-cultural encounters such as these can be much more successfully and artistically handled than is the case in "Lady Vienna". The same may be said about "Men and Bulls" which is essentially a description of the life of a bullfighter in Spain, full of long depictions of bullfights and the reactions of the narrator to the events which he witnesses and the people whom he meets.

The story of "The Black Soldier" suffers from some of the faults which we have just outlined. The desire to produce a work which will be a direct commentary on the human condition seems to have been very much in the forefront of the author's consciousness. "The Black Soldier" is undoubtedly the best of the works in this volume because it shows Idris, the committed Egyptian writer of fiction, addressing himself to a question which has only recently shown itself with full clarity to have been one of the central issues of Egyptian society during the decade of the 1960s, namely personal liberty, the psychological effect of internment on intellectuals and other members of society, and the generally reticent attitude of society at large to the seemingly random arrest of its members by the state security forces.

In "The Black Soldier" there is a heavy emphasis on description of past events at the expense of characterization of even the major figures in the story. What emerges therefore is a tale of immense power, one which fully reflects Idris's close involvement in the struggles for personal freedoms during the 1960s and shows his own considerable courage in even broaching such a theme, but, at the same time, one which lacks the artistic subtlety of some of his earlier works. Idris here allows his overwhelming concern for his fellow human beings to come entirely to the fore; we are therefore presented with an important document, but one which lacks some of the artistic qualities of his other fictional works.

Idris's next three collections of short stories appeared over a period of nine years: *The Language of Screams (Lughat al-Ay Ay, 1965)* contains stories written between the years 1957 and 1965; *The Clarion (Al-Naddaha, 1969)* contains those written between 1965 and 1969; and *The House of Flesh (Bayt min Lahm, 1971)* those written in 1970 and 1971, along with a couple from an earlier period.

For an author who had previously been so noticably prolific in his fictional output, this may seem to represent a considerable change on the author's part. The causes are no doubt as complicated as the personality of our subject, but they seem to be made up of some combination of the following factors. In the first place, Idris began to take an intense interest in the theatre during the 1960s. We have already noted that he had published two plays in the 1950s and that he advocated in a series of articles in 1963 a completely new approach to the drama and indeed the creation or revival of indigenous Egyptian dramatic forms. To emphasize his points, Idris composed his highly successful and controversial play, *Farafir* (in translation, *Farfoors* tr. Farouk Abdel Wahab, in *Modern Egyptian Drama*, Minneapolis: Bibliotheca Islamica, 1974), which was performed for the first time in 1964. It should also be remembered that Idris gave up his medical career during this period and, as many creative writers in Egypt do, turned to journalism, working first for *Al-Jumhuriyya* and then for *Al-Ahram*. On the more negative side, we have already noted the extremely difficult conditions under which Egyptians had to carry out their lives during the oppressive years of the 1960s up till 1967. The June War of that year was, of course, a setback for the Arab world as a whole and something which caused intellectuals in particular to indulge in a great deal of thought about the very bases of their society and its attitudes to itself and others. This general unease in the immediate aftermath of June 1967 continued until the death of Abd al-Nasir in 1970. The first years of the Sadat regime have seen some superficial freedoms restored to the press and other writers, but at the same time have witnessed the appearance or reappearance on the cultural scene of some extremely reactionary figures with whom Idris can feel little sympathy. In fact, he and several of his fellow writers were deprived of their jobs early in the Sadat regime. All these factors, positive and negative — to which can be added a debilitating heart condition — made the last two decades particularly trying ones for Idris, as for many creative writers in Egypt. This may perhaps account for the slower rate of publication during these years.

Some of the stories in the collection, *The Language of Screams,* reflect the wide variety of themes found in Idris's earlier collections. "Because Judgement Day Will Not Happen" takes us, like "Playing House", into the world of children. "Caught in the Act" is a particularly successful description of a brief encounter. The Dean of a university college is initially outraged when he sees a girl student smoking in secret as he looks out of his window. His anger is put aside as he watches the young girl enjoying every puff of the cigarette, and he almost comes to participate vicariously in her feelings of relaxation and pleasure. As she finishes the cigarette, he comes to himself again. The girl suddenly feels a sense of danger, and their eyes meet. She realizes that she has been "caught in the act."

Alongside these stories we find others (the most recently composed of those in the collection) which stress a new theme, man's lack of concern for his fellow human beings. The title story deals with a successful man who is made aware by the chronic illness of his old school friend, Fahmi, of his separation from the plight of other people less fortunate than himself. In an ending the implications of which are too clear to miss and in fact expressed with an insufficient sense of artistry, Al-Hadidi, the successful man, carries Fahmi out of the house on his shoulders; they are going on "another, more difficult path." His wife asks him if he has gone mad as she refuses to go with him.

If human indifference is the theme of "The Language of Screams", then "The Aorta" deals with the subject of human oppression and cruelty. In an opening passage of considerable impact, the author builds up a picture of the human herd instinct, as people swirl around a square like ants, following anyone who seems to have any goal and then reverting to their lemming-like rush to nowhere as the goal proves not to exist. In the midst of all this, the first-person narrator suddenly comes face to face with Abduh whom he suspects of stealing money. We are made aware of the narrator's total lack of any human feelings towards this man; as he contemplates the possibility of chewing him up while throttling him, all he can comment on is the man's "repulsive" habit of bursting into tears. The animal hatred and callousness of the narrator proves contagious, and the people around him join in the insane hunt for the money which, they believe, is hidden on Abduh's person. Abduh pleads in vain that he has had an operation to cure "a dangerous disease that threatened to infect all Egyptians", and that he has had his aorta removed. The similarities of the crowd in this story to those of a lynch mob are now further emphasized as they hoist Abduh up on to a butcher's hook and then proceed to strip him. When they discover that he is indeed covered in bandages, they still do not believe Abduh's story; by now, the herd instinct is at its fullest frenzy. Only when the bandages are finally off and Abduh's aorta dangles in the air does the crowd finally realize that Abduh was telling the truth. He has been done to death for something which he never had.

This story is one of the most impressive and forceful of Idris's more recent compositions, in some of which there is a conscious withdrawal from reality in order to address himself to various profound and disturbing issues of the day. Indifference and human cruelty were indeed apt subjects for discussion in Egypt during the 1960s, and they were not irrelevant elsewhere. Idris's treatment of them before the June War of 1967 is not a little prophetic. Many authors touched upon this theme in the aftermath of the war, including playwrights like Sa'dallah Wannus and Muhammad al-Maghut. Nagib Mahfuz devoted a considerable amount of attention to it in a series of compositions written immediately after the War. The impact of stories such as "Under the Bus Shelter" and "Sleep" may have been more noticable directly after such a defeat, but the implications of the often grotesque events which take place in their surreal environment find an earlier echo in these stories of Idris.

This combination of themes based on both the real and surreal is carried on into the next collection of short stories, *The Clarion (Al-Naddaha* — 1969). The title story again deals, like "City Dregs", with the impact of the big city and those who live there on the fate of a woman. Fathiyya, a country girl, is seen in her village by Hamid, who serves as a doorman in the big city. She feels attracted towards the metropolis and agrees to marry him. He takes her back to live in his small room in the building where he works. Hamid has to be away a great deal, Fathiyya feels alone, disoriented and bored, and the inevitable happens. Fathiyya gives in to another man, and they are caught *in flagrante* by Hamid. The latter takes Fathiyya back to the station, intending to send her back to her village. However, she manages to escape from him in the crowd and returns to Cairo. The conclusion of the story makes it clear that this time she is taking on the city on her own terms.

One of the stories in this collection with a nonrealistic frame of reference is "The Wonder of the Age" ("Mu'jizat al-Asr"), in which a midget mastermind with tremendous talents and potential is unappreciated by his own people, but finds encouragement elsewhere. Another is "The Point" ("Al-Nuqta"), a brief impression with no plot in which the narrator describes his relationship to his own environment. But the shortest story in the collection, perhaps Idris's shortest short story, is "The Concave Mattress" ("Al-Martaba al-Muqa''ara"), a telling commentary on the routine, even the monotony, of married life for certain couples. The sting is in the tail, so to speak, in that the wife only comes to realize the fact after her husband's corpse has bounced on the hard ground below the window beside which she has been standing.

The comment of Idris cited above about sex and the importance of the relationship between men and women continues to find an application in these latest collections of short stories. In those already analysed, we have seen the subject presented in a variety of contexts and through a variety of approaches, ranging from the bitter and sarcastic to the purely tragic. But Idris's repertoire on this topic is far from expended, and we find new examples in his most recent collection, *House of Flesh (Bayt min Lahm)*. Idris illustrates further the frustrations, the temptations and even the loneliness involved in the relationship between a man and his wife, and indeed between men and women outside marriage. The title story, "House of Flesh", is a very forceful case in point. Here the author takes his reader back to one of the themes to which he had addressed himself on more than one occasion in earlier stories: the problems of the family without a father figure, or, in more sexual terms, the emotions and tensions inside a house full of women, a widowed mother and her three growing daughters. Society here works in a vicious circle, since the mother does not wish to remarry before her daughters have settled down, and yet the lack of a man in the house means that no men ever have the pretext to go there. The only exception is the blind Qur'an reader. Anything is better than nothing, it is decided, and the mother marries him at her daughters' urging. The mother puts on her wedding ring at night as the couple go to bed and then make love. The daughters lie awake in the same room, following every sigh and groan. Even with a man in the house now, no men come to ask for the girls' hands. As they grow up and reach maturity, they plead with their mother to help them. In resignation, she lets them put on the ring. Each daughter in turn sleeps with her mother's husband, the ring becoming a passport for the relief of their sexual frustration. And, as the author tells us at the end of the story, the blind man knows nothing about what is going on; or does he?

In the story "In Cellophane Wrapping" ("Ala Waraq Silufan") we have another instance of sexual frustration. The gorgeous and bored wife of a celebrated surgeon visits the operating theatre where her husband is performing for the first time a pioneering operation. She is confronted by the fact that in this situation he is far from being the quiet, submissive creature which he seems to be at home; he is in fact an utter tyrant who loses his temper, throws things around and yells at his subordinates. Seeing this aspect of him which she has never seen at home arouses all the basic impulses towards him which she has been transferring, albeit diffidently, to another man. Idris here succeeds in conveying through the stream of consciousness technique the feelings of this spoiled and petulant woman as she enters her husband's working environment, her initial resentment at her husband's lack of concern for her and her gradual realization in the operating theatre itself that he does in fact become a completely different person at home, someone who allows her considerable latitude and freedom. Even though she really feels the need for him to exhibit at home the same character traits as he displays at work, she comes to be aware of her own selfishness. The "other man" vanishes into thin air as she watches the miraculous skill of her husband at work.

In two of the stories from this same collection, sexual relationships are treated in a more sardonic fashion. In "The Greatest Sin of All" ("Akbar al- Kaba'ir") Shaykh Sadiq becomes increasingly devout and this leads him to neglect not only his farm but also his wife, Umm Gad. She however finds consolation with the eighteen year-old Muhammad on the roof of the house, while her husband below is involved in his religious rituals. This story begins with a short commentary from the author to the effect that most people find the whole tale very amusing and burst into laughter, while Muhammad himself cannot see anything funny about it at all. The insertion of this tale-telling description at the beginning of the story lends a certain folkloric touch (presumably deliberate); this, we presume, is the kind of story which people like to be able to tell each other. The same is true of another story, "Lily, Did You-Have to Put the Light On?" ("A Kana La Budda Ya- Li Li An Tudi' al-Nur") . Once again we are told at the beginning of the story that this is the kind of anecdote which people like to gossip about, and we are even told that in this case certain types, when sufficiently stoned, like to improvise variations on the basic theme. This story also has an amusing side to it, and again the butt of the humor is religion, or the outward practice of it. The gradual build-up of the present shape of the story and the assumption that many tongues have participated in the process of its composition is further aided by the structure of the story. It begins with the description of the quarter and the kinds of people who live there and then proceeds to describe the scene as the newly attracted mosque congregation is stuck in the position of prostration during their prayers, not daring to move. We then retrace in retrospect the arrival of the young Imam and his initial failures, then his technique for scoring some success and his final defeat as he falls victim to the charms of the gorgeous Lily, a child of an Egyptian mother and English soldier father. This defeat, eventually acknowledged by the Imam, explains the terrible dilemma of his congregation whom he leaves stranded in the prostration position. That provokes the laughter of the listeners to the tale, but it is not the last laugh. The young Imam follows the Devil's lead and goes to Lily's room. But she no longer needs the lessons which she has previously requested on how to pray; the Imam is finally thwarted, since she has been instructed in prayer by a phonograph record.

If sexual themes are common in these stories, they are not the only ones; for Idris continues his wide choice of subject matter. "The Chapter on the Cow" ("Surat al-Baqara") presents us with an amusing, rustic tale, full of lively colloquial dialogue and touches of local description. In it we trace in simple chronological sequence the responses of a peasant who is leading a cow home from market to importunate questions from all and sundry as to how much he paid for the animal. These responses change from initial politeness to exasperation, anger, outright assault and finally the uncontrolled outbursts of a lunatic.

Two other stories show a continuation of Idris's use of a suspension of reality to paint an allegory of modern life. In "The Journey" ("Al-Rihla"), translated by the editor in the *Journal of Arabic Literature*, Volume 3, 1972), a man carries the dead body of his father around in a car. He proclaims his continuing love for him and his great debt to him for the way he has cared for him while a child. To those who ask, the son vehemently denies that there is an unpleasant smell in the car. However, the stench gradually becomes more pervasive, and even the narrator has to admit that his father's body is the thing which is smelling. He abandons both the car and the body on the road. One may interpret this story as a statement that the younger generation is rejecting the old, and such a literal interpretation may be all that is intended. However, in a country like Egypt in which any work of literature is minutely examined for its possible political and social implications, wider implications have been suggested for this story. These are further underlined by the publication date of the story in *Al-Ahram* (5 June 1970). According to such interpretations, the dead father is intended to represent Abd al-Nasir (rendered effectively "dead" by the June War of 1967 and its results), and the message of the story is thus that the time had come to abandon even such a beloved figure as one's own (the country's) father figure.

Another short short story (like "The Concave Mattress" discussed above) is "The Little Bird on the Telephone Wire" ("Al-Usfur wa al-Silk"). Here the style is more cursive and indeed almost poetic in comparison with the deliberate terseness of the dialogue in "The Concave Mattress." A little bird lives his life of flying, perching on a telephone wire and making love to his paramour, blissfully unaware of the electronic pulses of modern life going back and forth within the wire which he is clutching. Deceits, blandishments, love, hatred, heroism, cowardice, all these things are blended into the same electronic pulses which succeed in eradicating all differentiations. As modern technology reduces everything to the same level, the little bird, with its "innocent" claws, carries on unawares, and the picture which results presents the reader with a forceful contrast between the guileless values of nature and the normalizing reductions brought about by modern technology and the existence which it creates.

"The Chair Carrier" places the narrator of the story in a crowded street, as in "The Aorta". But this time, he is not participating in their activity; in fact, he is exasperated by their total lack of interest or concern. Once again, the theme of total indifference to others is introduced. A man is carrying a gigantic chair around. He has been carrying it since the Pharaonic period, even though a notice is pinned to it saying that the Pharoah has given it to him and he should take it home and sit on it. The narrator is almost beside himself with frustration as he reads the message to the porter. The latter listens patiently but with scarcely concealed annoyance. He tells the narrator he cannot read and in any case he needs the proper "authorization." The narrator has no such authorization, and so the porter goes on his way, grumbling that he has to earn a living and has been delayed for nothing. As the narrator watches him slowly disappearing into the crowd, and as people continue to speed by in total disregard of the man and his huge chair, the narrator is left with a vestigial feeling of guilt because he did not have the authorization. Perhaps he is implying thereby that the modern world feels no sense of the meaning of and need for a historical perspective, and thus the man and his chair must continue to wander in search of someone with the proper "authorization."

In the preceding pages we have placed the works of Yusuf Idris within a chronological framework. The content and structure of each composition has been analysed within the context of other works written at about the same time as the work in question. Such a diachronic presentation of this author's works runs the risk of viewing each work in isolation from others with similar themes, relying on the logic of chronological order rather than more literary criteria. However, now that we have described and analysed the works included in this anthology and other works from the same periods, an attempt will be made to essay some general remarks about the different facets of Idris's artistry.

The short story is the genre which constitutes the greater part of Idris's output. Indeed, we may perhaps go even further than that and suggest that the short story is the genre with which Idris feels most at home and to which he has contributed his most noteworthy works. His concentration on the short story has been of the greatest benefit to modern Arabic literature. After all, the genre must be considered one of the most difficult from the point of view of the use of language. Anyone who writes on a regular basis will know that it is much easier to spread one's thoughts over several pages with no constraints on space than to put on paper everything one wants to say in a restricted number of words or in some kind of precis form. The short story is, of course, in no way a precis, but it does involve the use of words to their maximum semantic capacity and the economical application of the various facets of the fictional art. It is in this regard that Idris's genius comes to the fore, and we become aware that his own experiments with language constitute a real contribution to the development of the short story in modern Arabic literature. Idris himself was always extremely modest about this and even described the process as an unconscious one:

Renewal of writing is a natural, spontaneous and ingrained process which the author pursues unconsciously, because that is actually what art is. Writing is not a process of abandoning one mode and starting another; it's an attempt to get at the real "me"... Put differently, my struggle with myself is the worst one I have; it's a struggle with my own inner, animal self... I try to get close to this inner "me" and write from the inside. Thus, I can say that development in writing does not come about one day through the dissemination of some specific (intellectual) school of thought, even though the experience of others can be useful to you because it shows you how other people view themselves. Development in writing will only occur as the consequence of this struggle with oneself, and of its receptivity to and desire for development.

(Mawaqif 9 [April-June 1970], 51 ff.)

From the beginning of his writing career Idris insisted on the use of the colloquial in written form to convey his dialogue. The descriptions meanwhile were written in a style which observed most of the grammatical and stylistic conventions of the written language.* To be sure, Idris's style was the object of criticism from the beginning of his career. In the Introduction to the collection, *Farahat's Republic,* Taha Husayn, that stalwart foe of the use of the colloquial as a literary language, suggested that Idris should abandon his use of the colloquial while complimenting him on his undoubted contribution to the development of the short story. Another critic, Fu'ad Duwwara, has the following to say about the use of language in the novel, *Taboo:*

I am one of those who have no doubts at all concerning Yusuf Idris's great talent and the excellence of his writings. However, I have the feeling, especially after reading this novel, that he is a lazy writer who does not write or revise his works with the care they deserve ... Among signs of laziness in this novel is a disjointed and poor use of style in a number of places. This is in spite of the fact that the author has demonstrated in numerous other works that he is quite capable of producing a neat and genuinely expressive style.

*(On the Egyptian Novel [Fi al Riwaya al-Misriyya],
Cairo: Dar al-Katib al-'Arabi, 1968, p. 86)*

* There are two excellent studies on Idris's style in English: Jan Beyerl, *The Style of the Modern Arabic Short Story,* Prague, 1971 (this includes linguistic analyses of the writings of other writers also), and S. Somekh, "Language and Theme in the Short Stories of Yusuf Idris," *Journal of Arabic Literature* VI (1975), 89 ff.

At this point in our discussion, we can gain further insight into the questions of the coherence of structure and use of language in Idris's works through another quotation:

> I personally regard the language problem as a burden on me. But I'm very content when writing in Egyptian Collo-quial. . . Personally, I cannot write in the classical written language *(fusha)*. I can do it and it may turn out fine, but at the crucial moment of composition, I am not in a position to choose between what is suitable and what is not. The writing is almost dictated to me. I am the means, not the writer himself. Introducing the force of will here impairs the entire process. Perhaps it is better to interfere later with a conscious mind and through the author himself. (*Mawaqif* 9, ibid.)

From this, it seems clear that Idris relies a great deal on the inspiration of the moment when writing. It is hardly surprising therefore that, of all the possible literary genres, the short story is the one which best suits his genius. In this respect, he would seem to differ widely from his famous colleague, Nagib Mahfuz, who readily admits to being the most methodical writer. His huge *Trilogy (Al-Thulathiyya)*, a group of three novels, involved years of planning and research followed by many years of writing. Furthermore, Mahfuz's writes for a specific number of hours each day and then stops. Everything we know about Yusuf Idris suggests that, when he has an idea, it keeps hold of him until he has finished what he wishes to say. This comparison no doubt contains elements of exaggeration or simplification, but the writings of the two authors seem to bear out its major implication. Mahfuz's works have passed through a number of phases, and yet his mode of writing and especially his themes have changed relatively little. He has continued to reflect the life-style, the values and the aspirations of the middle class of Egyptians to which he himself belongs. This he has done in a grammatically correct style which has made few compromises with the colloquial dialect. Idris, on the other hand, has gradually broadened the scope of his themes and has stretched written literary Arabic to remarkable limits.

In this context, Idris's remark about his discomfort with the written language and his preference for the colloquial is significant. For, as his writing career has developed, his short stories have shown increasing signs of the influence of the colloquial language, both in its structures and its vocabulary. As Somekh points out in his article mentioned above, this does not mean that Idris writes his stories in the colloquial, but rather that he is expanding the manner through which the written language may express accurately (and stimulatingly) the language, the thought processes, the interior monologues, the streams of consciousness of contemporary man, all these being most naturally conceived in the colloquial parlance of the country concerned. In a recent comment, the Egyptian story writer and critic, Sulayman Fayyad, suggests that Idris's ability to use language in this way to illustrate character is one of the main reasons for his mastery of the short story genre; by contrast, he finds Mahfuz's style almost bland by comparison. *(Arabic Books / Kutub Arabiyya / no. 1 [Jan. 1977], 1)*

Yusuf Idris was one of the most famous creative writers in the Arab world this century, and arguably its finest writer of short stories. We have suggested that some of his works show certain flaws, but that is comforting in its own way; the world might well be intolerable with too many Mozarts. Idris's fictional career was seriously impaired over his final years for reasons which have been mentioned above. He left behind a large oeuvre that is both provocative and often extremely moving, works that show a continuing concern for man and his existence on earth, and that arouse both admiration and opposition for their experiments in theme and style. Such was and is the essence of Yusuf Idris.

In the Eye of the Beholder, ed. Roger Allen. Minneapolis: Bibliotheca Islamica, 1978. Introduction, xi-xvi, xx-xxxix [revised].

The Later Stories

P. M. Kurpershoek

Part I. The Message

General

At the end of the fifties and in the early sixties, Idris' approach to the short story underwent a radical change. The simple, realistic depiction of life 'as it is' in the lower strata of rural society and in the slums of Cairo disappears and a more complicated type of story emerges. Gradually setting and characters become more indistinct and universal until his prose approximates to the abstractness of absolute poetry in a short story like *Halawat ar-Ruh* (The Sweetness of the Soul), published in 1970. An atmosphere of pessimism prevails, the protagonists are often given to introspection and fretting, the symbolic representation of moral and political themes supersedes the former outward description and brisk action.

New Emphasis on the Extraordinary

As early as 1957, stories like *ash-Shaikh Shaikha* (The Hermaphrodite), *Tabliyya min as-Sama'* (A Dining-table from Heaven) and *Shaikhukha bi-dun Gunun* (Old Age without Madness) show a less strict adherence to realistic portrayal and an increasing preference for bizarre and sometimes macabre events. The weird friendship between two human monsters of uncertain sex in *ash-Shaikh Shaikha* and the grotesque figure of shaikh 'Ali, the hero of *Tabliyya min as-Sama'*, who threatens to bring Divine wrath down on his village by renouncing his faith, already mark the transition to the later, more fantastic stories.

An even clearer departure from the principles of realism occurs in *Shaikhukha bi-dun Gunun*, so entitled after a legal expression indicating that someone has died a natural death. In this amusing story, a health inspector, whose main task is to issue birth and death certificates, proceeds to examine the remains of Muhammad, one of the 'corpse-washer boys' *(as-subyan al-hanutiyya)*, whom the local undertaker recruits from retired janitors and office messengers, most of whom are sixty-five years and over. On his way the inspector recalls how 'uncle'

Muhammad used to accompany him to the house of the dead, how he struggled to turn the body, raised the legs and vigorously pulled its hair in order to demonstrate that it did not come off, which proved that the man had not been poisoned. Now Muhammad is subjected to the same quick routine. But, as one of the other 'boys' tries to turn the corpse face downwards, the doctor sees 'uncle' Muhammad stir and distinctly hears his stock-phrases: "Be careful, man, may you tumble into your grave. Here I am. If you please, Sir. I turn myself over. But there was no need to take all that trouble, Sir." "I told you so. It's just old age without madness."

Social Morality

Besides this intrusion of the fantastic into the texture of the realistic story, there is a remarkable increase in the moral overtones, as a comparison between 'Ala Asyut (1953), Ahmad al-Maglis al-Baladi (1960) and Sahib Misr (1965) may illustrate. Purport and characters in these three stories are related: they feature vagabonds who are humorous and sensitive despite their poverty and who, after having briefly been in touch with modern civilisation, cheerfully abandon its mixed blessings. But when tracing these similarities, one is struck by the differences in presenting the subject-matter, especially the shift from the scenic representation of social contrasts to overt moralising in frequent asides by the omniscient narrator.

'Ala Asyut (To Asyut) is a sketch-like satire of the way a poor peasant who seeks treatment for his game leg is kicked around by the medical staff of a Cairo hospital. This character of the poverty-stricken, physically handicapped yet brisk provincial turns up again in Ahmad al-Maglis al-Baladi (Ahmad of the Local Council, 1960). But here the emphasis is not so much on social injustice and class differences as on the morally reprehensible and psychologically pernicious effect of the individual quest for material gain and social prestige. Ahmad al-'Uqla, a one-legged barber, Jack of all trades as well as a compulsive traveller, is a hot-tempered person, but kind to a fault and with a knack for doing odd jobs: he has built his own reed shack and, whenever the bridge over the irrigation canal is on the verge of collapse or the pump of the mosque out of order, he can be counted on to do the repairs, even though he himself never goes to the mosque for prayer. He is the one who clears the road of sand-heaps, moves the furniture into the house of the newly-wed and feeds the hungry; but when he in his turn is invited to a meal he bashfully looks away.

His Fall from this state of happy naivety comes when the health inspector of the district confirms to him that it is possible to have an artificial leg fixed free of charge at the Qasr al- 'Aini hospital in Cairo. Thanks to his resourcefulness and tenacity, Ahmad succeeds where the cripple in 'Ala Asyut failed. However, the artificial leg sets in motion a fatal succession of events which deeply changes his attitude to life. He is forced to buy a shoe and stockings to match those fixed to the artificial leg. As a result he has to abstain from horseplay, climbing palm trees, plunging into the canal and sleeping on the ground as he used to do, and this just in order to keep his new outfit clean. He seats his clients in a chair and, instead of running around with his self-carved stick as before, he moves with a slow and dignified pace. When roaming the country, he no longer takes the 'first upper-class seat,' i.e. on the roof of the train, but buys a ticket like other self-respecting passengers, and he even considers purchasing a necktie and braces. For the rest he keeps his purse strings tight in order to save money to buy the few square metres on which his shack stands. Therefore he discontinues his ancient habit of treating friends to unlimited glasses of tea. His aim in life now becomes to settle down and to get married 'like all decent people'. So the ebullient Ahmad, who used to laugh at jokes about his bodily defect, turns into a thin-skinned sour-face with self-important airs. When asked to repair the mosque's pump, he appears willing but actually never does, thinking: "Why should I repair it? I am just like the others who pray without repairing the pump or clearing the road. Why not begin to pray and act like other people, who eat, dress, get married and shield themselves against the blows of fate ?"

Nevertheless the burden of civilisation soon proves too heavy for Ahmad. He disappears for a while, only to turn up again with his wooden stick in place of the artificial leg. His lost innocence is regained. With one leap he comes down from his place on top of the carriage, bouncing and frolicking as in earlier days. Moreover, though his account of what has happened to the artificial leg varies from day to day, always he ends with his habitual stammer: "To hell with it. It was like walking with a broken leg."

Though Ahmad's lineage as a character goes back to the cripple of 'Ala Asyut, and in a sense also to al-Bar'i of al-Umniyya, two anti-heroes who, each in his own way, clash with the modern urban world, the reader is bound to feel that this short story does not merely aim at throwing into comic relief the contrasting values embodied in the cosmopolitan city and the Egyptian village. It is shown that Ahmad renounces one of the attainments of human progress, the artificial leg, because he comes to feel uneasy with a life of selfish and competitive individu-alism, and of regular habits, the leg's unavoidable companion.

Looked at from this angle the story conveys a moral message which is quite different from the social criticism implied in 'Ala Asyut: once man decides to further his own interests regardless of the needs of the community, he inevitably comes into conflict with his fellow-men, a process which ultimately leads to his social isolation. The material advantages thus gained from self-centred conduct are paid for with the loss of the warmth and spontaneity of a more natural, sociable way of life, whereas self-effacement is rewarded with an enviable peace of mind. Hence, the outwardly successful social climber is the one who is really "walking with a broken leg."

In Ahmad al-Maglis al-Baladi Idris achieves an admirable balance between the humorous realism of his early stories and the didacticism of some later works. In Sahib Misr (The Master of Egypt, 1965) Idris presents his views in a less unobtrusive manner. The scene of this story is set at a crossing of two desert roads somewhere between Ismailia and Suez with a military check-point and a tea stall (ghurza) as the only signs of human habitation.

The stall-owner, a vigorous old man named Hasan, shares many characteristics with the hero of *Ahmad al-Maglis al-Baladi*. His love of freedom and zest for life prove incompatible with the drabness of a settled existence. Like Ahmad he prefers to wander the countryside and he puts up his tea stall at remote places because "the profession he had chosen was to serve people where they did not expect it." At this particular crossing he soon makes friends with the soldier on duty, who is so enraptured by the innumerable stories of the old man that he comes to like his company even better than that of his mistresses in the city. But his thriving business attracts ever more tea stall proprietors to the crossing; the usual professional jealousy manifests itself and soon "the stench of the rotten human order" vitiates the air. Haunted by the ghost of civilisation, there is only one course open to Hasan. Turning a deaf ear to the supplications of the soldier, he loads his chattels on a passing truck and leaves for a new, unknown destiny.

Sahib Misr is a rather long story of thirty-five pages, yet Hasan seems less alive to us than the cripple of *'Ala Asyut*, a short story of not more than three pages. The tea-seller is not so much a character as the incarnation of what Idris holds to be the supreme human virtues. The tedium resulting from the icon-like idealisation of the characters is further increased by the incessant homilies so placed as to break the thread of narration. It is hard to avoid the impression that Idris uses Hasan as a peg, thinly disguised as a character, on which to hang an inventory of his moral ideas and pseudo-scientific theories about the evolutionary processes that transform the "centres of egoism *(marakiz al-ananiyya)*" in the human brain and "the base Self *(adh-dhat as-saghir)*".

The adage 'blessed are the poor of spirit', so harmoniously integrated in the texture of *Ahmad al-Maglis al-Baladi*, is elaborated upon in *Sahib Misr* in a ponderous digression. Ahmad has a man's craving for individual security and indifference to the needs of his fellows, which in Idris' opinion is the root of all evil. This is personified by the multitude of believers who, while paying lip-service to the teachings of religion, in fact only seek shelter from the misfortunes they dread. The hypocrisy of those who content themselves with the sterile observance of religious duties is brought to light by Ahmad's near-conversion, so that when he considers joining in prayer, he revises his altruistic habits and no longer volunteers to repair the mosque's pump, a job he had never thought twice about before.

There is no such subtle intertwinement of two levels of meaning in the corresponding passage in *Sahib Misr*: "Good old 'uncle' Hasan did not entertain such petty ideas. One wonders in what spaciousness his mind has its abode and what freedom his thoughts enjoy. What absolute sense of security protected him? Indeed, to obtain that security people move heaven and earth and entrench themselves in shelters and catacombs, seeking protection against known and unknown enemies, the vicissitudes of fortune, disease and treachery. The harder they search the more they are afraid, for they perceive that there is no effective remedy or refuge. And the more they fear the others, the more they frighten them, till all grow so apprehensive and terror-stricken that they run riot in a blazing frenzy . . . Unfortunately not everybody is like 'uncle' Hasan, so one day the problems will become intolerable.''

Political and Social Criticism

Political and ideological themes abound in Idris' short story works, but usually they have to be unearthed from under a mound of symbolism. If in *Mu'ahadat Sina'* (The Sinai Accord, 1963) the issue is plainly stated, it is probably because it concerns Egypt's position in relation to the superpowers and not the internal situation; but in a story like *al-'Amaliyya al-Kubra* (The Major Operation, 1969) the hidden sense can only be inferred, and in order to grasp the full meaning of *A Kan La Budd Ya Lili An Tudi' an-Nur?* (Was it Really Necessary to Turn On the Light, Lili?, 1970) one has to rely on the glosses of the author.

In one of the early political stories, *ar-Ra's* (The Head, 1958), Idris endeavoured to lay down a 'politico-biological law of leadership.' It tells how a boy discovers a school of fast-swimming fish in an irrigation canal. Surprised at the steadfastness of their course, he decides to test the fish. Indeed he repeatedly succeeds in luring away the leader of the school by feeding him bread-crumbs; yet this hardly influences the speed of the school. After a little confusion, a new leader emerges, changes occur in the other positions in the lead, and the fish resume their course. Moreover the boy notices that the former leader, once he has swallowed the breadcrumb, usually tries to regain his place at the head but is pushed back by the others and eventually has to content himself with being relegated to the tail of the school. The theory implied in this analogy with the animal world is that the human community instinctively recognises the qualities of leadership and pushes the possessor of these qualities to the fore (*ifraz gama'i*). When his devotion diminishes and he gives precedence to his individual interests, he automatically loses his mission (*risala*), and the command then passes to another member of the community.

Ar-Ra's makes good reading because its theoretical content has been harmoniously integrated into a poetical description of the quiet and charm of the Egyptian country side. On the other hand, in stories like *Qissa dhi-s-Sawt an-Nahil* (A Story with a Thin Voice, 1963), *Mu'gizat al-'Asr* (The Miracle of Our Time, 1966), *al-Aurta* (The Aorta, 1965) and *Hammal al-Karasi* (The Chair Bearer, 1969) the political bias of the author shows through so distinctly under the story-telling veneer that they seem rather to be intended as fictional illustrations of the political ideas that Idris has outlined in his journalistic writings than as artistic creations.

The first of these is a story Idris avowedly wrote in a possessed state of mind; the 'stream of consciousness' technique is employed to expose the reactionary mentality of the ruling classes under the *ancien regime*. The anxious ruminations of the inner voice (*al-'aql al-batin*) are so rendered as to make it a virtual self-accusation. The building in which the narrator lives follows the social stratification of Egypt, as appears from the story-teller's comment as regards his neighbours: "The people overhead are very nice, we get along well with them. But downstairs there are lots of people, about fifty to one room. They swarm all over the places like ants . . . and their wide open mouths swallow up whole water-melons, everything." The people downstairs symbolise the Egyptian revolutionary masses. He is scared of the hatred in their eyes and complains that they behave as if they alone have a right to the country: "Every day a new nationalisation . . . I don't care twopence for Egypt anymore, it has been robbed by thieves, or do they deserve another name ?"

Further on we learn that the narrator, who is represented as a paranoiac reactionary, had forcibly been given an injection with a serum concocted from the eye-fluid of the masses downstairs. A similar curious comparison of a certain political attitude to a mental disease requiring medical treatment occurs in *Mu'gizat al-'Asr*, where the hero discovers a new technique for brainwashing by using a chemical called 'anti-capital.'

Qissa dhi-s-Sawt an-Nahil smacks strongly of political propaganda, but its display of revolutionary rhetoric also provides Idris with a cover for smuggling in some trenchant criticism on the regime's high-handed way of running the country. According to the mechanism that is consistently applied throughout the story, the following passage amounts to a sort of inverted flattery, yet one cannot help feeling that for once it is the author who is speaking his own mind: "He (the leader of the people downstairs) thinks the world of himself. He thinks that he can do anything he wants to. He thinks that the people are a loaf of bread which he can cut into ever smaller pieces till he has finished it. He wants to turn us, human beings, into animals with no will in order to herd and bully us at his pleasure."

But Idris dropped whatever aesthetic considerations still restrained him in *Mu'gizat al-'Asr* (The Miracle of Our Time, 1966), a fictionalised survey of his moral and political ideas. The story opens and closes with an apocalyptic panorama of the collective hysteria which Idris seems to view as the logical consequence of the capitalist system. The horrid scene unfolds on the beaches near Alexandria where a seething mass of people grapples in search of a man, the 'miracle of our time,' a pocket-sized hop-o'-my-thumb named Nussnuss. The central part of the story is devoted to the adventures of this dwarf. A brilliant student who took a doctor's degree in fourteen different subjects, Nussnuss fails to find employment because of his Lilliputian stature. Thinking he is unwanted, he throws himself from the roof of the Mugamma' building, a huge structure in Cairo's central square that groups many government departments and is notorious for its Kafkaesque bureaucracy. However, thanks to his lack of weight, he flutters down like a feather and lands unharmed. For the same reason, he stays afloat when he jumps into the Nile. Carried along by this stream of life and hope, he takes courage and decides to accept the struggle to live. Thereupon he makes countless inventions and discovers solutions for every known and unknown problem of humanity.

But again his size (*hagm*, a noun that also connotes the social weight one carries) stands in the way of recognition, and his attempts to rouse interest in his scientific discoveries meet only with derision and insult. When he barely escapes from being fed by a peasant to a donkey, he leaves the earth in a self-built spacecraft and heads for another planet, one that is inhabited by a people equally puny in size. Here he is finally valued at his true worth, and his genius soon changes the planet into a paradise.

The planet-dwellers adore him as their saviour, but it is nostalgia that in due course drives him back to Egypt. There he vanishes in his native country's crowds. However, a fleet of spaceships soon approaches Earth looking for Nussnuss. Seized by panic, America prepares itself to receive the invaders with a shower of atomic bombs, but the astronauts land safely in Switzerland. There the world hears for the first time the story of the Egyptian scientist, and only then does a belated search start on the beaches of Alexandria, reportedly one of Nussnuss' favourite spots. Within this fictional framework a great number of digressions and generalities aim at facilitating the understanding of the theories the story is meant to illustrate. The need for moral reform is brought out by the contrast between the bleak prospects for human civilisation if the present free-for-all continues and the breath-taking progress which is to be expected from the spread of a more reasonable mentality.

The desolation of the existing conditions is reflected in the opening scene: "It was a winter day. The sun was yellow and its sickly rays made the sand look like one stretch of anaemic, pale colour." The beach is full of people, or rather "throngs of human flesh." Their great numbers only enhance their individual sense of alienation (al-ghurba): "The crowd was like a halter, about to be tightened around your neck." The dissensions which flare up as a result of the incessant jostling in the groups have a depressing effect: "The people stand in a stooping posture or they lie listlessly on the ground. All are too preoccupied with what seems an excruciating inner crisis to give you any attention. Their hands gesticulate nervously, they are engaged in fierce arguments which sound like gunshots;" others who thrive in this atmosphere laugh up their sleeves. The hunt for the neglected genius brings out people's lowest instincts. Each premature cry of joy is followed by a general scramble, and in the rough-and-tumble all are indiscriminately swept along: "Brawling, wrestling, crying, wailing, torn throngs of people."

The central part of the story, Nussnuss' quest for recognition, gives Idris ample scope to display his contempt for certain social categories, such as bureaucrats, capitalists, rack-rent landlords, highbrow intellectuals, the same who are stigmatised in the diaries. University professors are shown as an exceptionally obdurate caste. The integral approach to science of Nussnuss, a universal scholar who, like Ibn Sina' and Ibn Rushd, is seeking ultimate truths, proves the undesirability of over-specialisation. But instead of drawing a lesson from this, the professors plunge themselves into new hair-splitting discussions about the "Nussnussian phenomenon."

As a result of the divorce between these sterile, purely theoretical debates at the university and the social reality outside its walls, Nussnuss himself is left out in the cold when he applies for a job: "At private meetings with him the professors who spoke in such glowing terms of his genius only shrugged their shoulders, explaining that their hands were tied and pointing out the circumstances which prevented them from assigning a job to him."

In an interview, Idris characterised Nussnuss as the little man, the *farfur*, who builds up what the bigwigs pull down and who, in spite of his energy and capabilities, often remains unemployed, or is exploited, and in the end gets lost in the sands of life. But the story itself rather reveals Nussnuss as the underestimated, truly human and creative element that lies repressed and sealed up inside most people: "The miracle of the age, that small being which is present in our life from the very beginning. But since it is so small, all pass it without feeling any excitement or paying it the slightest attention."

Like al-Hadidi in *Lughat al-Ay Ay*, people are too engrossed in their own worries to notice the voice of reason and compassion: "We lost the free exercise of our own vision . . . The only reflections of our inner self which we (choose to) perceive are those that mirror our own interests, ideas and dreams. We have lost the pristine faculty of absorbing what is outside us . . . We just look for things which serve to show and to prove that we are right." In this perspective, the concluding words of the story take on their full meaning: "Perhaps (Nussnuss) is in your pocket, you never know."

Idris never tired of emphasising that as a prerequisite for any improvement, all forms of iniquity and exploitation should be eradicated. The absurdity of the social situation in Egypt, where in spite of the Revolution a minority maintains a leisurely life-style at the expense of the poor masses, is the subject of the stories *al-Aurta* (The Aorta, 1965) and *Hammal al-Karasi* (The Chair Bearer, 1969).

As in many of the stories Idris wrote during this period *al-Aurta* suffers from being encumbered with much abstruse symbolism and quasi-scientific theorising. Nevertheless, the story has the merit of showing also the reverse side of the wrong done to the poor. 'Abduh, the victimised hero of the story, submits passively to his fate. "He was thin and beggarly (*ghalban*). Never a glint of defiance shone in his eyes, he never faced anyone with the intention of asserting or defending himself. He was a kind man, kind in a colourless, negative way. Furthermore he was afflicted with a double hernia, and when alone he used to sing sentimental *mawwals* ".

Like *Mu'gizat al-'Asr*, the story opens with a scene which expresses moral chaos. The narrator nervously wanders amidst a huddle of people on a vast square. They run hither and thither as if in search of a starting-point—that is, probably, a guiding principle—for their real pursuit in life. Again, the gathering of large crowds only serves to accentuate human divisions (*at-tagammu' li-t-tafarruq*), and the continuous hustling causes explosions of blind violence. A scapegoat is found in the person of 'Abduh: "A petty thief who only steals a few piastres when he is desperately in need of them and even then he takes as little as possible. When caught, he is so bewildered that he can only stammer and swear false oaths. And woe betide the man who deals severely with him, for then he starts to cry and nauseates you."

Incensed by a new accusation of theft against 'Abduh, people form a menacing circle around him. 'Abduh feebly protests that whatever coins he possessed disappeared in the hospital where they have just operated on his aorta, a drastic step because the doctors diagnosed in 'Abduh a virulent contagious disease. Naturally his assailants take the story as one of his usual transparent fabrications: "The most important thing to all of us, none excepted, was that he had the money and, no doubt, kept it hidden somewhere on his body, for 'Abduh did not possess any other hiding-place in the world."

Accordingly it is decided to search him. But when they try to take off his gallabiyya, they find that it is glued to his body. Undismayed, they then hang 'Abduh from a meat-hook of a butcher's shop, amidst the slaughtered sheep, and proceed to strip off the faded garment "in the same manner as a rabbit is skinned." Under the gallabiyya, his chest and abdomen appear thickly swathed in white bandages. Since his oversize purse contains no more than five piastres, it is assumed that the rest of the money lies concealed somewhere in the surgical dressings. So, they carefully begin to unroll the bandages while 'Abduh's cries of distress gradually die down till he silently watches "as if he also with every winding expected the money to come out." Suddenly the end of the bandages is reached and all look aghast at the emptiness behind them.

"'Abduh was completely naked. A very long wound stretched from his chest till deep down in his abdomen. Both the chest and the abdomen were hollow as if they had been emptied of all their organs. The aorta dangled from the place of the heart, looking like a bamboo oboe. Thick, long, whitish and broken, it swung back and forth in his abdomen like a pendulum."

Here, as in other stories, Idris unfolds his general ideas against the specific background of his medical experience. *Al-Aurta* states that those who are in a position to know the causes of 'Abduh's ill-health, foremost his poverty, and who are supposed to cure him, in fact bring him to the verge of ruin through their indifference and disastrously mistaken policies. Left in that condition, 'Abduh is destroyed by the greed of the others who fail to understand that his powers of resistance have been fatally undermined.

In *Hammal al-Karasi* (The Chair Bearer, 1969) the plight of the downtrodden is treated in a different vein. As in the two preceding stories the discrepancy between the actual living conditions of most Egyptians and Idris' ideal of an egalitarian society is brought out symbolically by the description of a fantastic event. But whereas *Mu'gizat al-'Asr* comes close to science fiction in its evocation of a world governed by reason and justice, and *al-Aurta* exposes the absurd and undeserved maltreatment of the poor, *Hammal al-Karasi* represents Egyptian man, enslaved and oppressed since time immemorial, in his mythical, tragic grandeur.

The story simply describes the entrance and exit of a man carrying a tremendously large chair. The stage is again a square, this time specifically situated in the centre of Cairo. The man and his load are described as definitely Pharaonic. The chair is upholstered with leopard skin, its rear part is covered with silk, and the four legs end in gilt hoofs. What appears as a fifth leg is a gaunt man, wearing no more than a canvas skirt, who sweats profusely. Like Idris' favourite characters in the earlier realistic stories, he has a kindly, wrinkled face.

Questioned by the narrator, the man tells that he has carried the chair ever since the Nile has flowed through Egypt. Hearing this answer, the narrator invites him to put the chair down: "Chairs are made to carry people, not to be carried by them." But the man remains adamant. He replies that only an order from the ruler who saddled him with the chair, or from one of his descendants, can discharge him from the burden. The narrator confesses that he has no connections in ruling circles, but a small sign on the front of the chair informs him that it belongs to its bearer and his offspring. Overjoyed, the intellectual imparts the revolutionary message to the toil-worn carrier. But this enthusiasm fails to spark off a similar reaction. The man sullenly declares that he cannot read and that he places confidence only in an official warrant. Then, with a curt "People like you only hold me up," he proceeds on his way, watched by the stunned would-be liberator who is left wondering how to break the vicious circle of ignorance, suspicion and fatalism that keeps this beast of burden in servitude.

The Six-Day War and Nasser

A number of other short stories, most of them written between 1968 and 1971 and collected in *an-Naddaha* and *Bait min Lahm*, have a more immediate political bearing. *An-Nuqta* (The Point, 1968) was written when Idris' depression was at its worst. It is an almost static picture of a person standing motionless on a railway track which curves through the wilderness so as to encompass the entire globe. The whole decor is of a torpid bleakness, reflecting the stationary grief of the spectator: "A grief arising no doubt from what he saw, for it was definitely the sight of something approaching its end. The end of the world, the end of life on earth, the end of joy and hope."

Idris later explained that objectively there was not a ray of hope to be descried after the war of 1967, but since he had reached ultimate despair, he realised that whatever the future would bring could only be for the better: "I did not wait for the train to get on it, all I did was wait for it, or rather for the moment that suddenly— I was certain that it would take me completely by surprise—the head of the train would appear over the horizon. Perhaps its colour would be black, but it certainly would emerge."

This certitude of the man who scans the horizon is merely based on an inference: "Till then no train had passed . . . There was absolutely no relation between me and the train, except that I saw the rails. And where rails lie there must also run a train." Under such circumstances the mere emergence of a point on the horizon is a life-giving event: "That moment, at a thousand years distance from the next or following one, solely that moment keeps me attached to life."

In *al-'Amaliyya al-Kubra* (The Major Operation, 1969) Idris retrieved his old extroversion and incisiveness. His first reaction to the traumatic experience of the Six-Day War was, naturally enough, to withdraw into extreme pessimism and brooding introspection. *Al-'Amaliyya al-Kubra* marks the end of this phase as it constitutes his first attempt to analyse the causes of the defeat. The story shows that Idris thinks all blame for the disaster should be laid with Nasser, personified by Doctor Adham, whose vanity, despotism and reckless handling of the crisis are painted in glaring colours. 'Abd ar-Ra'uf, a medical student who has much in common with the young Idris, rues the day that he made Dr. Adham his idol, but otherwise does not seem to hold himself responsible.

'Abd ar-Ra'uf is the most accomplished, or at any rate the most ambitious student of Dr. Adham, who is the head of the section, the Dean of the Faculty, Counsellor to the Ministry of Health and the most reputed surgeon in the hospital. As a real surgeon Dr. Adham is a short-tempered man with prima-donna airs, who in the operating theatre puts on his act as if on stage. In his own domain he rules supreme. His assistants are but "instruments in the grip of his will," and "the reputation of Professor Adham as a merciless president (of the section) matched his fame as an excellent surgeon." 'Abd ar-Ra'uf, who hopes to build up a career under the patronage of Dr. Adham, considers him "the leader and the master brain . . . the great professor, his mentor, a real scholar." Therefore he puts himself out to please the surgeon, for "the approval of Professor Adham meant peace of mind and the approval of God, God incarnate in all His Power, Bounty and Perfection."

A vainglorious man, Dr. Adham has a predilection for rare cases. "He did not so much practise surgery in order to cure people but rather as an art in its own right, adding ever-new lustre to his glory." His special interest is in a woman who has been hospitalised with a lame leg, but in whom he has diagnosed cancer in the cartilage of the vertebral column. In doing this he did not rely on the outcome of an X-ray examination because, in his opinion, that would reduce surgery to a mere technician's job. Instead he decides to check his diagnosis by operating on the woman, not an unusual practice in his section.

At first the operation runs smoothly, only Dr. Adham's probing hand does not feel the expected tumor. A sample of the tissue is taken to the laboratory, but the specialist is not in and when finally tracked down he proves unable to analyse the substance. When his fury has spent itself, the surgeon stubbornly decides to go on with the operation: "What do you think of it, the wound is still open, the tumor is not big. It is easily removed."

Since no one ever dares to question his opinion, everything is put ready for the big operation while Dr. Adham withdraws into a corner of the room to smoke. Then a strange unconcern comes over the team and its leader. Preparations are made in a slapdash way: instruments are sterilised with alcohol, an oxygen bottle that does not open is kicked over, and it appears that the bloodgroup of the patient has not yet been determined. Even before the first drop of blood has flown into her artery, the surgeon loses patience and sets to work. But while trying to dislodge the tumor from the spine, his scalpel slips and cuts into the aorta. With might and main the bleeding is stopped and as soon as Dr. Adham has regained his composure, he declares: "The successful surgeon keeps his sangfroid under unforeseen circumstances, even when the aorta is hit. Surgery is a matter of nerves. Those who do not have strong nerves, they'd better look for another job, my dear fellows. As you saw, a problem like this is easily solved. We stopped the bleeding and the next step is to sew up the wound."

But eroded by the tumor, the wall of the great artery proves too fragile to support the stitches. As they struggle to ligature the aorta, it snaps completely, releasing an enormous fountain of blood. It spouts up from the open abdomen, staining the antiseptic masks and blinding those who wear spectacles. Even the white ceiling gets spattered with blood. "So much blood, one would say that ten men were bleeding at the same time. Amazing that its only source was this skinny, unconscious woman."

In the ensuing chaos, all medical rules are abandoned: "All available hands reached out for the abdomen of the patient—to hell with sterilisation—and finally, with the aid of a huge pack of cotton and under the pressure of eight hands the impetuous deluge was dammed."

Though obviously the fate of the woman is sealed, Dr. Adham gives orders for all the blood stored up in the first-aid centre to be brought and patches up the cut-off aorta with an artery which he removes from the thigh. His instructions are dutifully carried out, but in their heart the assistants have lost all faith in his ability to cope with the situation. For 'Abd ar-Ra'uf, "reality had turned into a nightmare in which the people and things around him appeared as mere symbolic figures."

Five hours after what had begun as a simple exploratory operation, the patient is dying. Yet Dr. Adham refuses to be impressed. Blaming the lack of proper thread and needles and the absence of air-conditioning for the fiasco he concludes: "She would have died from the tumor anyway. But science has gained by it and Egypt as well, never before this kind of operation has been performed here. As you see, the operation came off well. Look, the woman is still alive!" 'Abd ar-Ra'uf takes a different view: "Things went wrong from the day that the professor began to practise surgery for its own sake. Ever since that time, operations and patients, mostly poor defenceless people, became the arena where he demonstrated his prowess and mastery."

As in other stories mentioned in this chapter, the denouement seems primarily designed to point the moral and therefore leaves an impression of undue artificiality. Ordered to watch by the patient, together with the nurse on duty, 'Abd ar-Ra'uf releases his corked-up emotions and anguish by cracking cynical jokes and finally by copulating with the nurse in front of the dying woman.

Apart from the obvious similarities between al- 'Amaliyya al-Kubra and al-Aurta, there is also one crucial difference. 'Abduh, though aware of the danger, meekly bows to his slaughterers. In al-'Amaliyya al-Kubra, on the other hand, the entire responsibility lies with Dr. Adham, whose unjustifiable decision to embark upon a major operation without prior consultation with the patient constitutes a flagrant breach of confidence. The parallel between the surgeon's crime and Nasser's ill-fated brinkmanship in 1967 leaps to the eye, and one cannot but express one's astonishment that the similitude escaped the attention of the censors who allowed the story to be published in al-Ahram. The exaggerated picture of the confusion, the monstrous incompetence of the surgeon who piles one blunder on another, the seas of blood lost by the emaciated woman, in addition to some astutely concealed semantic clues, make it abundantly clear that the woman who is being sacrificed to the ambitions of Dr. Adham personifies Egypt. The picture shows the Egyptian people, in particular the lower classes, as always carrying the brunt of suffering caused by bungling politicians.

Idris takes Nasser equally severely to task for his despotic rule in the short stories *al-Khud 'a* and *ar-Rihla*. *Al-Khud 'a* (The Deception, I969) is a scathing satire on Nasser's omnipresence in the form of portraits in public buildings, in the press and so on, and through the interference of his security services with the private lives of citizens. In this story, official meddlesomeness and the personality cult round Nasser take the shape of the obtrusive head of a camel—Nasser's first name, Gamal, is derived from the same root as the word for camel (*gamal*)— which pops up in the oddest places, from between the curtains of the shower, from the newspaper, in the bus, in bed between the intertwined bodies of two lovers, and in offices from the wall above the door of the director's room, where the camel displays two tight-shut, serried rows of strong teeth, exactly like some official portraits of Nasser.

The camel's impertinence throws the narrator into a rage: "I revolt and refuse what the Revolution wants me to do (i.e. to idolise Nasser)." The ubiquity of the head extends back to the past and into the future: "At times I see it watching my mother when she delivered me or my father when he begot me. And sometimes when looking at the future, I perceive it through piles of projects and plans."

Unlike the narrator, most people have however gradually grown accustomed to the head's appearing everywhere. What is more, it has become such a standard feature of daily life that its disappearence would seriously disrupt the usual course of things: "What a disaster and a loss that would be! Which way to turn, for with us things have gone so far that we do not live by our free own will but because he is looking down upon us whenever we set ourselves to do some work or whenever we feel an emotion stir in us. If we were not constantly aware of his gaze, we would not undertake anything.

Ar-Rihla (The Journey, I970), one of those that Idris terms his prophetic stories, is the monologue of a person who makes a trip by car with, at his side, a dead body. Idris asserts that the story is to be considered a synopsis of his spiritual journey with Nasser of whose approaching end he seems to have had a premonition. This explanation corresponds with the scattered remarks about the features of the dead man and the whole tenor of the monologue.

The attitude of the driver towards his lifeless passenger fluctuates between awe, repugnance and affection, while his wistful tone betrays the light nostalgia of someone who looks back upon a wound-up love-hate relation: "Lean on me, it doesn't matter. How many times didn't I rely on you." But in retrospect the less pleasant memories prevail. Most of all he reproaches the man for having repeatedly encroached upon his freedom: "You are the only person in the world I used to fear. You were always present in our house, you tied me and pulled (the cord) taut . . . Why did we differ? Why did you press me and insist that I must renounce my own opinion and adopt your point of view? And why did I always revolt and why did I loathe you sometimes? Why I now and then wished you dead in order to regain my freedom?"

P. M. Kurpershoek, *The Short Stories of Yusuf Idris*, Leiden: E. J. Brill, 1981, pp. 125-30 and 144-58.

Questions on the World of Yusuf Idris's Short Stories

Sabry Hafez

1. Introduction

The short story. . . is the real gateway to the creative world of this great writer. Yusuf Idris began his writing career with the short story, and he has continued to devote a great deal of attention to it right up to the present day. Moving on from the short story, Yusuf Idris has also made contributions to drama and the novel, but he has done so in a way that enables one to say — and here I do not wish to anticipate the critical commentary below — that, in writing works in these other genres, he continues to use the methods and vision of a short story writer.

Anyone acquainted with Yusuf Idris's artistic world can appreciate that the origins of many of his plays and novels are to be found in short stories written earlier. And if only this were the sole reason for suggesting that the short story is the primary means of access to the dramatic and novelistic parts of Yusuf Idris's output! But there are others as well. Among them we would note that Idris's artistic and intellectual development is reflected most obviously in the short story genre; that the significant contributions he has made to our Arabic literary heritage on the twin levels of vision and structure serve to emphasize the importance of this genre in his output; and that his continuing emphasis on this particular literary genre has brought significant benefits in his contributions to other literary genres as well. The nine short story collections that Idris has written from 1954 till the present day [1974] can be used to illustrate the major issues that are dealt with in his story-world and to pinpoint the central themes they contain. . . .

When Yusuf Idris arrived on the short story scene in Egypt with the publication of his first collection, *The Cheapest Nights*, the genre had already had more than thirty years of development and maturation. The process of establishing the genre in Arabic literature had involved a number of important endeavors, beginning with the "New School" in the 1920s right up to the courageous experiments of Yusuf al-Sharuni in the late '40s and early '50s; in between come such eminent figures as Yahya Haqqi, Mahmud al-Badawi, Najib Mahfuz, Sa'd Makkawi, and

45

others. Even so, the emergence of Yusuf Idris remains a major landmark in the
genre's process of development and maturation right up to the present. . . .

2. The First Five Collections

Yusuf Idris's stories placed the genre firmly on the road towards development
and further maturation. In the space of five years Idris published five short story
collections: *The Cheapest Nights* (1954), *Farhat's Republic* (1956), *Isn't That
So?* (1957), *The Hero* (1957), and *A Matter of Honor* (1958). At this point Idris
was writing prolifically and with great sensitivity, as though he was aware that
he had a task to fulfill. In spite of the large number of stories, he never repeated
himself, nor did he rely on the experiences of other writers. . . . It's true that from
a reading of the stories in these first collections we come to realize that he is under
the influence of the mighty Chekov, reflecting the methods, the perception, and
the vision of the great Russian author. I use the words "under the influence" rather
than "imitates" because genuinely great writers never imitate others. Even so,
they may never realize the extent to which the logic, technique, and conceptions
of other writers infiltrate their subconscious. Because he is such a great writer,
Yusuf Idris soon escapes any Chekovian influence and separates himself from his
great predecessor. Idris discovers his own combination of ideas and expression
and embarks on the areas of concept and structure, in language and world-view.
Once we come to recognize this method and the different adventures on which he
has embarked, we begin to appreciate the features of his world as presented to us
in these first five collections that Idris published in one burst and almost yearly.

We will start our analysis with these five collections because they form a
single structural unit. This comes about not only because they were written so
close together and on the basis of a single short story concept, but also because
they serve to reflect the predominant facets of Yusuf Idris's world. They can be
of help in defining the features of the solution that he was able to offer to the crisis
in the development of the short story in Egypt, one that is manifested in a new and
profound understanding of the idea of realism. . . .

These five collections are . . . a clearly defined stage in Yusuf Idris's story
writing career, since with the collection, *The End of the World* (1961), he begins
to explore entirely new horizons and embarks on a new phase in his writing career
as regards both concepts and structure. Needless to say, none of this occurs
outside the realm of the modern Arabic literary movement in general and its
Egyptian component in particular, with its proclivities for development, experimentation with new styles, and exploration of untrodden paths. All this need not
be underlined. With that, let us now examine the features of Yusuf Idris's world
as presented in these five initial collections.

3. The Broad Range of His Story World

The first thing we notice about these first collections is that, in spite of the fact
that the people in them tend to belong to the lower or middle-class of society, the
world-view they create is very broad indeed and the scope of the experiences

involved is equally wide. On the evidence of these collections, Yusuf Idris does not concentrate on a narrow group of issues, as other writers often do . . . He prefers to range freely over a wide variety of themes so as not to repeat himself and be restricted by his subject matter. He writes clearly about a number of different experiences. He roams the worlds of the village and city with the same simplicity and openness. The village may be in the provinces or along the shore; it may be a large community or the confined environment of the country estate; the village may be proud of its long and illustrious past, or else it may be some hapless and unimportant hamlet. The simplicity with which the author moves through all these different venues is repeated in the different images of the city. This ranges from Cairo, large and menacing, to the provincial capital hovering on the brink between rural and urban life. All this spatial movement is accompanied by a wealth of sensual touches and a profound awareness of the experiences he is talking about and the characters with whom he is dealing. As a result, we get the impression that Yusuf Idris's stories represent a dose of sincerity where phrases interact to give the story a special flavor and intensity.

In his short stories Najib Mahfuz focuses on two strata of Cairo's broad social world: intellectuals and the inhabitants of the popular quarters. Yahya Haqqi chooses to concentrate on characters from Upper Egypt and on characters from the popular quarters. Mahmud al-Badawi tends to focus on the world of civil servants sent to work in remote cities, while Yusuf al-Sharuni and Edward al-Kharrat concentrate on the frustrations and alienation of the intellectual. Yusuf Idris uses all these worlds in portraying his principal and ancillary characters. Beyond that, he explores a totally new area within all these different worlds and offers insights into a domain that the Egyptian short story has never broached before, complete sections of life in the village, the provincial town, and the city. . . .

In *The Cheapest Nights*, for example, we find a peasant laboring under the burden of crushing poverty. He is trying as best he can to escape its clutches but finds that the burden is so great that he is unable to get out of the vicious circle which will drag him yet further into the abyss ("The Cheapest Nights"). We meet a young girl who against her will finds herself snatched from the dreams of childhood in order to spend her days of innocence as a servant in the homes of upper-class folk in the city, watching all the while as children frolic to their hearts' content in the streets ("A Stare"). We encounter a teacher who is burdened on the one hand by family problems and on the other by a group of fiendish students. In this story a side plot consists of the way in which a young student feels encouraged by the words from this teacher who is himself overwhelmed by his students but finds himself driven to stick things out and change his lifestyle ("The Certificate"). . . . We find a starving Bedouin who, in spite of his intense hunger pangs, refuses to have his honor impugned. He is therefore forced to accept an unfair bet as a result of which he suffers severe stomach cramps ("The Bet"). . . . We meet the shaykh of a mosque who is forced by need to agree to a deal with the undertaker whereby he accepts a fixed price for conducting prayers over the bodies of the dead he is burying ("The Funeral"). . . .We come to smile grimly as we pursue the details of the peculiar trip that Sergeant Shubrawi takes. Such is his longing to visit Cairo that he finds himself involved in accompanying a crazy woman, Zubayda, to Cairo. As we follow the details of the journey, we smile as the trip turns from a lifelong dream (as reflected in the final sentence, "I would sell my life for an hour in Cairo") to a horrendous nightmare. He finds himself hounded both by regulations and the crazy woman he is escorting; he eventually gets tired of the whole thing ("A Trip"). . . .We encounter 'Abduh who has gone from one job to another and is now unemployed. He is forced to sell his own blood in order just to carry on ("Employment"). In "The Machine" we see how Usta Muhammad is brought low. After working on a wheat-grinding machine for twenty years, he is fired by the machine's owner. Initially he watches in glee as a succession of other people hired by the owner are unable to operate the machine, but his delight turns to an outburst of anger when the machine lets him down; a young man arrives who is able to get it working.

4. The Range in Spatial and Temporal Dimensions.

All these examples culled from the very first collection illustrate the variety noted above: the aristocrat living a life of luxury and the poor in their destitution; the young child, the school student, and the elderly; the peasant, carpenter, policeman, teacher, doctor, officer, lawyer, patrolman, bedouin, shaykh, and laborer. . . .Such range and variety as this will not be found in any other Egyptian writer. Even though his primary focus may be the middle and lower classes, he still manages to encompass all the societal dimension of current Egyptian reality and to incorporate figures from every level of society in the provinces and cities.

This variety in social stratum and individual experience is not the only indicator of this great writer's breadth of range. There are a number of others. The most significant is that with Idris the range goes beyond the broad spatial dimension that we have just described and extends into the realm of time. I do not imply by this the historical mode of time, something of relatively minor significance in Idris's short story, but rather that the tableaux created by his stories cover the whole Egyptian day. Yusuf Idris's day is not all daylight as is the case with Yahya Haqqi, nor is it all nighttime as we find with Edward al-Kharrat. Idris's stories contain variations on combinations of day and night: the vile emotions of daytime, the subtle diversions of the night; the cruel events of daytime and the gloomy dark of night; the overpowering gleam of the midday sun and the pale light of sunset announcing the day's demise and the onset of night with its remorseless gloom. These variations on day and night serve to expand the scope of Idris's fictional world. We find that the gloom of night kills off man's craving for freedom, the same dread night when resentments are nursed and feelings of failure and poverty are intensified. Then we encounter daytime, with its brilliant, clear light, a time for hard labor and crude ritual, a daytime full of misery that harbors terrors far worse than all the obscure worries of the night, worse precisely because they are the relentless terrors of daytime, of a reality that cannot be changed, a reality full of failure, frustration, and uncertainty. . . .

5. The Nightmare World and Ambiguity of Vision.

The hero in Yusuf Idris's stories from these five collections is overwhelmed, frustrated, and weighed down by a long tradition of oppression and persecution. In reading these five collections we have a clear sense of this oppressed human being looking over our shoulders, however different the individual features or experiences being presented may be. True enough, the hero may be frustrated in one story, overwhelmed in another, a failure in another, and powerless in yet another. However, in spite of the variations, the unifying factor in all of them is failure or defeat. Defeat is a cruel word; it may be an impossible concept in the context of mankind's experience. As Hemingway says: "You can crush a human being, but you'll never defeat him." And yet it still manages to rear its ugly head from within the images conjured up within the fictional world of this great writer. . . .

Before I go into detail about these elements of frustration, oppression, and defeat as they emerge from Idris's stories at this phase in his writing career, I shall talk about the nightmarish sense of reality that is to be found in a large number of the stories. Discussion of this sense of mood will serve as a useful introduction to the analysis of frustration, oppression, and defeat. In many of the stories we get the impression that moments of human discovery or suffering serve to transform ordinary trivialities into weird, nightmarish entities that crush mankind into the dust. The broad expanse of an open space then becomes a gloomy cave filled with failure and frustration. "The Cheapest Nights" is a good example: for its hero, 'Abd al-Karim, the open night-world is transformed into a narrow cave that fences him in on all sides. In "Farhat's Republic" the author gives us details of a truly nightmarish vision of a world, one whose features begin to have their impact on the reader from the very first words of the story.**

In this extract we can feel the author's keen eye transforming the trivialities of daily life into a truly gruesome nightmare; the openness of life is constrained till mankind finds itself overwhelmed. We get the same feeling in reading the passage describing the "discovery" in "A Matter of Honor"; in that case it cannot be claimed that the transformation occurs under cover of darkness since the event occurs in broad daylight. . . .

This nightmare world is not just that of adults; it extends to children as well, young children, boys and girls. Yusuf Idris's world is full of children, to an extent unparalleled in any other writer with the one exception of Ibrahim 'Abd al-Qadir al-Mazini whose stories are also full of children and infants. The nightmare world I have been describing besets children too. Even though they may be tender in age

[**At this point, the entire first paragraph of this particular story is reproduced. For an English translation, see *Modern Arabic Short Stories* selected and translated by Denys Johnson-Davies, London: Oxford University Press, 1967, pg. 1.]

and body, they move around in its shadow, seemingly embodying the foulest aspect of reality with all its oppression and falsehood. . . .

There is in fact an ambiguity in Yusuf Idris's vision as encountered in these stories, or, to be more precise, two parallel visions that operate in tandem in this initial phase of Yusuf Idris's artistic development, visions that only coincide and coalesce in his second phase. The first is an intellectual vision that stems from the mind, qua ideas and concepts; the second from the realm of emotion, qua images and intuitions. The first endeavors to impose its concept of reality and the way it operates on to the world of Idris's artistic experimentation, while the second prefers to make use of intuition and the world-experience locked in the author's own subconscious. . . .Let me cite some examples so that this notion can be made more specific. In the collection, *Isn't That So?*, for example we can point to the existence of the phenomenon in a number of stories. In "People," artistic vision is embodied in the collection of events and tales about the tamarisk tree, the possibility of its being used to treat eye diseases, the villagers' trust in its properties, and the fact that such trust goes back many generations. We also see it in the long and futile struggle between a group of boys from the village who have received an education and the rest of the village; the boys try in vain to do away with superstitions and to convince people that it does more harm than good. The intellectual side of the vision in this story lies in an attempt to confirm the fact that "the majority of the community will never agree on a falsehood." Scientific analysis has confirmed that the leaves of this tree contain elements of copper sulfate from which medicines are manufactured. The end tries to show us that life is in a constant state of change in spite of everything and that development cannot be stopped. People have stopped using the leaves from the tree; instead they have started taking medicines dispensed by the hospital. Even when the young men tell them the results of the scientific analysis, they still refuse to go back to using the leaves. It is almost as though the story is confirming that life has to move forward, never backward. . . .

I will not cite any more examples of this phenomenon from the other collections; suffice it to say that *The Cheapest Nights* alone has nine stories which illustrate this ambiguity as I have explained it. What I do wish to point out is that, were such ambiguity to exist in any other writer, it would completely destroy the value of those stories in which it occurred. With Yusuf Idris however, it is another matter. He is a very gifted writer who is able to conceal this ambiguity; it lurks within certain sensual details, often so well hidden that only the eye of an experienced critic is able to spot it. Even if it does emerge, it never manages to spoil the story itself. This can be traced back to an essential point, namely that with Idris the sheer power of the artistic aspect of his vision makes the intellectual side seem muted and less obvious. It is an artistic vision to rival the exceptional gifts of Tolstoy whose artistic genius in the great novel, *War and Peace*, has been beyond the power of any number of critics to describe adequately. . . .

6. From Frustration to the Edge of Defeat.

We shall now discuss the frustrated and overwhelmed individual, the discussion of which we postponed till we had treated the nightmarish world of Yusuf Idris and the ambiguity of vision involved. This kind of person is the predominant type to be found in all the stories of these five collections; in some of them, the character starts that way and remains so to the end; in others, the character ends in ruin, most especially those stories that address the topic of death as an overwhelming metaphysical force as well as those that deal with coercion and terror. None of this should be taken to imply that the characters in Yusuf Idris's stories are puny or lacking in resolve. In fact, among the principal features of his characters are a pugnacious instinct, a willingness to take on intolerable burdens, and an ability to survive in the most impossible circumstances. But, even with all these sterling qualities, Yusuf Idris's characters are destined to suffer the very bitterest kinds of defeat. This makes the principal characters in his stories at this stage not a little akin to the epic hero, but epic in a peculiar way because the heroism involved here does not involve achieving miracles but is rather the heroism of the simple man who is able to put a brave face on poverty, austerity, and frustration; a heroism of patience, silence, and pugnacity, all coupled with an amazing ability to put up with pain and agony. In the same way, the defeat that these characters suffer is like the heroic failure we encounter with the figure of Santiago in Hemingway's *The Old Man and the Sea*. . . .

Let us take as an example one of Yusuf Idris's finest and most poetic stories, "Summer Night," a story that manages to embody frustration in its most characteristic form, one in which the sensation acquires a number of suggestive resonances. The story tells us about a group of young peasants inwardly bursting with that cauldron that is adolescence. They all find themselves swept along by the sheer impetus of the gathering, only to discover themselves early the next morning confronting a world full of frustrated urges, shattered dreams, and crushed hopes. When the story ends, their failure to find any kind of fulfilment of their fantasies leads to a violent and bloody confrontation and to a tense series of events and actions. In spite of the restricted nature of the core group and the decision to select them from a specific segment of the village community, the scope of the evening gathering is expanded to include the village as a whole, with all its suppressed longings for materials comforts and sensual pleasures that can never be realized. There is a bitter irony in the gap between the dull, harsh reality they live and the dream they all entertain of transcending it. In the story all this is revealed to us through the medium of these young men sprawled out after dinner on a big pile of straw one summer night, each one of them showing off his masculinity and prowess. The living embodiment of their frustrated desires is to be found in the tales that Muhammad, one of the villagers, has to tell them. He travels to the provincial towns. He sees things and tries them out; every night he fires their imaginations with stories of his adventures. For every person present the story is the embodiment of their sexual and social desires (and their economic ones too, if the term can be applied in this context); in the rustic imagination it represents paradise, a world with a plump white houri — and slender village girls as well, delicious food ("and turkey, lads, stuffed with pigeon, potatoes, and mutton"), and its own sexual appetite to stir the passions of the deprived. I said earlier that the story seems like a private dream for everyone present, so much so that it leads them to egg on Muhammad in his narrative adventures, to respond to that woman's gesture, to go into the house and sit down on the plush cushions, and then to devour food and woman all at once. The story makes them urge Muhammad to do in the story he is telling precisely those things they long to do themselves but will never be able to.

At the end of the story, they come to realize that the story Muhammad has been telling them is a reality, not a fantasy; in the city of al-Mansura, there really is a woman that beautiful, food that plentiful, and sex that good. With that, they force Muhammad to go with them to al-Mansura and show them the woman's house and let them all go up to her one by one so they can have their fill of her sexual hunger and slake their burning passions. The journey itself takes up more than ten pages of the story; they proceed on their way amid much conversation and commotion. However morning dawns before they are even within sight of their dream. They are nowhere close to their goal when cold reality hits them, along with all the frustration and sorrow it brings. They all start worrying in case their families come looking for them. They realize all the things they have to do when the day fully dawns. Throughout the journey we become fully aware of the shattered hopes, the suppressed urges, and the reality that can dash even the sweetest of dreams. The story finishes with a poetic description of their return along the very same road as they took at night. They have been thwarted; daytime has come, brandishing the huge, brutal cudgel of reality that can so easily frustrate all dreams. . . .

Taking a look at the collection, *A Matter of Honor*, we can find other images of frustration that border on a sense of defeat. There we discover new angles on the frustrated man who impinges on our consciousness in all of the seven collections, however much basic features and experiences presented may differ. In the story called "Bus-stop," frustrated man takes the form of someone who almost suffocates because there is some fresh air in the world for other people to breathe; there really exists the possibility of a love relationship between boy and girl. This passenger on the bus wants to turn the world upside down when he suddenly discovers that there are people who make love and that his own life has been wasted in vain; that the world that for him consisted of visible and invisible bars on a cage actually allows for a good deal of spontaneity and openness. Here is this poor man who has, without even realizing it, allowed external pressures to infiltrate into his inner being so that he has himself become one of the very instruments of that pressure within whose clutches he has managed to waste his entire life. At the end of the story his words emerge almost as a scream of agony: he is not crying, he tells us, because values have collapsed, but rather his life has been wasted; he has never been able to enjoy himself, and he has spent his entire life as a prisoner of those visible and invisible bars. . . .In "A Tray From Heaven" the feeling of frustration rises to such a pitch that the hero, a shaykh, feels impelled to yell out to the heavens and to forget all about the years he spent studying religion at Al-Azhar and the awe with which one is supposed to regard religion. One failure after another forces him to the very brink of despair and rebellion both at once. Poverty, weakness, loneliness, and failure lead him to raise his voice against the heavens and the entire village; the disgrace of defeat removes all veils of pretense from his eyes and forces him to confront the unknown head on. . . .

7. Variations on the Idea of Oppression and Defeat.

If the factors involved in the way Yusuf Idris's stories depict frustration at this stage are mostly the product of society and aptitude, they are linked to a number of other more metaphysical aspects which also contribute to the way defeat is framed in the stories. When societal and metaphysical oppression combine, we discover that defeat is the inevitable consequence; Yusuf Idris's characters may be able to avoid one, but not both. . . .In the story, "A Matter of Honor," the defeat in question finds itself bolstered by a variety of factors — the prevalence of poverty and frustration and the way in which these two phenomena combine to stifle innocence and vitality. In this story Fatimah's fall, the bitter event which sounds a death knell for her sense of spontaneity and innocence, does not result from her inability to confront an oppressive societal or even metaphysical force. Rather it is the consequence of, on the one hand, a prolonged conspiracy on the part of the men in the village who find themselves frustrated in the face of her startling beauty, vivacity, and sheer sweetness, and, on the other, of a corporate desire of all the frustrated women in the village to spoil her beauty and sully her innocence. . . .In "Farahat's Republic," the defeat is found in the profound irony implicit in the gap between dream and reality, man's pathetic inability to transcend the bounds of the reality in which he lives and to achieve his dreams on his own.

8. The Concept of the Circle and the Seeds of Inevitability.

The themes of oppression and defeat are linked to another main idea that manages to link the vision and structure of the stories from this phase in Idris's career. This idea suggests that the circle will continue spinning and that the events of each story are merely a temporary ripple on the surface of life after which everything will go on its own way again. With this notion in mind or maybe as a response to its structural demands, Idris eschews any endings that smack of de Maupassant's technique, even though there are occasions when the way in which the particular story is structured would seem to demand such a technique. When one of Idris's stories comes to an abrupt ending that sheds a good deal of light on the events that have preceded, he fully intends to keep the story going in order to confirm that the circle will keep spinning and that life will carry on to the same rhythm. Everything that has happened has either already slipped out of the character's consciousness or is about to do so; any further attempt to transcend reality is doomed to failure. These then are the principal seeds in the concept of inevitability that are so clearly delineated in the recent stories; man as individual will never manage to change the direction taken by events or to stem their flow, no matter how abundant the resolve and awareness may be. . . .

Taking as an example the story, "Camel Corps," we discover that, even though Idris portrays the arrival of the Camel Corps at a village as a purely temporary matter, by the end of the story the image has taken over. It becomes clear that the delight the villagers feel when the Camel Corps leaves is the thing that is temporary and not the reverse. It is one of the short periods of respite that they can enjoy away from the Camel Corps before falling into their clutches all over again. Everything is inverted: whereas the Corps' dominant presence used to be the temporary element in their lives, it is the events on the road, events that manage to liberate the villagers for just a short time, which turn out to be temporary. A group of young men have kidded themselves that they can alter the course of events, defeat the personnel in the Camel Corps, chase them away, and send them packing. The story goes to great lengths in describing the overwhelming feelings of joy the villagers feel when the Corps is driven off and the restored pulse of life that vibrates throughout the village that night. It envelops everyone, old and young, boys and girls, men and women; several men lose all their inhibitions and start dancing around. The story describes all this in detail, but at the end of the story the bitter words "Just tonight, my love; tonight, and that's it" intrude like a knife-point to remind the reader that this entire night of joy is just a dream and that things will soon revert to the grim existence that the village is used to expecting, one whose laws they have tried valiantly to flout so that they can break out of the vicious circle of their lives. . . .

These two features, circularity and inevitability, are not confined to the semantic level in Yusuf Idris's stores, but operate on the structural plane as well. We find them reflected in the structure of a number of stories. In several, events begin from the end, or end where they began. Indeed a number of stories begin and end with the same sentences and words. "The Treasure," for example, ends with the same quiet piece of reportage with which it begins. "Isn't That So?" ends with the identical words and sentences, so much so that we can turn the pages back to the start and read the same words over again, finishing where we started and beginning the journey all over again. It is as though we are faced with a story that, like life itself, never ends, but instead carries on with the same pulse and in the same style. This is not meant to imply that the idea of circularity in these stories is turned into a kind of cheap trick or a piece of structural decoration, but rather that the structural form itself is loaded with significance. That "The Treasure" starts and ends with the same words confirms that everything that has happened in between is just a slight tremor on the face of life; soon everything will return to normal. The events remain within the circle of the imagination, or rather the realistic depiction of the events in the story is used to achieve and validate its imaginative status.

9. The Sensual Aspect and Paternal Authority

Let us now consider Yusuf Idris's celebration of the sensual aspect of life, something we have touched on slightly above in discussing ambiguity of vision, along with the power of his artistic vision and the way it predominates over intellectual factors. What I want to discuss here is . . . Yusuf Idris's celebration of the sensual side of life, his concentration on sensual pleasures and the detailed way in which he depicts them. It almost seems they are a kind of sacred rite everyone believes in, vigorously resisting any attempt, however weak-willed or well intentioned it may be, to leave out or pass over the tiniest detail. These are sensual feelings of the very subtlest kind when placed into a world that is so harsh and callous. And yet, however slight they may seem, they manage to deepen our awareness of the very harshness of existence on the one hand and on the other the overwhelming desire to transcend such a life and to enjoy a little material and sensual pleasure. The heroes in his stories no sooner sense an opportunity for even the slightest sensual enjoyment, be it food, drink, laughter, or even friendly conversation over a cup of hot tea, than they launch themselves into it with complete abandon. So involved do they become that it seems as if they are embarking on an elaborate sacred ritual with its own ceremonies and procedures that cannot be ignored or overlooked at any stage.

We can easily appreciate this phenomenon when we come to read the description of life's rituals in the story "Ramadan," along with all the details of daily life, ways of eating and drinking, the noise of chewing, and so on. For example, when we read the way Yusuf Idris describes the early morning meal before the fast begins, we come to realize how such an ordinary operation has been transformed . . . We sense that the meal has been changed into a kind of sensual oasis of shade on a boiling hot day. The depiction of the sensual is not focused merely on eating alone, nor on sex and gluttonous desires. We get precisely the same feeling when we look at the course of the conversation and hear the bursts of laughter when the villagers gather for an evening chat in "At Night" or a similar conversation on top of a pile of straw in "A Summer Night." Even involvement in a simple game of backgammon in "A Glare" is turned into a sensual ritual that takes the heroes of the story away from the world and helps them forget all the futility and hardship of the difficult life they have to lead. We get this same sense of ritual whenever we read about eating, as in "Diverting the Bride" and "A Table From Heaven." In these and other stories we get to see the extent to which Idris celebrates the sensual aspect; it seems almost as though time itself has come to a standstill or that the characters in the story are completely oblivious of time as they relish these few moments of meager sensual pleasure. This leads in turn to the impression that time has been frozen and will remain in a state of suspended animation until these minor rituals are at an end. And then we find ourselves suddenly confronted with the fact that time actually was in motion all along. This leads to a sad conclusion whereby that tiny magical spark that represents all the characters have left after such wonderfully sensual rituals is completely extinguished.

Let us now consider the authority of the father figure, something that looms large in several of the stories of this phase. It emerges as an absolute societal edict that reverts to the paternalistic societies of primitive times and is an omnipresent aspect of Idris's stories. Every single societal thread is governed by the iron grip of this authority that controls the course of the entire family's existence. The father comes to represent protection and oppression, affection and fear, at one and the same time. As a consequence, when the father figure is absent, life loses its sense of proportion, and along with it its flavor, legitimacy, and sense of elan. When fate in the form of death, disease or some other agent brings this authority to an end, everything quickly falls to pieces: the wife soon goes to the bad (as in "The Seesaw"), and the child feels the loss of security, protection, love, and even the innate sense of being alive (as in "The Big Hand"); any ambiguities that may have existed regarding the father figure are of necessity resolved even though some private cravings may have been kept suppressed (as in "The Wallet"). In Yusuf Idris's stories paternal authority is not something to be disregarded; it comes to represent security, understanding, and protection, even if once in a while it also signifies oppression too. . . .

10. Resort to Irony and Other Features.
The final feature of Yusuf Idris's story world at this phase is his resort to irony as a structural principle; irony in its broadest sense as a synonym for art in general terms: the process whereby dozens of disparate elements can be fused together and the production therefrom of a new composition whose particulars are not merely the sum of everything that went into it but rather different features that are at one and the same time more distinctive and comprehensive . . . We find such irony in every great work of literature. All Yusuf Idris's mature stories are steeped in it; in fact, it is the quality that gives them their maturity, profundity, and poetic quality. He loves to focus on the bitter irony between dream and reality, between what people would like to happen and what actually does, between the aspirations, dreams, and desires of human beings on the one hand and on the other a reality where parameters allow for no escape or crossing the rigid constricting boundaries it sets up. . . .

In "The Incident" the level of irony is intensified in that its range stretches all the way to the minutest detail. Beyond the total irony involved between the simplicity of the villager and the complexity of city life, we also sense a further bitter irony between what 'Abd al-Nabi Efendi imagines reality to be and what it actually is. We come to feel the same irony between 'Abd al-Nabi with his hang-dog personality and his wife, Tuffahah, who is extremely domineering; she feels that the gap in age between them — she is many years younger than he is — gives her the right to boss him around and scold him with or without cause; between 'Abd al-Nabi Efendi with his subservient personality and total inability to quell or control his wife's recalcitrance, and the four year-old boy with his innocent laughter and complete control over his little boat and his own world. . . .between the reality of 'Abd al-Nabi's existence and his dream of either himself or his son being like this serene, confident and secure little child. It is through these ironies and other narrative threads that cross or run parallel to each other that Yusuf Idris constructs his story. In "The Queue" this irony assumes a new aspect which carries it beyond that between dream and reality or the actual and the possible. In this case the irony is between the inevitability of natural law or something similar to it, and the will of the individual who aspires to challenge that natural law or at the very least imagines that he can face up to it and force it to change direction. Such is the author's insistence on these features that the queue of the title acquires a variety of aspects and images that convert it into a societal phenomenon in its own right, a natural law that the land-owner tries in vain to challenge, destroy, and domineer. The story shows us the two forces in savage conflict, each one trying to impose its will on the other . . .

Alongside these features there are other Idrisian touches that can be identified, such as a close linkage to the authentic Egyptian spirit. They can be seen in the story style and the narrative technique: an insistence on choosing names that will reflect aspects of Egyptian humor or spirit; the use of a bitter, sarcastic humor even at the bleakest moments; the way in which characters, aware of their own impotence, resort to self-deprecation as a way of purging themselves of the feeling of impotence and of transcending the sense of frustration. Idris is able to make use of his medical specialization when, in "The First Practice," he describes the way the students get drunk as follows: "They started to feel high, as though they had inhaled some freshly prepared ammonium hydroxide." At some points he also provides the reader with certain suggestive images that do not in and of themselves create the story nor do they necessarily further the story's structural complexity or richness, but rather serve to suggest, to brush over certain sensitive aspects on the body of reality and point to some of its maladies. "To Asyut," for example, provides us with an intensely focussed vignette of the sufferings of the human body and spirit, while "In Passing" is a bitterly sarcastic portrait of certain features — and enigmas — of the human soul.

11. The Four Most Recent Collections.

Having covered most of the issues and observations regarding the first five collections of stories by Yusuf Idris, stories that give us a good overview of his artistic world, we should now turn our attention to the most recent four collections: *The End of the World* (1961), *The Black Policeman* (1962), *The Language of Screams (1966)*, and *The Siren (* 1969). This will allow us to discover the kinds of change that have taken place in his approach to vision and structure. In dealing with these most recent collections there will be no need for the same detailed discussion that was adopted for the first collections; to do so would be to indulge in a large amount of repetition. We will begin by focusing on the nature of the changes that have affected the story-world created by the first collections, something whose most significant aspects we have already identified, and then move on to consider what may be the new elements that these latest stories offer to that world, be it from the point of view of vision or of structure. These recent stories do, of course, offer us examples of the author's continuing development and illustrate many of the changes that have affected his understanding of both art and mankind, but they still maintain a close link with the world as found in his earlier collections. In fact, they can be considered an extension of them, and on more than one level. In dealing with most of the new additions to his repertoire in this second phase of his story-writing career, the discriminating researcher can find seeds for them in the earlier collections. . . .

12. Constants and Changes.

The most important feature that remains the same in this second phase is the broad canvas that we acknowledged at the beginning of this study. It remains as broad and comprehensive as ever: the city, villages, desert communities, open country, desolate tracks. The stories are still situated in hospitals, prisons, schools, and colleges; inside company offices, villages, popular quarters, on deserted roads, in fields, city streets, alleyways, and even mining areas in the desert. The places are the same, and yet the human experience, for all its apparent variety, begins to focus on a limited number of issues and to revolve around particular poles. Taking just one of these collections, *The Language of Screams,* we notice that the twelve stories, for all their different experiences, revolve around two basic issues: the first is the discovery of the essential futility of life as lived by the character, a realization that usually comes too late, after the character in question has discovered that the opportunity to change things has passed. The sheer impotence engendered by this realization becomes a kind of masochism, with the character wallowing in his own misery and relishing the sensation. None of the heroes in the eight stories that revolve around this theme can turn the clock back or find any compensation in the way things have turned out for him. The discovery of the brutal truth manages to ruin even the illusory satisfaction which kept him alive. This is the case in "Caught in the Act," "Sinai Treaty," "Ten Pound Note," "Beyond the Bounds of Reason," "Language of Screams," "The Game," "Because Judgment Day Never Comes," and "The Aorta." The other four stories revolve around another theme, a never-ending feeling of loneliness, harassment, uncertainty, and insecurity. Man feels beset by a staggering burden of doubts, intrusions, and anxieties ("Story with a Thin Voice" and "This Time") and strange misgivings; he will close in on himself, alone and helpless (as in "Visitors") or else he will be compelled to submit to sinister threats that dog him wherever he happens to be ("The Master of Egypt").

If the breadth of Idris's canvas is only subject to relatively few adjustments that focus and refine his method, the same cannot be said for the second feature of his technique, the nightmarish world he creates and the ambiguity of vision. Here there is an enormous change. The nightmare atmosphere is transformed into a kind of abstraction aimed at lessening the impact of the nightmare itself and achieving a different way of generalizing the experience. Previously he had moved from the general to the particular by focusing on the nightmarish details of the particular realm alone, thus revealing to us the broader aspects of the general nightmare that society is suffering at that period. In this later phase he prefers to broach the general level directly, sometimes through abstraction, at other times through the use of dreams, and still others through a process of using a realistic experience to express something that is exactly the opposite. In "The Aorta" from the collection *The Language of Screams* we find Idris resorting to the abstract directly and completely avoiding anything to do with the senses, something that is reflected in the use of language. Sentences are direct, sharp, and curt. The story itself leaves the realm of reality altogether and narrates a series of events that have absolutely no relationship whatsoever with the norms of realism. Instead it creates an image of reality through what we might call contemporary myth, something that manages to convince us only because we ourselves are prepared to accept its premises (as Dr. Shukri 'Ayyad has noted) and because its style — short sentences with extreme concision — succeeds in numbing the reader's consciousness into accepting the myth as a possibility. That myth is presented to us by the author in a mere six pages, and yet we come to feel that he has managed to say in those six pages something that he could not possibly have said in sixty. A man walking around with no stomach, accused, yet with no evidence of guilt and no court . . . this man with his severed aorta, encased in thousands of ropes like strips of old parchment, he and the humanity who gather around him evoke dozens of potential meanings, even though the frame in which he is presented is frozen in time; this man's fate succeeds in commenting graphically on the problems of the civilizational moment from which he stems and in conveying the author's own vision of that period.

In "The Game" the author resorts to the dream style once again in order to present his nightmarish vision to us, or rather to place us directly into the core of his nightmare. He makes use of the same style, one that relies on a terse and direct mode of discourse, eschews all detail, and avoids any justification for events that might seem illogical or incomprehensible. In fact, he goes to great lengths to highlight for readers those elements that are peculiar and illogical and in such a way that the hero of the story becomes "everyman" and the peculiar and deceptive "game" of the title turns into the game of life itself. . . .In the story, "The Demon, from the collection entitled *The Black Policeman* the author imposes a realistic imprint on a narrative that portrays an experience that is surrealistic or even abstract. A highly realistic scene — an army truck overturns on the Kornish, and the hero, abruptly jolted out of his daydreams, is almost killed — is used by Yusuf Idris to present a comprehensive realization of all the incredible potential hidden inside every human being, all those intangible faculties which only reveal themselves at moments of crisis.

By using these three modes — abstraction, dreams, and applying elements of the realistic to the expression of unrealistic and abstract ideas — Yusuf Idris has found a substitute for the nightmarish vision that so characterized the works of his first phase; or, more accurately, has reformulated the vision so that it appears in a new guise. . . .There is no room any more for a sensory perspective that pays attention to all the details and particulars of reality nor for a cerebral approach that attempts to impose its own understanding of the workings of reality and its particular vision of the nature of its development on those same details and particulars. The two elements are now united and blend together in a fashion that precludes any differentiation; the sensory and cerebral are completely merged. . . .

13. From Vanquished Man to Miracle Man.

We now turn to consider the changes that have affected the defeated hero, the character that so dominated the scene in Idris's stories from the first phase. We notice from the outset that the hero displays essential changes that serve to reveal and crystalize the hidden aspect of the stories from the earlier period. The average, simple human being is now transformed into man the wonder, capable in spite of all appearances of bringing about the most unlikely of miracles and of directly confronting the impossible. As a result the construction of character in this phase no longer makes use of a logical progression, preferring instead a more arbitrary one of a particular type, one that plays a larger role in building the miraculous dimensions of the character in question. Each story tries to bring together the features in the new logic of its character in the events that transpire, logic that needs to be distinguished from the traditional Aristotelian kind and from the usual societal conventions. Since common man has now been trans- formed into man the wonder, he is also changed into man the riddle. . . .However the appearance of man the wonder does not imply that the frustrated or van- quished man from the earlier stories has disappeared from Yusuf Idris's story world; to the contrary in fact, he is as much a part of the stories in this phase as he was in the previous one. If we take the collection, *The Black Policeman* as an example, we find that frustrated or vanquished man makes up the hero of every story except one ("The Demon"). He is Shawqi and 'Abbas al-Zunfuli in "The Black Policeman," Mustafa in "Al-Sayyidah Vienna," Isma'il and the narrator in "Triumph of Defeat," the narrator in "The Head," and man in various guises and under different names in all the stories in the collection. . . .

As we analyse the way that man the wonder looms so large in the stories of this phase, we notice that he comprises aspects of frustrated or vanquished man. However, that person has now managed either to transcend the frustration and defeat, or else to clothe his defeat in a heroic mask. "The Wonder of the Age" is a small text, little more than a thumb-nail sketch. Here is a puny, fragile human being, ignored by everyone, the kind of person that lurks inside each one of us; all he really represents is the frustrated, defeated individual who tries to transcend his frustration and move beyond his sense of defeat. The process involves channeling his feelings of frustration into new positive directions, helping him to overcome society's unawareness of his existence; the never-ending routine of the job he holds forces him to reconsider his whole attitude to his own function vis- à-vis society and everything else. . . .

In this second phase the notion of defeat does not make itself quite as obvious as in the stories of the previous phase, except, that is, in "Triumph of the Defeat" where time itself comes to a stop in one long moment of confrontation with death . . . In the collection, *The Siren,* we find frustration portrayed in a variety of guises. Here sex seems to provide a soft pillow in which to bury the tensions it raises and lessen the violence of its impact. The *Language of Screams* gives the reader different examples of transformation involving continuing encounters between fulfillment and failure, encounters that show us that, even if life fails to provide fulfillment in one way, it soon does so in another. . . .

14. Time Stabilized; Inevitability in Control

In this phase we find a large number of the structural elements that have already been noted with regard to the previous phase still present. Irony continues to occupy central position in the author's artistic and semantic vision. The third person narrative mode continues to be his preferred style, although there are rare excursions into the first-person narration. Authorial intervention almost completely disappears, except, that is, for story endings. The concept of the circle, something on which we focused above, still predominates in his vision of reality and story. However, even though he may have preserved many of the new and outstanding features of his initial style in this new phase of his writing, he does adopt a new method to deal with and indeed construct events within his narratives, one that dispenses with a lot of detail and goes straight to the core of the topic without any of the usual preliminaries. Such is his focus on the core of the topic that he occasionally finds himself pushed close to abstraction and forced to stabilize the time element by suspending it. By suspending time here I do not imply the philosophical process that would refute the manifest essence of things so that they come to seem outside both time and space or on the edge of the absolute, nor the more abstract process that we come across in a number of modern works of art such as Strindberg's play, *The Ghost Sonata,* and Ionesco's *The Bald Madonna,* nor the suspension of time that we encounter in Halim Barakat's excellent novel, *Six Days,* where the stopped clock in the square in Dayr al-Bahr is a symbol of the community's continuing cultural backwardness, something that all Arab countries suffer from and that was to be a contributing factor to the June 1967 defeat.

This suspension of time is something different from these other categories. Here time is fixed in a motionless state akin to perpetuity, so that the narrative moment stands absolutely on its own, unconnected to anything else; its features emerge and shine with tremendous clarity. The entire process acquires a lyrical texture that makes the story the kin of great poetry. As a result, this process of stabilization does not put either the narrative moment or the story's topic into an ironic position vis-à-vis the external world, but rather permits both of them to become the purest conceivable expression of that external world, with all the vision and conflict that operate within it. This becomes a style that allows the artist to make maximum use of the smallest possible moments in the life of man to express the entire spectrum of human existence, past, present, and future; to describe dreams and frustrated youth, aspirations for a new reality and feelings of impotence not merely about achieving that new reality but even simply dreaming of it — for, after all that has happened, even dreaming is an impossibility. This method of freezing time cannot be compared with usual chronological methods of calculation; the only way of comprehending it is as a kind of surveillance from the outside. The author never lets his readers become aware of this suspension of time, but rather gets them in his grip and then uses this technique to show them events, characters, and incidentals.

There is one collection whose stories rely completely on this process of stabilizing time and freezing the moment, namely *The Language of Screams*. From the very first story, "Caught Napping," we can detect the way in which the fleeting moment has been transformed into an actionless permanence through which events and characters are brought to light; we discover how the potent quiescence of this moment is able to neutralize any attempt to rupture its atmosphere or to use action — whatever kind of action it may be — to curtail the moment's continuity. In this story the personal moment — that of the Dean of the College — steals from itself in order to provoke a self-confrontation and reveal some of the secret recesses of the life involved. Thus, hardly is the moment over before we come to realize that the Dean is panting, as though he has had to expend a lot of energy on some major endeavor or has embarked on a long trip that has made him short of breath. No wonder, for he has indeed traversed an entire lifetime in that fleeting moment! If we look at the story from the point of view of the other character involved, the young girl, we notice that she lives the self-same moment in a different way and from a point of departure that is completely opposite to that of the Dean. She steals this moment from time, society, and life; as a result she enjoys its apparent permanence and relishes its continuity. Without expressing her feelings in any direct way, she clearly wants this moment to last for ever. Clutching her cigarettes for all she is worth, her young body is totally devoted to the task of using every puff to savor the nectar and sheer essence of this exquisite moment. In her case, the moment is hardly over before she is brought back to reality with a severe jolt, a hammer blow that destroys this momentary world of beauty and restores her to reality with its concomitant fears, terrors, and miseries. . . .

In "The Language of Screams," the suspended moment becomes the equivalent of the suspension of life as a whole, the complete collapse of all values: suspension of that breathless quest for life and illusion, suspension of that particular illusory game that the hero, Doctor Al-Hadidi, has been running between himself and Fahmi who, as the story is being narrated, is in the kitchen screaming as he endures the savage onslaught of the pain of bladder cancer. When the game is suspended or rather comes to an end, reality is revealed in a foul and unexpected light. The moment is extended for a nightmarish eternity that causes Doctor al-Hadidi to review his entire life. He comes to realize that it has all been a waste; everything has slipped between his fingers without him even realizing it. Illusion has dogged him at every turn and drained all his faculties, making him run breathlessly from one stage to the next without pausing to gather breath, review his life or enjoy it. Turning to "This Time" or "Because the Day of Resurrection Never Comes," we find that the suspended moment is transformed into a nightmare, but one with a gentle touch and light tread, something that slinks in surreptiously and grabs its wretched victims by the neck with a brilliant contemporary smile on its face. . . .

The majority of stories in this collection and some of those in the one that follows it point clearly to the extremely evocative qualities of the title *The Language of Screams,* not merely with regard to the content of this collection and its successor, but also to the style through which the content is treated. For this particular artist "the language of screams" represents pain; a language that, faced with the sheer rapacity of existence, turns into a series of vivid, fragmentary symbols. The word, or actually the whole elongated sentence with its bitter message, assumes the phonesthemic qualities of the scream itself, encapsulating the alphabet as a whole and comprising the extensive world of pain and bitterness. Since pain is a sharp, tangible, and fiercely real organic sensation, it demands a particular kind of expression that suits its characteristics. As I noted above, the title of this collection betrays from the very first instant the mode of expression that will succeed in encapsulating the bodily pains with which the stories are replete. . . .

Turning now to consider the notion of inevitability in the world envisioned by the stories of this phase, we note from the outset that the seeds of inevitability mentioned with regard to the first phase have developed and born fruit in the second phase. The notion of inevitability has now become one of the principal ideas permeating the fabric of most of the issues discussed, to such an extent that it becomes part of the fabric itself or a thread that is clearly visible among its principal features . . . In "The Siren," for example, inevitability takes on a fresh flavor to become that mysterious and ambiguous call that keeps importuning the heroine and forcing her towards it with an irresistible power. Every event and detail in the story becomes an attempt to justify the merciless onslaught of this cry and the heroine's surrender to its dictates. . . .

These then are the most significant features in the second phase of Yusuf Idris's story writing. No doubt they will be subject to further change and addition as Yusuf Idris continues on his arduous adventure in art and life. The reason for this is that anyone who looks at the majority of stories from this second phase can recognize the yeoman efforts that Idris has made to enliven the story structure, so much so that they can in truth be said to constitute a group of real attempts to search for an Egyptian story form and for the most appropriate modes of expression in which to couch them.

[EDITOR'S NOTE: In making a number of cuts from this lengthy article concerning Idris's short stories, I have retained the sections which discuss theory and technique; the omitted sections provide further illustrations of the stories themselves.]

Sabri Hafiz, "Qadaya al-'alam al-uqsusi 'inda Yusuf Idris," *Al-Mawqif al-adabi* vol. 3 no. 9 (1974): 57-85.

The Search for the Authentic Self Within Idris's City

Mona N. Mikhail

Al-Qahira, Cairo, and le Caire are magic words which resonate with medieval splendor and mystery. Cairo, the city of a thousand years and more than a thousand minarets, has never ceased to fascinate artists and writers both indigenous and foreign. The cultural capital for more than one hundred million Arabic-speaking people, it is also a prominent religious center to millions of adherents to Islam, harboring the great theological center Al-Azhar. Cairo stands today as a modern cosmopolitan center and heir to all the ills of its western prototypes. Najib Mahfouz and Yusuf Idris are the two leading modern chroniclers of that great city. Mahfouz has immortalized its streets and alleys in his famous trilogy and several collections.

The Cairo recreated in the works of Idris and Mahfouz is very much the thriving bustling city of the middle ages. A city that has not changed much over the centuries, it remains in their works furrowed with ever narrowing streets, overcrowded alleys dazed by the pounding of metal and the din of brass. The Cairo of Khan Al-Khalifli and Al-Qal'a (The Citadel) and its neighboring city of the dead —a palpable reality of the presence of death —are all aspects of the city which serve as metaphors to Egyptian writers. The modern metropolis with its traditional symbols of wealth, power, and oppression is usually an image which appears in their works only to contrast with its lingering medieval soul.

The title story of the collection *Qa'-al-Madina* (Heart of the City) is one of Idris's best treatments of the subject, a novella for which he chooses as his protagonist a stereotype of the modern city, a young, arrogant bachelor judge. His counterpart is the young woman victimized by the city, who seeks a living by working for him as a maid. Mr. 'Abdallah (Slave of God) is more likely to be enslaved by other deities, "the things" which make up a life in a modern metropolis. Idris describes him thus:

> He is a judge, as yet unmarried but however, owns a luxuriously furnished apartment. His life is filled with serial numbers: 3445. 399876, 10031, 66, 8345, which in chrono-

> logical order are his license plates, his refrigerator policy, his
> life insurance policy, his apartment number and his bank
> account number in no special order of priority to him.

From the very beginning he is presented as one trapped by modern life and completely conditioned by the machinery of the great metropolis. The sense of loss and alienation of the characters is effectively given by the recurrent negations in the story. The theme of loss of innocence is insightfully examined and rendered through a series of images and metaphors all through the narrative. The outline of the narrative is one that has been a favorite with Egyptian writers in recent decades. The young bachelor who has achieved some success and social status abuses and exploits the innocence of an attractive peasant girl who usually works for him. She in turn becomes something of a *"putain respectueuse"* who is drawn into the current unwillingly at first, then seems to accommodate herself quite well to that new way of life. At the beginning she is ready for any sacrifice provided she can fend for her ailing children and unemployed tubercular husband. At the end of the story prostitution becomes her life-style. In the hands of Idris these seemingly socio-economic factors or, one could say, invariables of the Egyptian scene, acquire insightful literary dimensions.

In conveying the sense of the loss of innocence, Idris hints with great discretion and caution. This awareness is shown through the eyes of the wary judge who at first is bewildered at the change that has come over his maid servant:

> And it seemed to him that he could detect in her face things
> that weren't there before, or rather that her face was missing
> something that used to be there.

Our young man scrutinizes the face of the woman and it seems that he reaches his moment of illumination at the end of a process of accumulation of significant details. He examines, in character, his woman as if she were a series of "state exhibits."

> He sees her now as it were with parts of her features
> completely obliterated, while others seem to stand out. Her
> eyes had become deep set in her face enclosed by uninnocent
> circles . . . even her smile was no longer simple, naive . . . and
> suddenly he was scared of the change.

This alteration in a person he thought he knew unnerves him. Here it is not merely a loss of virginal innocence as much as a loss of something fundamental. The shock of recognition of 'Abd-Allah is the more unnerving when he realized that he was, in the ultimate analysis, to blame for that appalling discovery. His mounting interrogations to himself heightens the effect and reality of his guilt. "Is he responsible for what has happened? Has he really brought out that change in her? Is he the one who has violated her faithful marital features?" Moving thus from an impressionistic level of interpretation of a situation to a conscious one merges the different elements of the story into a coherent whole.

In that part of the story where our protagonist sets out on a journey through the streets of Cairo trying to locate his maid servant who had presumably stolen his watch, we are again presented with another of Idris's *coups de maître* at merging several levels and visions. Here Idris quite literally uses cinematic techniques in narrating his impressions of a journey to the undersides of a city. This odyssey brings together many elements that may have seemed disparate and focuses them to the point of culmination.

Through his skillful use of language, Idris creates an impression of immediacy which is most effective as cinematic devices usually are. His use of an active present tense secures the effect of events and scenes taking place before our very eyes in the experience of reading the material. The distinct impression one gets is of an eye of a camera placed on the hood of the taxi he rides, searching for his servant. The focusing eye of the camera seems to select significant details which help create the overall effect of disintegration.

> . . . as they advance the streets become narrower and their importance diminishes, the houses losing their numbers and their upper stories, the doors turning yellow and the windows losing their shutters; the shops become stores run by their owners, whose hands are the machines, and the faces of passersby become paler and their clothes bleached and worn out; language disintegrates and becomes words and shouts and insults; the smell of spices and glue and sawdust rises; and they keep advancing and the streets become lanes carrying deafening names and the asphalt is replaced by blocks of rock and the pavement ends.

This metamorphosis of a city before our very eyes is symbolic of the changes that are taking place on several levels in the story. They certainly parallel the change that has overcome our heroine and to a larger extent the deterioration and disintegration of 'Abd-Allah himself. For as the streets and houses lose shape and faces and clothes lose color, the deeper he moves towards the heart of the city, so does our man's whole personality disintegrate in his attempt to falsely accuse his maid servant of the theft. The disintegration of language here is also very significant; for it symbolizes a break in the very essence of things, a loss of formulated values, a loss of the truth traditionally sought by a man of law, usually through the medium of words.

Idris in this passage and the ensuing ones seems to be carried away by a verbal mushrooming of ideas. At points we are tempted to believe that he is not in control any more but is rather led by these images unreeling at a dizzying speed. Along with his hero, Idris seems to lose a sense of direction:

. . . and from that moment he started feeling himself slip-
ping away, getting lost.

This sense of incoherence and loss of a sense of reality is reinforced by that
vagueness that follows and his inability of determining a beginning to that
episode.

A reconstitution of the fading scenes is given in flashbacks which contrast
sharply with the former images. The cinematic technique here is, as it were, a
quick playback. These are scenes of the large avenues, clean streets lined on both
sides with trees. Here the streets are occupied by elderly dark-suited men, while
the other streets which are gradually transformed into narrow constricted winding
lanes are confusedly populated with masses of human beings. These lead to a
place of no "being" where everything commingles with everything else:

and the color of the earth is muddy and mixes with the color of
the dust and the tattered rags; and the smell of people mingles
with that of the earth with that of houses and the interrupted
hummings with the barking of dogs with the squeaking of
opening doors.

He thus creates that unmistakable feeling of an undifferentiated mass throbbing with life of, and from, the earth. Here he appeals to our senses individually
and collectively, making us aware of smells, noises, of certain textures and, of
course, of visual images.

As mentioned earlier Idris seems to indulge in these side developments of the
central theme, but as we have tried to show they contribute to the whole by
reinforcing it. All through the story he uses at different points the various
techniques of close-up, rapid and slow motion. These cinematic techniques are
thus cleverly used to further Idris' thematic designs. His constant preoccupation
with life and death is forcefully shown in this story. The co-existence of the two
principles of existence is so vivid to him that he rarely passes an opportunity
without elaborating on it:

and the low dusty dwellings stand by the graves that spread to
infinity.

He provides variations on the theme by giving specifics:

and the old man leans on the young lad, and the blind one is
led by a boy and the sick person is upheld by a wall and (the
prophet taught us to take pity on the seventh neighbor), and a
thin hidden thread links them all and ties them as beads on
"worry beads" as one soul living in different bodies and time
has no value.

This oneness of an organic whole is thus effectively demonstrated. The components of this throbbing city are thus made to partake in the eternal cycle of being. The rhythmic re-cycling of life into death, through these cinematic techniques, is thus translated into visual realities.

Our hero is not totally swamped in those swarming crowds although at times we get the impression that Idris may have been tempted to lose him being himself so deeply immersed and overwhelmed by this totally new and different world he encounters once out of his select and walled residential areas. Emerging from this inferno of many circles our judge is certainly a different man. Although the change that has come over him is not clearly detectable, we are led to believe that his odyssey has humanized him, has rendered him a person more aware of his surroundings, of the human beings who are less fortunate than himself, who are so close and yet so remote from his own experience. Idris takes these very simple *données* and through the medium of his art turns them into a forceful statement. This story is also to be noted for its language. The prose here is molded into forms rarely used before. It is rendered flexible and resilient to a great extent. The imagery and immediacy of events are not hampered by traditional similes and stock metaphors. Here Idris very clearly locates new meaning into old words, revitalizes the language and rejuvenates the storytelling art.

The Image of Woman, and the Search for a New Identity

> To the religious and the humanist solutions of man's plight in
> the universe must be added the Existentialist. The basic ques-
> tion here is still one of freedom, the search for identity under
> the aspects of violence or alienation.

"Al-Naddaha," ("The Siren") is a merging of the effects of the glamor of the big city on the future of the life of a peasant couple, and the assertion of the individuality of the peasant woman, irresistibly attracted by her newly found personality within the framework of the huge, engulfing city. The story also offers innovations in technique and delineation of character.

Fathiyya is like thousands of other peasant girls who dreamed of marrying someone who would take her away from the native village into the exciting city life. Unlike the other peasant girls, Fathiyya not only dreamed about the exciting prospects but actually worked towards realizing them. For when two eligible young men from the village asked her hand in marriage, Fathiyya did not hesitate in choosing Hamid —the poorer of the two —but the one who was to take her with him to the city. Thus we see how very early she had already made a choice, asserting a certain strength of character not too common among submissive peasant girls. However, what really drives her to that choice is not so much her reasonableness, as much as a certain sense of inexplicable doom. Fathiyya somehow "knew" that inevitably she was destined to live in Cairo, this huge, fascinating, luxurious place, "where callous dry skin disappears, and is replaced by attractive smooth beauty."

Hence, led by this mysterious call from the unknown, Fathiyya rationalizes her life and the "meaning of every sign." Now she feels that she was destined for something better and higher than being stuck in mud from sunrise to sunset. Her beautiful white skin was made to flourish in the city. For "she was as white as one of the rich, beautiful girls from Cairo. Tall and slender and bound to eventually gain good weight, if she ate enough bread and butter." This inner voice kept her going, goading her as it were towards her doom. So she marries Hamid. Although he is only a modest janitor of a house, yet she is proud of the fact that it is a ten story building. Her one room apartment in the basement of that house, under the stairway—although not one of the beautiful apartments she had dreamt of—yet was more than she ever had, with a bed and mattress and a chest of drawers and above all, electricity.

In spite of her fascination with the city she could not quite explain how so much poverty could exist in the place of her dreams. This however did not dampen her spirits, and she was still completely taken by it, yet fearful of it. This ambivalence is shown consistently in the story:

> And to a certain extent she and her husband Hamid not only could not resist giving in to the great motion of the city and have it treat them like the others, . . . but also this great fomenting motion only managed to frighten them, drive them to reclusion, or more specifically, drove her to seek seclusion.

She felt that the new surroundings to which she was confined, namely the room under the stairway, and from which she peeped into the outside world, was her only protection from what she termed a "sea without a shore or fathomable bottom" and imagined herself walking on its edge, and if her foot slipped but once she would be done for. It was a sea:

> which had a thousand hands stretching out, and with thousands of smiles like the smiles of sirens or mermaids deceptive, inviting her, luring her into the waters. Yes they were all cunning hands and cunning smiles, even that tenant eager with the money in his hands and (the grocer's store so close by), petrified her, froze her in her place, while she would turn her head trying to avoid the piercing looks, hoping for some kind of a miracle to save her from this situation.

So little by little Fathiyya becomes aware of that other version of life in a big city. She learns through her husband and through observation about the shady underground happenings in their building as well as in the city at large. She becomes conscious that behind the beautiful facades there is another Cairo full of scandals, shameful things and goings on.

In spite of these discrepancies and deceptions Fathiyya's dream remained intact. Cairo remained that great coveted place, and as for evil, well, after all she thought it was to be found everywhere, for according to her "if evil and slime and ugliness were in the bottom, safety lay in floating or swimming."

And so she continued to "float" until she inevitably hit the iceberg. To the young tenant next door, an avowed Casanova, she at first seemed as if she was going to be his easiest conquest. Actually she was to be quite a variation on his regular victims. But he soon discovered that he was not dealing with a common case. Fathiyya was not to succumb to his charms all that easily; he realized that this time he would have to wait and would have to plot cunningly. He became completely obsessed with Fathiyya, and, the more she avoided his looks and the longer she remained confined to her room, the more he had to resort to all kinds of machinations to get to see her. Fathiyya on the other hand became even more fearful, and her sense of doom became the more haunting. After having adopted the colorful dresses of Cairenes, she reverted to her long black gallabiya and the refuge of its respectful protective folds.

So our young bachelor tenant became more intrigued and more obsessed by this untouchable fruit. He resolved to either have her for himself or kill her and her Hamid if either one opposed his decision. Meanwhile Fathiyya had felt confident in her newly self-imposed seclusion. She even thought that she had triumphed over her sense of doom and that haunting vision of an affandi seducing her. But the inevitable was to happen; he intruded into her cloister. Idris discusses those intensely lived moments with great perception. She stood there astounded, paralysed as if struck by lightning. From being a sentient creature she turned into one who had lost complete touch with life. In her state of shock she instinctively managed to hold her child from falling and sought the bed's poster for support. Anger replaced fear as for the first time she looked her seducer in the face. She examined that "white smooth skin, those long, thick lashes hiding deep green eyes, those regular shining teeth and that mouth which any woman would have desired to kiss." His smile was triumphant, inviting, a smile she had dreamed about for so long, a smile that invited her to sink to the bottom where the slime and the ghosts were. Yes she had feared the 'affreet all her life, and now he had made his appearance, and the whisperings of her inner voice had finally come true.

Idris succeeds in charging that one evanescent moment with myriad impressions experienced in a stream of consciousness. Everything converged in that one moment, her fears, her dreams, her determination to avoid the inevitable doom— they all were charged in that moment crowded with thousands of vibrations and emotions. All she could do now was to beg him for mercy, to shed tears, to humiliate herself before him, but this did not last too long. Idris traces the change coming over her in an interesting correlation between the effects and impact of the city on her whole psyche. She began experiencing strange things—it was as if the shimmering lights of the multi-colored city blinded her. Beautiful shaven faces, expensive elegant clothes, numbing perfumes, wide open avenues, people gaily walking in and out of theatres, clean healthy children with their mothers, all this conglomeration of sights, sensations and emotions stole into her being while she attempted to resist—a resistance she soon had to abandon out of exhaustion and despair. She despaired that a miracle would take place, but what was unbelievable and incomprehensible was for her to realize that her surrender would turn into a pleasurable one. That which was impossible to believe even while it was happening had happened, and then Hamid opened the door and stood there, stricken. She lay there expecting, hoping that Hamid would kill her, and thus fulfill all her premonitions. yet she somehow knew that he would not put an end to her, that she was destined for yet another life.

The author tells us how, like a wounded animal, Hamid spent the night in a vigil after having lost all the driving force behind his decision to kill her. Would he have done the same had he been still living in his little village? Has Cairo totally defeated him, was he really shedding tears out of pity for her humiliation? With the first rays of dawn the family stealthily groped its way through the darkness, a small caravan in flight making its exit from the indifferent cruel sleeping city, seemingly innocent of what it had brought about. Hamid was seized by a wave of fury and would have wanted to smash those glittering facades of lighted shop windows, he would have wanted to uproot its asphalt—anything to lessen his pain. Hamid bought tickets on the train heading back to their little village, but he alone took the ride back home, for Fathiyya disappeared in the hustle and bustle of the crowds flowing into Cairo through its Grand Central Station. This time she was returning to Cairo out of her own accord, and not in answer to a mysterious call. Thus Fathiyya at the end of the story evolves as a woman who has come full circle, who has stepped out into the world, the real world to assume the full responsibility of her destiny. The city had helped crystallize her personality and emancipation.

Ibsen's Nora, in *The Doll's House,* comes to mind as well as some of Henry James' heroines. These heroines had at one point believed that they were destined for modes of life other than the ones they had heretofore led. Nora decides to leave her husband and to search for her identity and place in society, putting aside all other considerations. Fathiyya, the peasant, illiterate girl, initially mesmerized by the call of the big city, after undergoing her initiating harrowing experience, at the end decides to turn around and face her destiny and assert her individuality. Idris thus gives us the growth of Fathiyya in actual process, while he sets it in a background of the evil city, as the catalyst which accelerates her development. His treatment of Fathiyya is quite innovative in that he does not merely recount to us the common events in the life of a transplanted peasant girl; he succeeds in closely showing the initiating changes she undergoes, in actually *changing* her before our very eyes. Our heroine detaches herself from the gallery of those women who determinedly forge their way through. Fathiyya does not have much to draw upon, but her dream. For in spite of her disillusionment, the dream, which she can now face more realistically, will keep her afloat in this sea of tribulations.

A Search for the Authentic Self

In the collection *Lughat al-Ay-Ay (The Language of Pain)*, the title story is an existential experience of pain and death. With almost clinical accuracy Idris examines and dissects an acute state of pain suffered by a man ailing from cancer of the bladder. On one level we have the description of the symptoms of that disease; on a yet deeper level it is the experiencing of the objective correlative of pain.

The story is that of a famous specialist and college professor who after long years of separation from a childhood friend he had left behind in the village is sought by the latter and is asked to ease his suffering. The doctor is all the more deeply affected when he realizes that he himself could have very easily been the ailing man if it had not been for a stroke of luck which brought him to the city to continue his higher education — coupled with his own gift of strong determination since his early childhood. But more decisive was that very friend who arrives more dead than alive seeking his help. For this very friend was his inspiration and incentive to go on with a career; as a child he was brilliant and at the top of his class, and Fahmy was always secretly competing with him. He had been with him, in spirit, all these years in the city, goading him, competing, forcing him to continue to excel. Today he sees him as a heap of bones, squirming in his pain, writhing and wriggling, crying out in pain "Ay! Ay! Ay!" with an ever rising pitch. Al-Hadidi takes his friend home, overruling his wife's objections and threats, and spends the night in mental torture with him. Here there is a parallelism between the unbearable physical pain of Fahmy and the doctor's more excruciating moral and mental suffering. Lying beside his insensitive wife who embodies and represents the kind of life he has espoused, Al-Hadidi goes through a series of epiphanies which reveal to him his true self, what he really wanted from life. He first experiences a pressing need to scream with all his might, just like Fahmy who could not control his pain. Al-Hadidi then thinks of all the times he felt like standing in the middle of Tahrir Square (the main square in Cairo) and just letting go, screaming with all his might:

> and he felt a faded comfort; and voices reaching an internal fathomless point in him, refreshing him with a touch of refinement and sweetness. Yes right here is the spot where he felt it assembling . . . his Ahat (Ouch's) he hadn't let go of . . . for they are not of the language of this world of this life, but it is the language of the depths and the Ay Ay.

This realization leads him on to others and eventually culminates in the total rejection of his actual life. He lies there, dissecting in his mind those cries of pain rending the air, and he comes to the conclusion that if they mean anything at all then they are to be equated with a sense of life. He reflects — to be alive is to feel, to feel intensely, and Fahmy out there is more alive than he ever was. For all through these years he had kept his feelings under control, and had "lived" according to the rules of society and had been "successful." Now he realizes how dead he was all along, his life a series of "amputated" friendships, "parts" of relationships and interrupted contacts. He, more than Fahmy, carried in himself the cancerous, malignant tumor. A cancer which ate away the very essence of life, which froze feelings and made him a non-sentient being, unable to share in any form of exchange, unmotivated to give or receive love. Thus he sees the light: "From here the tragedy began which transformed him into a 'living' dead man."

Al-Hadidi at this moment of illumination ironically turns to his friend Fahmy and asks for his help, his forgiveness and acceptance. For a brief moment Fahmy overcomes his gnawing pains and becomes to his friend what he once was—a comforter and inspirer. But this does not last long, for his unbearable pains resume and his uncontrollable cries awaken the whole neighborhood. Eventually the police are summoned and Al-Hadidi in a final gesture of rejection of unauthentic life offers his wife the chance to leave her old life behind and follow him. She, of course, misses the whole point of his transformation and unsuccessfully tries to keep him, but he sets himself free, carrying his friend on his back, walking proudly for the first time, unashamed of his modest peasant background—at long last liberated. Al-Hadidi for the first time feels alive, and sees the people around him as "corpses," just as he himself had in a sense so recently been. In this heavily suggestive story, Idris succeeds in intermingling two levels of meaning. The symbolic thrust for liberation is enhanced by the literal sense of the story. Al-Hadidi's search and finding of himself is a process he had apparently been experiencing all along, but which comes to a point of culmination when he encounters Fahmy. He becomes a forcible catalyst for change, whereas previously he had been rather a helping agent in the furthering of the character, personality and career of Al-Hadidi. Thus Fahmy is not merely the social alternative, the embodiment of sickness, poverty and ignorance that Al-Hadidi escaped being; he is in a sense his alter ego, that other self he always was, the "living" principle he had suppressed for so long. Fahmy becomes, ironically, in his death what Al-Hadidi had always assumed, wrongly, he had been in his life. It is doubly ironic that Idris should choose a fatally sick man to embody that principle, but on the other hand it may be that he merely was pointing to the fact that "life" in the figurative sense was ebbing away from Al-Hadidi, just as it was from Fahmy, and both were desperately trying to hold on to it. This process takes place through a language emanating from the depths, a language of pain and suffering—universal expression of pain. the language of al-Ay-Ay. Idris' approach to this story and others is reminiscent of Joseph Conrad's, particularly in *Heart of Darkness*. Here, too, Conrad fuses two levels of meaning, the literal (the story of a journey through a real wilderness in search of a real man), and the symbolic journey through a wilderness found at the center of the human psyche in search of some center of the self concealed inside the soul of each of us. Conrad's emphasis and extensive use of symbols, symbolic scenes and structural subtleties afforded to him by the length of his story help him secure a certain detachment and impersonality which enables him to operate more freely.

As Conrad descends provisionally into the heart of darkness and emerges crying "the horror, the horror," having probed the dark corners of the human soul to find it plagued with evil, but also capable of some good. so does Idris when he delves into those regions of "fathomless internal depths" and emerges crying "Ay, Ay, Ay. . . ."

The interest of Conrad's story for us lies in its technique of a tightly knit story. Conrad employs the literary device of using two narrators to recount his story, one of whom turns out to he a dubious authority, for in the process Marlow becomes the embodiment of the meanings the novel requires of him. In having a nameless narrator introduce Marlow, who will proceed to reveal the mystery of Kurtz in the heart of Africa, Conrad twice removes himself from his creation to view the denouement of its drama from a perched privacy. This same device is often used by Idris in his stories, with appropriate variation. In "Farahat's Republic," another of his stories, he is twice removed from the scene by giving us a spectator-narrator, who in turn gives his own point of view, his impressionistic insights of the dramas unreeling before him. Marlow and Idris' narrators in "Farahat's Republic" fret about reality and unreality. Like Conrad's hero, Idris' Fahmy seems to be the "secret sharer" of Al-Hadidi.

The confrontation with the authentic self as examined in these stories takes place at a moment of extreme tension—sometimes at a moment of death—and it is at this crucial point that the existential man comes to grips with his *condition humaine* and tries to redefine the meaning of life.

Mona Mikhail, *Mundus Artium* Vol. X no. 1 (1977): 89-99.

Sex and Society in Yusuf Idris:
"Qa' al-Madina"

Catherine Cobham

Yusuf Idris shows his most shrewd understanding of Egyptian society and its changing values through his stories of sexual relationships and his exploration of the nature of love, need, desire, repression, frustration, and masculinity and femininity themselves within these relationships. In his tales of village life, like 'Hadithat Sharaf', he demonstrates with lucid simplicity the workings of the process by which the community forces its members to conform to accepted standards of behaviour. Sex is the touchstone of social intercourse, and the attitude of a community to sexual relationships is most expressive of its culture; in the village masculinity and femininity are prized but, to appearances at least, they must be put to their designated uses in work and marriage. In a city the sexual code is more complex, and it is more difficult to confine the subject of sex within narrative patterns, but in 'Qa' al-Madina' (and also in 'al-Naddaha' and 'Halqat al-Nuhas al-Na'ima') Idris describes specific sexual relationships between men and women from different social backgrounds in a way which shows the interrelation of their positions in society with their attitudes to sex, and so imposes a pattern on elusive but crucial aspects of Egyptian life and creates a starting point for thought and understanding. . . .

'Qa' al-Madina' is the story of the judge 'Abd Allah who loses his watch, suspects his servant Shuhrat of having stolen it and makes a journey to "the bottom of the city" to catch Shuhrat red-handed with the watch and accuse her face to face. The plot itself is ironic: a judge who sits in court and passes judgment on all kinds of people every day, who has it in his power to adjourn a sitting to suit himself when the defendant pauses "to swallow his saliva", rarely leaves the green riverside quarter of Cairo where he lives, but when the crime is committed against himself he is intoxicated by the idea of confronting the criminal in her own house in the poorest area of the city. He rejoices at the opportunity to point to guilt in an individual who has personally threatened the ideas with which he protects himself and justifies his way of life. 'Abd Allah is a skilfully drawn caricature:

"His life was filled with the numbers 3445, 29987G, 10031,

66, 8345. They were the numbers of his car, his refrigerator, his life insurance his flat and his bank account. . . He was a man of medium estate, and was in fact average in all things. He was not tall, but you could not possibly have called him short. Similarly he was neither thin nor fat and his skin was neither white nor brown. In brief, if we took the average height, weight and colouring of a hundred men . . . we would have before us 'Abd Allah. Even in the sweetness of his tea — Mme. Shanadi would say to him as she put sugar in the cups: 'How many, 'Abd Allah *bayk*?', then normally she would supply the answer herself and say: 'Ah, I know. You like it medium... One and a half, isn't it?', whereupon he would smile and say, as he prepared to play trumps, for they were in the middle of a game of bridge, 'You know, Madame, I am a moderate sort of man.' Everybody would laugh then as if he had made a joke, for the judge's jokes were themselves always average, and moderately funny."

His behaviour is portrayed with delicate satire, not with facile or clumsy sarcasm, so that the reader is led to stand back with the author and understand it, not to join with him in ridiculing the judge. Idris describes 'Abd Allah searching for his watch when he first discovers its loss:

"During the search operation he had taken off his trousers and jacket and remained only in his shirt and shoes and socks so that he could bend down and look under beds and chairs . . . and in all those places that always spring to a man's mind the moment he loses anything . . . although in the majority of cases all that he finds there is dust and spiders. . . Then he sat down on a chair and placed one bare white leg on top of the other and began to think and wonder. A man like 'Abd Allah is confronted by problems of every shape and size, but to lose his wrist watch is an unusual problem which only sizes—if it arises at all—once in the whole of his life."

'Abd Allah is so perplexed by the loss of his watch that he decides to smoke:

"[He] did not smoke, but he had a packet of cigarettes which he kept in the desk drawer to offer to visitors, and very occasionally he smoked, once a month perhaps or every two months. He stood up to get a cigarette and returned to his former position, sitting with one leg crossed over the other. This movement revealed to him that he was almost completely naked and he hurried to put on his pyjamas before

anyone saw him. Not that there was anyone else in the flat, for
he was a bachelor and lived by himself, having decided upon
his thirty-fifth year as the appropriate time to get married."

With descriptions like this the author accumulates details which gives
indications of 'Abd Allah's attitude to sex. His pragmatic reasons for his
abstinence from sex are in retrospect an ironic comment on his relationship with
Shuhrat:

> "'Abd Allah was upright, not because it was forbidden
> (haram) not to be upright, or because these 'things' were not
> right . . . but because on one ill-fated occasion he had gone
> with a student friend and they had picked up a girl from the
> street in his friend's big car and had taken her on to the
> Alexandria road, and the next day he had been terrified by the
> appearance of ominous symptoms. Of course he had been
> completely cured but he had sworn to himself never to go near
> a woman until he got married."

By the time he is thirty his resolve has weakened and he determines to enjoy
the five years before he gets married, but although he takes the initial step of
ordering his manservant to come only in the mornings, still the flat does not "fill
up with women", and he has recourse to Mme. Shanadi's salon to meet girls in
keeping with "the dignity of his position" as a judge. The author's very brief
sketch of Mme. Shanadi and her salon is like a vivid cartoon for a situation in a
novel by Mahfuz: Mme. Shanadi is "a widow in her fifties whose passion for
bridge reached the bounds of madness." Among her friends are "great men of the
state" who meet in her salon where she skilfully directs the conversation and
"excels in listening to troubles and giving understanding smiles." She is significantly different from the delicate pale-skinned girls and women who frequent her
salon, although she partakes of some of their affectations: "her skin was deep
brown and she could have come from the heart of the Sa'id, but she said herself
that she was Turkish." At her soirees and card parties 'Abd Allah gradually learns
the conventions of behaviour with girls of his own class and is surprised to meet
girls from the families of other judges when he visits a cabaret, but secretly these
conventions, the need to be "polite and refined and say nice things to them," irk
him and inhibit him, and he is constantly insecure in their company and in the
places where he is obliged to go with them. He chooses a place far from Cairo and
makes sure that none of his friends or acquaintances or the lawyers from the court
knows it, but still he is perpetually ill at ease and "he does not breathe freely until
the girl gets out of the car, after tweaking his hand and saying 'Bye Bye' [in
English]". The most disturbing aspect of his relations with these girls is that he
only has to touch their hands and they start away from him, and finally need forces
him to try Mme. Shanadi herself, who "responds to him as if it were a routine

procedure, and treats him like an overgrown naughty child", so that his shame and resentment at his unjust deserts increases.

The circumstances in which he engages Shuhrat are themselves satirised. In what is described ironically as "one of the revolutions which 'Abd Allah made against himself, or more precisely against his friends", he makes an arbitrary decision to try and change the pattern of his life and his relationships, quite unaware of the real nature of his dissatisfaction. This expresses itself in a complaint about "the crisis of servants" and an attack on their bad ways to the accommodating Farghali, the doorman at the court, "who inclined his head, and sometimes his whole body, as a sign of his complete agreement with everything that the judge said." He asks Farghali to find a woman willing to work for him and, perhaps hardly acknowledging his intentions to himself, he starts by stipulating that she should be old, and finally decides that she should be young, "since the servants' staircase was steep and the flat was on the seventh floor", at which Farghali smiles, "realising the implied meaning" of the judge's conditions.

The satire, with its sporadic levity, fades when Shuhrat enters the story, and the meaning of the confrontation between her and 'Abd Allah stands clearly on the page. He interrogates her, as master to servant, but she is "polite rather than humble and submissive", and he is disconcerted by her assurance and independence. He remembers his real interest in her: "Would he be able to? He was frightened. It needed a hard struggle to overcome innocence." He stares at her impudently, perhaps searching for "that thing which experience had taught him to look for every time he met a woman, which meant she had no objection, but he did not find it", and she returns his look without embarrassment. Although he recognises her innocence instinctively he cannot acknowledge it for long, and is almost jubilant when he thinks he has found out dissimulation in her. When she tells him that she has never worked for anyone before, he thinks disbelievingly that she "must want to appear in his eyes like the lady of the house whom need has forced out to work". Again he cannot believe that she does not partake of the hypocrisy of the girls he is used to, when, shortly after he has finally forced her to submit to him, he returns to her to "look at those strong features, to see what had happened to them", and finds her "with resentful eyes and shining cheeks", upset by her first rude experience of infidelity to her husband. Roughly, he presses her to tell him what is wrong, but she remains silent until he insists:

> "He shook her shoulder with some pity and much irritation: 'What's the matter?'
> She said, 'I've never done it before', and the tears sprang into her eyes. He did not believe her for a moment. That was an old trick . . . she must be trying to make him look ridiculous, if she thought she could convince him that this was her first time. She must think him stupid and naive, or no doubt she wanted a rise for it."

After Shuhrat had refused to submit to him at his first diffident sallies, he had felt the ignominy of his weakness: "A woman like her and he wasn't strong enough to get her...and the flat was empty, and although he was young he had social standing, and yet he couldn't do it!", but when he has succeeded, he is seized by an unprecedented awareness of his physical power, for "it had not been his money or his manners or his standing in society which had got her, but his own strength."

For a time he enjoys this new consciousness of his virility which he had never experienced with prostitutes, nor in the emasculated intercourse of Mme. Shanadi's salon, but soon the spectre of Shuhrat's husband rises to the surface of his consciousness, and although he barely allows himself to consider their respective relationships to Shuhrat, he is forced to consider the differences between their ways of life. Momentarily he desires equality with her, and wants to convince himself that she submits to him and tries to please him "for himself and for his manhood". Not knowing whether he is serious or in fun he asks her if she loves him, and the exchange which follows his question is a set-piece between the intellectual who has forgotten how to respond to his feelings, but has "read about love. . . and been deeply involved in discussions about the meaning of love. . . with other educated people like himself", and an illiterate woman who knows what love is intuitively, but when forced to give an explanation answers: "Love is sent by God".

He is consistently preoccupied by the financial aspects of their relationship, although only when he has determined to get rid of Shuhrat and she has faded to the peripheries of his experience does a distant, elegiac sympathy for her poverty become possible, as it occurs to him to wonder how the family will live when she no longer works for him. As his confidence in himself and his contempt for her increases, he changes from proving himself to testing the nature of her dependence upon him, unscrupulously, by lowering her wage. This has the unexpected and undesired effect of bringing her world closer to his imagination, because when she complains to him he learns details of her poverty, and his jealousy of her husband turns to distaste: "His disgust reached its limit when he learnt that her husband worked in the tannery. Many impressions merged into one another in his mind. . . dirty hide, the smell of cattle and glue, Shuhrat's embrace and his bed."

The signs of the change that Shuhrat has undergone at 'Abd Allah's hands begin to irritate him, and as he was instinctively aware of her innocence when she first came, he begins to notice signs of a loss of her former naivety and honesty, "even in her smiles" and in her "languid, theatrical gesture" as she looks at herself in the mirror. He determines most firmly to dismiss her when she changes her *milaya* for a cheap blouse and skirt and goes bare-headed, with a light red colour on her lips "perhaps made by a red biro". He explains his distaste to himself with unconscious hypocrisy and puritanism mingled:

> "Why did she insist on wearing clothes like these when she
> looked much prettier in a milaya?. . . What would she do when

>she had stopped working for him, and how would they eat?
>She would have to go out on the streets, and the ones that wore
>*milayas* couldn't be worth so much, so that was why she
>wanted a skirt and blouse, to raise her price."

He does not want to pursue his thoughts too far, and besides, "Shuhrat as far as he was concerned was finished. Only a few days and he would drive her out for good, then let her do whatever she pleased." He is aware that he is responsible for the changes in her, but his recognition of his guilt is short-lived because he, the judge, has no fear of punishment or recrimination for what he does in the privacy of his flat. Since Shuhrat has changed into "a woman who can be bought and sold", he is preoccupied by feelings of jealousy "not of the lover for his beloved" but, since he has reverted to identifying his virility with his social status, the jealousy of "the master for his servant, or the master for himself. He had a terrible fear that Shuhrat would put him on the same level as a youth who did the ironing or sold bread on the street."

The emphasis in the description of 'Abd Allah's journey from the pleasant areas of Cairo by the Nile to the poorest areas behind al-Azhar is strikingly different from that in, for example, Yahya Haqqi's description in *Qindil Umm Hashim* (Cairo, 1944) of Isma'il walking through the square of Sayyida Zaynab, or al-Manfaluti's account of his hero wandering in "a lonely, desolate quarter. . . the dwelling place of *jinns*" in the story 'Ghurfat al-Ahzan'. With a powerful, evocative conceit Idris describes each stage of the journey in terms of the width and surface of the roads, the age of the houses and the type of windows they have, the shops which are replaced by booths and eventually by hand-barrows, and the features and clothes of the people and the way they speak and move, as all these things are modified, and degenerate; the reduction of humanity suggested by the description of the change in the people's language and movement is particularly effective. The complete interdependence and unity of life at the last stage of the journey, potentially a source of strength to the people, and a dramatic contrast to 'Abd Allah's way of life, is represented as a desperate clinging on to subsistence:

>"The houses leant against one another so that they would
>not fall down, and so did the people. The old man struggled
>along helped by the young man, the blind man was led by a
>youth and the sick man was propped up by a wall . . . and a
>hidden thread joined them together as if they were the beads
>of a rosary, one spirit inhabiting many different bodies."

'Abd Allah, accompanied by Farghali and a friend, becomes the centre of apprehensive attention and "women sitting in doorways weaving gossip out of their boredom...saw them and wondered, and heads were bent together and the whisper passed from doorway to doorway and they said to one another, 'Police'."

'Abd Allah's expedition to Shuhrat's quarter of the city is as much to restore his dignity and to assert his superiority over her to his own satisfaction, as to find his watch. He has a fleeting, ecstatic vision of asserting his physical power over her again: "if only he could strangle her . . . yes, if he could entwine his fingers around her neck and press and press upon her throat", but as he descends through the city, growing subdued and then benumbed by the unfamiliar surroundings, the gulf between him and Shuhrat becomes increasingly apparent. When he finally confronts her, "he assumes the role of the prosecuting attorney, and she that of the accused. . . and he shouts like the robbed master and she cringes like the thieving servant", but all savour of victory has gone out of the occasion and he is "like a sleep-walker", anaesthetised to the poverty and misery around him, as well as to any sensation of triumph at the sight of his rival, "something moving on the mattress . . . a tall, brown-skinned man, with a head like the tall clay jar that stood beside it, sleeping there...his clothes loosened and his worn, grimy underclothes showing through the opening in his trousers."

'Abd Allah's bemused relief as he emerges from the "nightmare" and returns to familiar sights and sounds is conveyed by the imagery which the author uses, and by the description of the intense contrast of the sensuous experience as they leave the poor quarters and approach the Nile and 'Abd Allah's flat:

> "Breezes began to blow and faces revived from the day's heat, and the bridge was filled with groups of people strolling along. There was so much water, and the distant white buildings were like dovecotes, and the city was so beautiful, more beautiful than he had ever seen it . . . He took avid gulps of the air and his head spun."

That evening he sits on his balcony as the sun sets:

> "Night would have engulfed the city if millions of tiny lights had not been sown over the surface of the earth, and these grew and changed the darkness as they bloomed, shining and twinkling. Then they burst into flower, and red and green and blue and yellow lights of different shapes and names and varieties suffused the air of the city, and the darkness was transformed into a carnival."

Still he has not quite regained his peace of mind and "he tries to concentrate his eyes on a spot wavering in the shadows of the night, far from the lights, behind the minaret of al-Azhar." . . . .

'Qa' al-Madina' takes the shape of a detective story: the judge discovers the loss of his watch, eliminates the suspects until he decides that Shuhrat must be guilty, and then plans his journey to recover it, with the help of his friend Sharaf, an impoverished actor who is to pretend to be a policeman, and Farghali, who comes from the same area as Shuhrat. The description of his sexual relationship with Shuhrat only forms the recapitulation in the centre of the narrative but it explains, most pertinently, the exact nature and extent of his separation from Shuhrat and all the people like her, and demonstrates the emptiness and hypocrisy of his own values. The natural climax of the story is not in the death of their sexual relationship, but in their confrontation in Shuhrat's house, when he "takes her to the window, and he looks out, and she looks out, and he says, 'Officer', and Sharaf says, 'Yes, sir' . . . and almost laughs", and then they go back into the room, and he threatens her with "a year in prison" if she does not hand back the watch, and in the end she takes it from a broken glass in the cupboard and gives it to him.

Idris traces the intricacies of cause and effect in the details of the relationship between Shuhrat and 'Abd Allah, a relationship which is more a confrontation, and has its blueprints in stories like 'Al-Hala al-Rabi'a' (where a complacent young doctor has his first contact with a woman "criminal"). Then with a skilled and delicate sense of proportion he steps back to describe the complete and tragic division between their ways of life with the dispassionate intensity of one who has been involved with, and has identified with, both sides and is able to create an image which does not impart a subjective impression, but forces the reader to imagine those aspects which he does not know from experience, and to share in the conflict.

Catherine Cobham, *Journal of Arabic Literature* VI (1975): 78-88.

The Language of Pain By Youssef Idris

Nur Sherif

This volume contains twelve short stories written over a period of eight years. *The Ten Pound Note,* the earliest of the stories is dated 1957 and *The Aorta,* which is the most recent is dated 1965. With the exception of three or four these stories were written during the period 1962-1965, and it is these relatively more recent stories that show Youssef Idris (1927—) at his best. They reveal an artist who has developed considerably towards a greater depth of feeling, a broader humanity and a more skilful mastery of the exacting technique of the short story.

The dominant note of the later stories is one of bitter disillusionment at man's engrossment in himself and his indifference to others. The pain referred to in the title of the collection is the physical and mental pain which unfortunate man suffers the pain which he should but seldom does share with his fellow mortals. Above all it is the pain through which he may redeem himself. There is little joy in these stories, if we exclude the brief happiness of the child in his close relationship to his mother during his early innocence in *Because the Day of Judgment does not Come.* In this sensitive study of the child's growing pains as the facts of life are revealed to him, jealousy, hatred and aggressiveness emerge with his sense of dispossession and loss of love. Unadulterated joy and complete abandonment to the pleasures of the senses are still possible in the world of the adolescent in *Caught Red-handed.* Here the situation is a simple one: a young university student of seventeen, smoking a cigarette in a quiet spot, is caught by the Dean who sees her from his office window. At first he is outraged, and his immediate reaction is to have her punished. Gradually, as he watches her surrender to the purely sensual enjoyment she derives at each puff that she takes, he is fascinated by the sight of every movement of her graceful body. The man, long past his prime and weighed down by the responsibilities of life, is slowly rejuvenated by sharing the same experience of uninhibited pleasure, an experience so intense that it almost amounts to a perfect physical union. At the end of the story, however, the voice of duty and authority ring clear in his ear, reminding the dean of his official role as enforcer of the law. The link which had bound him to another human being snaps.

Man not only fails to share joy, destroying it in others as well as in himself, he fails to share the suffering of others in his preoccupation with his own little world

85

of self. In the allegorical story called *The Language of Pain*, al-Hadidi, who is a professor, husband and father, is a success in the eyes of society. But his ambition and feverishness to reach the top of the ladder have cut him off from people, and he has led a life of loneliness and separation. Only when he recognises another man's physical pain does he suddenly realise how empty his existence has been. Throughout the story reverberate the agonised screams of Fahmy, al-Hadidi's old schoolmate whose poverty had destroyed all promise in the child, and who is now dying of cancer of the bladder. Everyone wishes to be rid of Fahmy because his presence is too disturbing, but al-Hadidi, who has suddenly come to life by feeling for the man, will not let him go. This contact through pain amounts to almost a mystical experience. Through it al-Hadidi is able to reach out to every human being on earth and every object in creation, and to gaze into the depths of his own soul without fearing what he sees there. The deeper he descends into the realm of pain the vaster and all-embracing his world becomes. In pain, as well as in joy, there is release for the pent up feelings and from the deadening effect of frustration.

At the end of the story al-Hadidi carries Fahmy over his shoulder out of the house. " I'm going another way, a difficult way, " he says to his wife, " will you come?"' But she refuses to join him, thinking he has gone mad. The people all around nudge each other, making fun of the man in this Christlike situation, carrying all alone the burden of suffering humanity. As he leaves, he sees "the windows and doors, thick with corpses," the stench of which has now become unbearable, and he hastens away from the place where he too had lived a corpse.

Mere indifference is not all. There is yet the story of positive cruelty and violence, the only forces which ironically bring people together. *The Aorta*, written in the form of allegory, is the most powerful of the short stories in this collection. Unlike *The Language of Pain* which is diffuse and too obviously didactic, *The Aorta is* an example of the compactess of the short story at its best, presenting the central idea through a concrete situation which speaks for itself. Here the writer's disillusionment reaches a savage intensity, expressed in images of horror which have an immediate impact.

The story is a nightmarish vision of humanity shown in all its inhumanity. The opening lines give a bird's eye view image of multitudes madly hurrying and scurrying, first in one direction, then in another with no obvious goal in sight, as though the rat race itself were the be all and end all of existence. No sooner is one black speck seen running in one direction than thousands are seen to follow rapidly, in the hope of getting there first. As soon as they realise that he is as much at a loss as they themselves are, they hurriedly dash to another spot. The whole face of the earth is shown from above, pulsating with these swarming creatures, rushing, crowding and then dispersing in all directions, with occasional clashes which nobody notices and occasional casualties dropping out on the way, heeded by nobody, so long as the others are safe.

Youssef Idris then slows down the action to give a close-up of a situation that is representative of the whole. The panoramic view of life seen from above

suddenly takes on the reality of flesh and blood, and the absurdity and meaning-
lessness of the former scene turn to one of horror. The horrible secret of this blind
mad rush of humanity is revealed as the first person narrator of the story sets eyes
on Abdou his fellow traveller, a poor weak living corpse of a creature whose very
defencelessness brings out the savage in the narrator. He wants to flay Abdou
alive in search of the few piastres he claims the poor man has stolen and is hiding
on his person. Then Abdou tells a terrible tale. He was found suffering from an
infectious disease which threatened to spread, killing the whole population. To
treat him an operation was performed, cutting the aorta, the artery of life. But no
one will believe his story and the crowd, which has found a common pursuit in
the name of justice, feverishly joins in search of the money hidden somewhere in
the clothes of the guilty man. But who is the guilty? The answer becomes clear
once the crowd starts the butchering process. Abdou is hung up on a hook, his
gown is torn off his back, and his bandages are mercilessly wrenched from his
body. To the horror of the reader, an ugly wound is seen reaching down the whole
length of his naked body. His chest and abdomen are hollow and the aorta dangles
loose from where his heart had been, as though it were a long thick reed pipe
oscillating inside his abdomen like a pendulum." Abdou had spoken the truth; he
was one of the millions of living corpses still tortured to death for the little that
might yet be obtained from them. His mere survival was a miracle. This is the
terrible story of man's cruelty to man and his exploitation of his fellow beings.

   Allegory is not the only method that Youssef Idris employs in his short stories.
In *This Time* he writes in a different vein, entering deep into the feelings of a
prisoner who waits for his wife's monthly visit. At every meeting we are made
to feel, through the hurried sentences, the acute sense of the passage of time. At
each visit a complete relationship has to be reestablished, by picking up the
broken threads which have snapped during the intervening month. Detail by
detail we follow the prisoner's sensations through his stream-of-consciousness
which runs wild under the calm surface of commonplace everyday speech. Each
time the man and woman meet, some sort of union is achieved after the first
anxious searching glance of exploration to discover any change that may have
taken place in the woman. With reassurance, contact is brought about and a whole
world of experience is condensed in their few moments together, when the senses
and thoughts are sharpened to a point that is painful. In the particular situation
"this time" in the short story, however, the prisoner senses a change which the
woman denies, and contact is lost. The man is left alone tortured by his fears and
anxiety and, above all, by the fact that he may never know the truth.

   Seen in the context of the whole volume of short stories, the concrete situation
of the prisoner may be interpreted symbolically. The prison here is the prison of
self, whereby the individual finds himself cut off from his fellow beings unable
to share with others either joy or pain. The prisoner who spends his life behind
iron bars, incapable of penetrating to others, is not the only frustrated character
in these stories. And no wonder, if life is the nightmare of savagery and cruel
indifference that Youssef Idris conceives it to be in *The Aorta*. On no level does

contact appear to be possible. But, through the impact of his own powerful images, at least the author has succeeded in communicating with the reader.

Nur Sherif, *About Arabic Books*, Beirut: Beirut Arab University, 1970, pp. 94-100.

Blindness and Sexuality:
Traditional Mentalities in Yusuf Idris'
"House of Flesh"

Fedwa Malti-Douglas

The related areas of gender and sexuality have become major preoccupations in contemporary criticism.(1) But much of the importance of these concepts derives from the fact that, in any given culture or literary tradition, they do not operate in isolation but dialectically combine with other cultural foci. Thus, they become part of the configuration of mental structures distinctive to every culture. In Arabic civilization, and therefore also Arabic letters, the topic of blindness has become closely intertwined with concepts of sexuality.

This is certainly the case with modern Arabic literature. But the mental structures pervading twentieth-century Arabic letters are not, obviously, all of recent origin. Arabic novels, poems, and stories of the past century draw not only upon the literary but also the more general cultural heritage of classical civilization. It is, therefore, not surprising that continuing classical and traditional Arabic mental structures should be central to the understanding of modern Arabic writing. The relations between the areas of sexuality and blindness can best be understood as the expression, in a contemporary literary medium, of traditional, but still viable, mental structures.

What better place to isolate these structures than in a text by the master of the Arabic short story, the contemporary Egyptian writer Yusuf Idris (b. 1927)? Trained as a physician, Idris has nevertheless devoted his life to literature, concentrating on the short story.

"Bayt min Lahm" [House of Flesh] is, without doubt, one of Idris' most finely-crafted literary pieces. It tells the story of a widow and her three daughters whose only male contact is a blind *Koran* reciter. On the urging of her daughters, the mother marries the sightless man, and, eventually, through an elaborate game of exchange of the wedding ring, the reader is made to understand that the blind man is dispensing his favors to the entire female section of the household.(2)

The art of Yusuf Idris derives not solely from an entertaining plot, however, but also from a variety of factors conducive to an effective story. Critics,

including Sasson Somekh and P.M. Kurpershoek, have identified some of these
in the Idrisian corpus. And, invariably, in these discussions, "House of Flesh"
holds a major place.(3)

But Yusuf Idris, like other Arab writers, is embedded within a tradition whose
mental structures continue to dominate his work. Such is the case with "House of
Flesh." The first, and obvious, relation to traditional mental structures is the
occupation of the blind protagonist. The role of *Koran* reciter has been traditionally relegated to the visually handicapped. (4)

Such links, however, go deeper than the mere occupation of the sightless
character. One of the most pervasive Idrisian subjects, as critics have noted, is
sex.(5) In fact, "House of Flesh" embodies classical Arabic mental structures on
the relations of blindness and sexuality.

These two come together in the medieval sources to create a specifically
Eastern perspective: blind men are seen as particularly virile. A classical Arabic
proverb, for example, states: "More Virile than a Blind Man."(6) This is, of
course, meant to indicate, as proverbs on that pattern do, that the blind individual
possesses that characteristic to such a degree that he becomes the model against
which other individuals are measured. The geographer and cosmographer al-
Qazwini (d. 1283), in his work on the wonders of creation, notes that the sightless
individual is the most virile of people, just as the eunuch is the one whose vision
is the most correct. That is because, al-Qazwini explains, the two functions,
vision and sexuality, represent two opposite but complementary poles: "what is
deficient in one is increased in the other."(7) The *Koran* reciter in "House of
Flesh" fulfills this role splendidly, as he moves from one female to the next,
satisfying them all.(8)

But the narrator of Yusuf Idris' story extends this traditional, Islamic perspective in yet another way. The female characters in "House of Flesh" are four in
total: the widow and her three daughters. As is well known, according to a
Koranic injunction, a Muslim can have up to four wives, if he can treat them
equally.(9) And our blind *Koran* reciter is quite at home in this injunction as well.
Though he does not marry all four women (which would be illegal in Islamic law),
he is effectively playing the role of a polygamous male by 'treating them equally,'
on the sexual plane.(10)

Part of what gives "House of Flesh" its symbolic density, however, is the fact
that blindness is not limited to the plot, or to the Koran reciter as referent. The
interrelated linguistic signifiers of blindness play a large rhetorical role in the text
as well. In this regard, blindness is exploited not only on its own but also in
combination with other perceptual categories. This can be seen in the enigmatic
prologue. The text begins: "The ring is beside the lamp. Silence descends and ears
are blinded." And these sentences are repeated towards the end of the text.(11)
They frame the story (though not the narrative, since this extends beyond the
repetition). While the first of these sentences is clear, the second is not, if taken
literally. On a basic metaphorical level, however, since the ears are the subject
and blinded the analogue, the phrase signifies inability to perceive, deafness, or

silence. But, like all metaphors, this figure associates two conceptual categories, here, ears with eyes, deafness with blindness, silence with darkness. And the prologue adds: "In the darkness, too, eyes are blinded."(12)

The prologue, therefore, establishes three things: [I] a cross-sensory tendency, categories from one mode of perception being used with another; [2] the notion that blindness can apply to situations other than the visual handicap and to individuals other than the blind character, and [3] an equivalence between silence and blindness (after all, it was "the silence" which "blinded" the ears).(13)

Though it begins the narrative, the prologue represents events at the end of the story.(14) Hence, the reader does not understand the significance of its imagery. Elements in the narrative, however, lead the reader progressively to the meaning of the prologue. Among them, are continued cross-sensory references. On the wedding-night, the widow and the blind reciter did not come near one another and from the three sleeping girls came a pair of "searchlights" directed at them: "Searchlights of eyes, searchlights of ears, and searchlights of senses."(15) When the husband confronts his wife with the change he sensed in her in the nuptial bed between midday and evening, she has an inkling of what has gone on. "She was silent. And with her ears which she had turned into noses, and senses, and eyes, she began to listen.(16)

As our examination of the prologue has shown, the phenomenon of cross-sensory perception is linked to a relationship between blindness and silence. In the most far-reaching study of Yusuf Idris to date, Sasson Somekh analyzes the evolution of silence in "House of Flesh." Taking off from the indications provided by the narrator, Somekh shows the development and progression of the concept of silence in the text, linking it to the psychological states of the five characters. He notes the "conspiracy" of silence taking place as each of the characters becomes initiated into the sexual game. By the end of the narrative, silence, according to him, means "sex in its existential, primitive meaning," one which does not take into consideration the licit or the illicit [halâl, harâm]. (17) This last point, silence representing a sexuality beyond morality, is an important one to which we shall return.

But silence must be seen in relation to blindness. By the end of the story, there is no question but that the silence is that of sexual complicity: "But it is the deepest kind of silence. For it is the silence which is agreed upon by the strongest kind of agreement, that which is concluded without any agreement."(18) Blindness, however, also represents sexual complicity. After all, it is the blindness of the hero which permits the four women to play their game, just as the reciter uses his blindness to pretend ignorance of what transpires. Blindness is his complicity as well.

Thus, by the end of the story, both blindness and silence represent complicity. Logic demands then that silence equal blindness. It is only by understanding this equivalence that the full import of the metaphor of the ears becoming blind can be exhausted. The link between silence and blindness, therefore, goes through sex, in effect, through the sexuality of the blind, itself reflecting a classical mental structure.

Linking sexuality, blindness, and silence, however, raises another question: the association of the latter two with an absence of moral responsibility, with a sexuality which transcends, as Somekh put it, the *harâm* and the *halâl*. This association finds its basis in two places in the narrative. The first is towards the end of the story, when the blind reciter, noting the transformations of his sexual partner(s), associates his uncertainty with a silence. The second, and more important, development of this theme comes in the epilogue. The narrator tells the reader that the sightless reciter "began to assure himself that his partner in bed was always his wife." She may be young or old, smooth or rough, slender or fat. "This is her affair alone," the affair of the sighted "and their responsibility alone." Only they can be certain, all he can do is doubt. "And as long as he is deprived" of his sight, "he is deprived of certainty, since he is blind."(19)

Does blindness take the sexual encounter outside the realm of moral responsibility? Certainly, this idea is posed. It is placed in the consciousness of the blind reciter. But the passage as a whole makes it clear that the reciter is using his blindness as a rationalization. He 'assures himself,' he washes his hands of the problem—it is the affair of the sighted, not his. His statement of unconcern is not credible because it is associated with "doubt," not with indifference. All these are gestures within a moral universe, not outside one. One who insists upon his doubt and who takes refuge behind his lack of knowledge is not unconcerned with the morality of his acts. Were the moral viewpoint truly transcended, the contrast between certainty and doubt would be of no importance.

Further, the emphasis in the epilogue on the physical variations in the blind man's sexual partner(s) reminds the reader of the unrealistic nature of the proposition that the blind man could truly ignore his sexual polygamy. It is well known that the sightless can determine the identity of individuals around them by their walk, by the sounds of their movements, and by their smell. This is especially so if the individuals are familiar ones, as is the case in "House of Flesh." Hence, at the very least, if Yusuf Idris has introduced the idea of the non-responsibility of the blind man (and, hence, of the silence associated with this situation), he has also invited the reader to question it.

Both the distinctiveness and the sophistication of Idris' psychological presentation can be seen clearly when it is compared with the more naive treatment of this same problematic of blindness and sexual morality in Andre Gide's *La symphonie pastorale*. Gide links blindness and innocence. Once his heroine regains her sight, she understands the immorality of her relationship with the pastor. Only with vision can she see the pain that she has caused his wife.(20)

That Yusuf Idris' text does not simply posit a sexuality beyond morality or blindness as moral non-responsibility can be seen even more clearly from the last words of the narrative. As Somekh himself noted, the text ends with a Koranic reference.(21) In fact, the penultimate phrase is a direct quote from the *Koran* and the final one is a recasting of this quote into an interrogative form.

Coming at the end of the text, this quote effectively redefines the material which precedes it, creating an intertextuality between "House of Flesh" and the most ubiquitous of Arabic texts. The notion of the *Koran* was already present in the story through the occupation of the blind hero. Reproducing parts of the *Koran* is his stock in trade; it is, therefore, not a coincidence that "House of Flesh" ends with a reproduction of a Koranic text. The *Koran* functions throughout the story as a subtext and the narrative as a whole can, thus, also be read as a discourse on tradition.

The phrase in question is an important one, since it appears twice in the *Koran,* once in "Surat al-Nur," verse 61 and once in "Surat al-Fath," verse 17. In his translation of "House of Flesh," Denys Johnson-Davies has given the Koranic phrase and its transformation as: "No moral responsibility attaches to a blind man? Or does it?"(22)

This is not, however, an optimal rendering of the Koranic text, *"laysa 'alâ al-a' mâ haraj,"* followed in the Idrisian text by: *"am 'alâ al-a' mâ haraj"* (23) The passage is translated correctly by Arberry as: "There is no fault in the blind."(24) The next phrase would then be rendered: "Or is there fault in the blind?" The key term is, of course, *haraj,* which can refer to a narrow place, a restriction (physical or moral), a prohibition, a crime, or something sacred or taboo.(25) Moral responsibility would not be lexically correct.

Nor would it fit the context of the Koranic passages. For "Surat al-Nur," both the context and the commentators agree that the passage is meant to indicate the absence of any negative or improper association with the blind and to enjoin eating with the blind and other handicapped.(26) What the *Koran* here provides is undoubtedly the rejection of the primitive notion that the visually or other physically handicapped are in some sense accursed or punished (an idea present in the Western tradition).(27)

The usage in "Surat al-Fath" is less immediately evident, but the commentators have interpreted it as releasing the blind (and other physically handicapped) from the obligation to perform the *jihâd.* (28) In neither case, does the *Koran* suggest an absence of, or a realm beyond, moral responsibility, an idea that would be doctrinally foreign to it in any case.

Of course, by writing "no moral responsibility," Johnson-Davies is linking the last phrases to the preceding paragraph which discusses the blind reciter's doubt and moral responsibility. As such, it is a stylistically effective translation. Further, it cannot be denied that some of the sense of the debate on moral responsibility which permeates this paragraph is transmitted also into the last phrases, forming one layer of their signification. But, to interpret the end of the story in this way is to eliminate the Koranic intertextual reference, and, with it, an additional layer of signification which has been added to the debate on moral responsibility contained in the paragraph. Otherwise, why include the Koranic reference, since the question could have been posed in other terms?

What then is the "fault" of the blind which is being questioned? In the context of "House of Flesh," and of Arabic mental structures generally, it is their superabundant sexuality, a sexuality which, far from being outside the realm of moral judgment, is capable of breaking moral rules. That is why the "no fault" clause is questioned at the end of the text. "House of Flesh" becomes a dialectical commentary on tradition. One traditional mental structure, that of the viriiity of the blind, is used to question another Koranic one, that of the absence of a special moral status for the blind.

In a typically Idrisian manner, a *Koran* reciter is drawn into an illicit relationship; as a result, it is the text of the *Koran* itself which is subverted. The progress of the sexual conspiracy has also been the progress of silence, an illicit silence which is the opposite of the law-establishing word, the oral word of the recited *Koran*. This subversion is achieved not only through the plot but, most dramatically, when a Koranic dictum is called into question, in the last words of the text. Is it any wonder that this should be the case when other rules have been subverted as well: rules of marriage, rules of sense perception, and, as critics have pointed out, rules of syntax?(29)

If the sexuality of blindness subverts on one level, it integrates on another. As we noted above, "House of Flesh" freely crosses sensoral boundaries. Silence becomes equivalent to blindness. In the prologue, ears were "blinded," and "in the darkness, too, eyes are blinded."(30) The condition of blindness does not inhere only in the *Koran* reciter. By the end of the story, it, like the silence, has enveloped all the characters. Instead of isolating the male character, his blindness links him to the women. This makes perfect sense if that blindness is also understood as superabundant sexuality.

This integration, too, recapitulates essential Arabo-lslamic attitudes to the blind. Taken as a whole, and especially when compared with those of the West, classical Arabic approaches to the visually handicapped (both mental structures and social roles) are remarkably integrating. Occupations like *Koran* reciter are an excellent example.(31) Indeed, it is the interaction of the mental with the social structures of integration which provides "House of Flesh" with its literary density. The integrated social role creates the setting for the story, just as the integrating mental structure creates its psycho-sexual dynamics.

Footnotes

1. See, for example, Elizabeth Abel, ed., *Writing and Sexual Difference* (Chicago: The University of Chicago Press, 1982); Elaine Showalter, ed., *The New Feminist Criticism: Essays on Women, Literature, and Theory* (New York: Pantheon Books, 1985); Nancy K. Miller, ed., *The Poetics of Gender* (New York: Columbia University Press, 1986). For the Arabo-lslamic sphere, see, for example, Fatna Ait Sabbah, *La femme dans l'inconscient musulman* (Paris: Albin Michel, 1986).
2. Yusuf Idris, "Bayt min Lahm," in Yusuf Idris, *Bayt min Lahm* (Cairo: Dar Misr lil-Tibi'a, 1982), pp. 3-11. This story has been translated by Denys Johnson-Davies, "House of Flesh," in Denys Johnson-Davies, trans., *Egyptian Short Stories* (Washington: Three Continents Press, 1978), pp. 1-8; and by Mona Mikhail, "A House of Flesh," in Roger Allen, ed., *In the Eye of the Beholder: Tales of Egyptian Life from the Writings of Yusuf Idris* (Minneapolis and Chicago: Bibliotheca Islamica, 1978), pp. 191-198. All translations in this study, however, are my own.
3. See, for example, Sasson Somekh, "Language and Theme in the Short Stories of Yusuf Idris," *Journal of Arabic Literature,* 6 (1975): 89-100; Sasson Somekh, ed., *Dunya*

Yusuf Idris (Jerusalem: Matba'at al-Sharq al-Ta'awuniyya, 1976); P.M. Kurpershoek, *The Short Stories of Yusuf Idris* (Leiden: E.l. Brill, 1981), Sasson Somekh, *Lughat al-Qissa fi Adab Yusuf Idris* (Acre: Matba'at al-Saruji, 1984). See, also, *Adab wa-Naqd* 34 (December 1987), special issue on Yusuf Idris.

4. Fedwa Malti-Douglas, *"Mentalités* and Marginality: Blindness and Mamluk Civilization," in *The Islamic World from Classical to Modern Times: Essays in Honor of Bernard Lewis.* eds. C.E. Bosworth *et al.* (Princeton: Darwin Press, 1989), pp. 211-237. For other manifestations of this traditional role for the visually handicapped as it relates to Taha Husayn, see Fedwa Malti-Douglas, *Blindness and Autobiography: al-Ayydm of Taha Husayn* (Princeton: Princeton University Press, 1988), Chapters 2, 3 and 5.

5. Kurpershoek includes "House of Flesh" with other examples of "deviant sexual behavior," in the writer's later corpus. Kurpershoek, *Short Stories,* pp. 132-133. For Somekh, sex in the later Idrisian volumes is "treated existentially... sex rules supreme. It is the end of all ends and the way of human salvation." Somekh, "Language and Theme," p. 93. See, also, Somekh, "Introduction," to Somekh, ed., *Dunya,* pp. 14-15. See, for example, in addition to the previous critical work cited, Ghali Shukri, *Azmat al-Jins fi al-Qissa al-'Arabiyya* (Cairo: al-Hay'a al-Misriyya al 'Amma lil-Ta'lif wal-Nashr, 1971), pp. 239-265; Catherine Cobham "Sex and Society in Yusuf Idris: 'Qa' al-Madina'," *Journal of Arabic Literature,* 6 (1975): 78-88. Yusuf Idris himself, in an interview, made it quite clear that sex for him equalled life. See Samir al-Sâ'igh, "Yusuf Idris: al-Kitaba, al-Thawra, al-Jins," *Mawâqif,* 9, May-June (1970): 54.

6. *Ankah min A'ma.* 'Al-Safadi, *Nakt al-Himyan fi Nakt al-'Umyân,* ed. Ahmad Zaki Bâshâ (Cairo: al-Matba'a al-Jamaliyya, 1911), pp. 21-22. Al-Maydânî, *Majma 'al-Amthâl (Beirut:* Dâr Maktabat al-Hayât, n.d.), v. 2, p. 412.

7. Al-Qazwînî, *'Aja'ib al-Makhluqat wa-Ghara'ib al-Mawjudat,* ed. Faruq Sa'd (Beirut: Dâr al-Afaq al-Jadîda, 1981), p. 348. Cf. al-Safadî, *Nakt, p. 54.* On the full ramifications of blindness and sexuality in Islam and a comparative analysis with attitudes in the West, see Malti-Douglas, *"Mentalités* and Marginality."

8. My colleague, Hasan el-Shamy, Professor of Folklore at Indiana University, has informed me that the special virility of blind men, and particularly blind *shaykhs,* is a familiar topos in Egyptian folklore.

9. *Koran,* "Surat al-Nisâ'," verse 3. Cf. Farida al-Naqqash, "Bayt min Lahm bayn al-Jins wal-Dîn," *Adab wa-Naqd,* 36 (1988): 28, which despite its title is a comparative analysis of two of Idris' short stories, "House of Flesh" and "Lîlî."

10. According to Islamic law, marriage to the daughters of the wife is forbidden. See Joseph Schacht, *An Introduction to Islamic Law* (Oxford: Oxford University Press, 1964), p. 162.

11. Idris, "Bayt min Lahm," pp. 3, 9.

12. Ibid., p. 3.

13. Much of the psychological and symbolic sophistication of the story derives from the fact that the equivalence of the paired elements is not logically complete. The paradigmatic partner to blindness would be deafness. Instead, what Idris has done is to relate an absence of sensory data with an inability to perceive, therefore creating an equivalence of situation between the perceptually handicapped (the blind reciter) and those struggling with an absence of perceptual data (all the characters).

14. This follows Genette's distinction between the story, what took place in the fictional world, in the order it took place, and the narrative, what is related in the text, in the order it is related in the text. See Gérard Genette, *Figures 111* (Paris: Editions du Seuil 1972), pp. 72, 146.

15. Idris, "Bayt min Lahm," p. 6.

16. Ibid., p. 8.

17. Somekh, *Lughat al-Qissa, pp.* 128-131.

18. Idris, "Bayt min Lahm," p. 10. Cf. Kurpershoek, *Short Stories,* p. 179, who, when discussing the prologue, states: "In this example, the inversion serves to focus the attention on the keywords *samt* [silence] and *zalam* [darkness], which, according to the author, stand respectively for 'conspiracy of silence' and the 'neglect of one's consciousness' [*ihmâl alwa'y*] ."

19. Idris, "Bayt min Lahm," pp. 10-11.

20. Andre Gide, *La symphonie pastorale* (Paris: Gallimard, 1925). William R. Paulson, *Enlightenment, Romanticism and the Blind in France* (Princeton: Princeton University Press, 1987), pp. 209-210, prefers to stress the doubts created by the pyschological naivete of the narrator. In this context, however, it seems to me that the mental structure in question is present, even though mediated through the narrator.

21. Somekh, *Lughat al-Qissa,* p. 18, writes that "the story 'Bayt min Lahm' ends with an allusion to the Koranic sentence 'Laysa 'alâ al-A'mâ Haraj' (Sûrat al-Nûr, verse 61)."

22. Johnson-Davies, "House of Flesh," p. 7. Mona Mikhail, "A House of Flesh," p. 198 translates it as: "You cannot reproach the blind. Or can you?"

23. Idrîs "Bayt min Lahm," p. 11.

24. A.J. Arberry, *The Koran Interpreted* (New York: Macmillan Publishing Co., 1974), v. 2, pp. 54, 227.

25. Ibn Manzûr, *Lisân al-'Arab*, (Cairo: al-Dâr al-Misriyya lil Ta'lîf wal-Tarjama, n.d., v. 3, pp. 56-61; al-Zabîdî, *Tâj al-Arûs*, v. 5, ed. Mustafâ Hijâzî (Kuwait: Matba'at Hukûmat al-Kuwayt, 1969), pp. 473-482; Ibn Sîda, *al-Muhkam*, v. 3, ed. 'A'isha 'Abd al-Rahmân (Bint al-Shâti') (Cairo: Matba'at Mustafâ al-Bâbî al-Halabî, 1958), pp. 50-52.

26. *Koran*, Tafsîr al-Jalâlayn (Jalâl al-Dîn al-Mahallî and Jalâl al-Dîn al-Suyûtî) Cairo: Matb'at Mustafâ al-Bâbî al-Halabî, 1966), v. 2, pp. 79-80; al-Qurtubî, *al-Jâmi' li-Ahkâm al-Qur'ân* (Cairo: Dâr al-Kitâb al-'Arabî lil-Tibâ'a wal-Nashr, 1967), v. 12, pp. 311-319.

27. In the West, blindness is frequently a punishment for sexual transgression. See, for example, Donald D. Kirtley, *the Psychology of Blindness* (Chicago: Nelson-Hall, 1975), pp. 20, 27; G. Devereux, "The Self-Blinding of Oidipous in Sophokles: *Oidipous Tyrannos,"The Journal of Hellenic Studies* 92 (1973): 36-49.

28. *Koran*, v. II, p. 255; al-Qurtubî, *al-Jâmi'*, v XVI, pp. 273-274. Cf. W. Montgomery Watt, *Companion to the Koran* (London: George Allen and Unwin Ltd. 1967), p. 234.

29. Somekh, "Short Stories," pp. 93-94; Kurpershock, *Short Stories*, p. 179; Somekh, *Lughat al-Qissa*, pp. 153-157.

30. In effect, in the structure of sense perception in "House of Flesh," auditory, olfactory, and visual senses become combined and are set off in opposition to the tactile sense. When the women see knowledge, the first three senses become entangled. They are effectively defeated by the silence of sex. The tactile sense, by contrast, is only employed by the blind man during sex and its conclusions are set aside.

31. Malti-Douglas, "*Mentalités* and Marginality."

Fedwa Malti-Douglas, *Critical Pilgrimages: Studies in the Arabic Literary Tradition*, Austin: University of Texas Press, 1989, pp. 70-78.

The Short Story Collection,
Vision at Fault

Abu al-Ma'ati Abu al-Naja

Even if we overlook the explanations that Yusuf Idris has proffered in a number of newspaper statements regarding the reasons for his preference for writing journalistic articles in recent years, the reader of this latest collection finds himself — perhaps unintentionally — posing himself a question as he considers the stories included: Is there a connection between the current small output of this story writer and the kind of experiments which he now considers worthy of being couched in short story form? Expressed differently, has short story writing, as far as Yusuf Idris is concerned, turned into a kind of quest for a rare pearl, however much time and effort may be involved?

Everybody realizes that the writer's career — any writer's — may take a number of different directions. It may take the form of an exploration of new positions on the larger map of society, the mind, or life in general; it may happen as the natural result of a growth in experience and knowledge and everything that that implies by way of a change in the mode of comprehending the human experience and crafting it into an artistic entity, even though it be on the basis of the self-same old situations!

Whatever its method, what does this new collection, *Vision at Fault,* have to offer that is new? Does it offer any kind of explanation for the small output of this short story writer who built his reputation in Arabic literature on his brilliant creativity in the genre?

General Features of a Notable Journey

Anyone who follows the course of Yusuf Idris's long journey with the short story — starting with *The Cheapest Nights* in the 1950s and then a whole series of other excellent collections, of which the most important are *An Affair of Honor, The End of the World, The Sin [sic], The Language of Screams, The Siren, House of Flesh, Kill Her,* and so on, will notice that at first his particular artistic vision sprang from his powerful and explosive sense of the profound effect that social problems have on the behavior of his heroes and the way that their fate is determined. In later collections however, the horizon broadens to reveal the effect of more psychological and cosmic issues on the heroes' behavior. As a result, his technique has developed from an initial sharp focus on societal issues, in which the vision relies on a good deal of conviction, to something different, with a considerably reduced element of certainty. Confronted with deep-rooted psychological issues and a larger, cosmic intellectual vision, the story-telling technique prefers to suggest, to disclose, to allude. Sometimes it makes use of the language of images and symbols, but, for all that, it remains within the general framework of a realistic vision, if one can use such a term!

Anyone following Idris's long journey, be it through his short stories, plays, or novels — and, however different the forms may be, it is still essentially one and the same journey — will, I assume, be confronted with its immense wealth, its breadth and depth, and will come to realize the seriousness of the challenge that faces a writer who is determined to transcend his own oeuvre with every new work he produces. Has Yusuf Idris, I wonder, fallen into the trap presented by such a challenge? Every time he has been on the point of writing a new story or approached the narrative moment, has he remembered that he has written the story before or already come to the same point in one form or other? Has he ever felt that all the good stories have been written already, either by him or someone else, and that searching for new sources in the recesses of the human mind or on the horizons of society, the cosmos, or nature, all this represents a dilemma exactly like the one faced by the hero in the superb story in this collection, "Way Out"?

About this hero, Idris has the following to say:

> "For a long time he had had the impression that life was no longer synonymous with happiness. This had all occurred a long time ago, after he had savored all the first fruits available, first success, first pound, first flirtation, first night with a woman. There had been a time when his ultimate dream was to have a monthly salary of a hundred and fifty pounds; when he spent that amount on a single day, the goal had increased to five thousand. He had wanted a son; he now had three of them, and a daughter too. He had wanted them to get an education and be graduated; they had. The goal had been changed again: for them to get married; now he had grandchildren."

He had everything he wanted, but life was no longer synonymous with happiness.

> "He used to be able to face the world with a pocketful of piastres. Now he went into a panic if there was a figure missing from the check. When he had threatened to leave home, he had done so in the absolute confidence that he could start life afresh; now he was scared even to go out of the house."

This then is the serious existential dilemma facing the hero of "Way Out." How can a man over fifty recover his sense of surprise and confidence at the same time? Lurking behind every new sensation he lives and experiences there lurks the specter of the old. He learns the lesson from a new-born chicken which bores at the shell of its own egg. Feeling constricted by its environment it keeps chipping away at the shell without even realizing that, beyond the narrow prison in which it is confined on all sides, there lies a wide cosmos that is stupendous and formidable. The hero manages to assert himself when he realizes that he will only be able to find this stupendous fresh resource — life being synonymous with happiness — when he can learn to respond to the same internal call that motivates the new-born chicken. He too must keep on chipping away until he breaks out of the walls of prison, whether that prison consist of family, society, or even nature itself if that becomes a prison!

While reading this story, I do not know why I kept having the strong feeling that the author of this collection is placing himself at the ultimate edge of things. He bores at the walls of the impossible, searching for a way out of this wide formidable universe, somewhere that life can be synonymous with happiness! I am not suggesting that I know why a great writer should stop writing for a while, nor indeed what the secret of writing is. Even so, let us endeavor to take a comprehensive look at the stories in this collection and see if the author really has tried to bore through the walls of the impossible, to place himself at the beginnings and ends of things in a quest for wonder or an aperture through which to survey a wide, formidable universe, something we can hardly see even though we are only separated from it by a thin shell, something we have to smash through. After all, you will never get anything unless, when the moment of decision comes, you are prepared to risk everything!

Unusual Experiences

In the title story, the narrator meets the old peasant who asks for his help in making some spectacles for his donkey; its eyesight has gotten very weak. The problem, which is a real joke at the start, is carried to a conclusion. In theory a weak-sighted donkey can see better if a way can be found to put the appropriate strength spectacles in front of its eyes. Practically speaking however, how can you measure how weak the donkey's vision is without any indications from the animal itself? Horse, donkeys, it makes no difference. The solution to the problem emerges from its point of origin. The donkey's owner finds out that the animal's eyesight is weakening when it does not respond to the sight of the neighbor's female donkey as it has always done in the past. Now, if we can put the donkey at a certain distance from the neighbor's female donkey and then put a series of different strength lenses in front of the donkey's eyes, the most appropriate lenses will be the ones that make the donkey respond to the presence of the female! All this takes place, of course, in front of a crowd of folk from the village, old and young. Using the plot development in this story that begins with an utterly weird and comic situation, the author cajoles his readers into discovering a moment of explosive and spontaneous sex that impinges not only on the animal world where the social conventions regarding sex do not apply but also on the group as a whole. This is how Yusuf Idris records the effect of the surprising turn of events on the crowd:

> "Nature unabashed, in the raw, yelling out in a loud voice:
> You put the earthquake inside our bodies, and within us the
> volcano burst. Disorder in the universe, or is it providing
> order? Sanity or madness to the utmost degree. Bodies thrash-
> ing excitedly, nectar pouring forth with all the primitive power
> of sun-spots, the pull of the full moon, hurricanes at their
> savage height. If human spectacles can help donkeys, I won-
> der if donkey's spectacles can do the same for humans"?

Here the author breaches the walls of societal convention; through the aperture we are given a look at the world of explicit sex. He places himself at the extreme edge between man as social and natural animal. The basic question is this: when did social man lose the feeling of innocence towards sex and why? But there's another question; in fact, two. Was humor the only and inevitable reason for selecting such a weird event as the vehicle for this story? Was the colloquial dialect in which the story is couched the only possible choice for an experience which lies on the extreme edge between social and natural man?!

"His Mother."

In this story we approach a rare moment in an unusual relationship between a vagrant boy and a tree. First the boy loses his father, and then his mother too, when she marries someone else. Hunger is not his most dogged foe either, since he can fend for himself by pilfering in garbage cans. No, his worst foe is the long, cold, rainy winter night when he is chased away from any place where he might be able to find some shelter. Every place has an owner, even the rusty, abandoned railroad waggons from which the police keep chasing him away. Then one night he comes across this tree, called "Mother of Feelings." It's a huge, non-fruit-bearing tree; its long branches hang down and come together at the base to form a trunk. Naturally enough, this trunk has apertures in it and is hollow on the inside. The boy takes refuge inside the trunk and discovers that this time there is no owner to throw him out. So he becomes the owner; it becomes his home in the big city. If Idris had written this story in the 1950s, he may well have given us a wonderful portrait of this boy's personal tragedy, but here the story is presented with no background. The real story starts when the boy senses that the tree has also become his friend, as though it is a mother with no children who then finds her child. He is scared he will come back one night and find someone else occupying his home inside the trunk, but removes his fears by lowering fresh branches to cover up the aperture so that no one else can see it. The tree keeps him warm, and, since the inside is cold, his breath also keeps the tree warm. The sharp protuberances inside the tree turn into blossoms to form a soft cushion.

Idris handles skilfully this rare relationship between boy and tree, the attractive connection between the different levels of life that stem from the kinship bonds between them. The boy grows up and becomes big and strong, too large to fit in the space inside the tree. He goes out into society, now able to argue with it on equal terms. He gets a house and a job. One day, he walks past the tree again and sees that it has become withered; the leaves have all dried up. For a few moments, he stands in front of it crying for his "mother."

Here too, we are placed on the edge of a society, with no place for a young boy who is unable to protect himself. By boring through the shell, this boy manages to open a crack in nature's prison and emerges into a wide universe of affection hiding in the trunk of a tree!

"Leader of Men."

If the story "Way Out" represents the key to this collection, then "Leader of Men" is the jewel. It's a story about a man who starts at the bottom and reaches a summit he never even dreamed of; in this long journey the secret password is man's ability to face challenges and make decisions. Through a long journey of fifty years,

> "he proceeded like a genuine colt, never tiring or running out of steam. He had set himself no particular goal, just the sheer process of moving ahead. He was not after money. Political ambition was not his motivation, nor was he seeking some place in history. Some of this, even all of it, might come to pass because of his perseverance and insistence. His goal was that his society should be a just one, not one filled with wronged people none of whom had anything more than the single gallabiyyah their father had had."

When had the first breakdown in his life come? He could not remember the time. It's certain there was such a time, but he couldn't recall it now. There had been a man, a call for help. The person who made it realized he wasn't directing his cries to the wrong man. He had had to make a decision on the spot. In no time at all he would have considered the odds. For him, sedate, reasonable behavior was not the sensible way of doing things. There were times when, if circumstances dictated, the craziest and most unusual decisions had to be made.

The assault had happened in front of everyone; the people who did it must have been mad. The response, everyone realized, would be instantaneous and brutal.

But, in spite of all that, he remained silent for a long time while he made a number of mental calculations. In place of the usual roar his voice came out sounding puny:

"This time I think we should withdraw and allow ourselves
to select the best time and place for the confrontation. Everyone — above all, he himself — was fully aware that this very
hour, high noon, was the best time (he could remember it in
every detail). Getting his men together for the face-off was
best done on the spot.

How had it all happened? For several years, day and night,
he had been analyzing the recesses of his own mind. He had
been wheedling his interlocutors into telling him why, in their
view, he had done what he had."

Let's leave this question, which represents the core of the story, and follow the
path of the hero's fall. It had all happened in phases. He had started off as a major
boss in the capital city, but then Sultan — that is his name — had returned to his
birthplace in order to become the "leader of men," leader of a group of considerably less import; an illegal gang to be sure, but at least its existence was enough
to preserve his self-esteem and give the appearance of being in charge of
something.

But then comes the major fall, in his own village and among his own kith and
kin. This time the challenge comes from a young boy who scarcely knows who
he is or anything about his legendary strength and brutality. This young man
refuses point blank to allow Sultan to insult him by making crude remarks about
his uncle who, according to the wagging tongues in the village, is a pervert. The
young man starts a fight with Sultan, and this time the result is a foregone
conclusion. The young man is in his twenties, while Sultan is in his fifties. The
young man throws Sultan to the ground, puts the blade of his scythe on his neck
and utters a solemn oath not to take it away until Sultan has admitted in front of
everyone there that he is a woman. If anyone comes too close, he will bury the
blade in Sultan's neck!

Then comes the end, or rather the beginning of the story. We find that,
perhaps as a result of the public acknowledgment he has made in order to save
his own skin, Sultan has in fact turned into a kind of woman. His relatives can
think of only one way to rid themselves of the scandals he is causing, and that
is to kill him.

Structure of the Story.

How does Yusuf Idris present this story, one that manages to cover a complete
lifetime, a journey to the top and back down again? He starts it at the end, from
the point where Sultan is scraping bottom, when he begins to feel the urge actually
to become something like a woman, his discovery of this cataclysmic sensation
in the presence of the nephew who is most impressed by his uncle's personality.
Sultan had called him "the bull," but, when he invites him that night, he has no
idea why. The young man sits in front of his uncle, waiting to see what he would
ask him to do. The events in the story begin from this meeting and almost finish

there too. Sultan resists his deadly feelings, and it is to the pulse of their ebb and flow that the story is constructed.

As Sultan resists these perverted sensations we live through some moments of his rise to power; when he surrenders, we see aspects of the downfall as well, as we share Sultan's secrets with him. In fact, the skillful way in which Yusuf Idris spreads them through the story affords the reader a greater perspective on Sultan's downfall than he himself has.

Significance of the Downfall.

Sultan's personality is that of a noble dictator or a just tyrant who is carried to the top by a formidable rebellious power. But he comes from the bottom, and the journey is long and hard. As a result, he has no time to catch his breath or look around him. His first point of weakness is that his strength refuses to come to terms with his own weaknesses and fears, nor is it prepared to compromise with the strengths and fears of those around him. In his arrogance he refuses to consider minor details and intermediate goals on the long journey; he is for ever plunging ahead "as though continuing was everything, in quest of a distant obscure goal named justice."

The second point of weakness is that he is content to rely on the sense of power that stems from the legend of his power. It does not come from his own internal strength, something that has already been exhausted by self-reliance and ignoring everyone else. When he finds himself confronted for the first time by someone who believes for a moment that he has nothing to fear from his own legend, indeed who senses that deep inside he is scared to death and exhausted, he suffers his first fall and fails to make a firm decision. After that, he can no longer be either noble dictator or just tyrant. Instead he turns into a mere dictator who conceals his own internal depravity by humiliating an innocent young man who is in no way to blame for the imputation that his uncle is a pervert!

With the second fall Sultan realizes that he has been stripped bare; all he can do now is to punish himself, a totally just punishment by becoming just like the boy's uncle whose perversion he made public and laughed at.

Between The Two Ways Out.

Isn't the journey of Sultan, "the leader of men," a kind of "way out" from the bottom to the very top? How is it that the hero of "Way Out" manages to make a decision to leave the prison of his own family and the role of father when he suddenly discovers he no longer is a father or has any real role, whereas Sultan fails to find a way out and actually returns to a bottom level that is even lower than the one from which he started? It may be because, while the hero of "Way Out" is an ordinary kind of person, he allows himself to talk, sometimes to himself, at others to people around him. When the main event happens, it is not a complete surprise to him; he has been spotting warning signs for some time and has even come to terms with them. His strength has not dwindled to the point of utter exhaustion. So he is able to take the "way out" and grab life's most valuable prize — even for someone over fifty — when life becomes synonymous with happiness.

Sultan by contrast prefers to be a dictator and to carry all the burdens of the journey up (or the "way out") on his own. The burden wears him out. His initial triumphs for which he alone wins the laurels give him exceptional power. However, when the first breakdown occurs, he finds himself, by sheer logic, bearing the burden of shame on his own. The weight crushes him, and the long journey down has begun. His attempts to conceal his own weakness lead him to expose the weaknesses of other people and to despise them, even if they themselves are not responsible for the point of weakness (for example, the way he scoffs at Al-Tahhan's nephew). A hidden force explodes inside the young boy, just like the force he himself used to feel and applied whenever people made fun of his father when he was a boy. He sinks so low that there is only one way out, and that is for his closest relatives to kill him.

Abu al-Ma'ati Abu al-Naja, *Al-'Arabi* 362 (Jan. 1989): 153-8.

The Function of Sound in the Stories of Yusuf Idris

Sasson Somekh

I

During the last three decades, Yusuf Idris (b. 1927) has established himself as a major figure in Arabic literature. He is first and foremost a writer of short stories, of which he has published twelve volumes between the years 1954-81.[1] The bulk of his work undoubtedly constitutes a landmark in modern Egyptian fiction; and the influence of his art is very much in evidence in the writings of younger Arab storytellers.

Regrettably, his works were for many years beyond the reach of readers who have no command of Arabic. It is therefore gratifying that in 1978 two volumes of his stories were published in English translation.[2] Furthermore, a scholarly work dealing with several aspects of his life and art appeared in English in 1981.[3]

II

Idris' mastery of storytelling is manifest in many ways, not the least of which is his handling of the language. Admittedly, critics with a partiality for classical stylistic norms often complain that Idris' language is "lax" or "untidy".[4] Others regret the excessive use of the dialect in his dialogue, as well as in the narrative sections.[5]

However, the art of fiction is not commensurate with linguistic "tidiness" or on its texts being written in an "exemplary" language. The ultimate test of the language of a story is in whether it is conducive to the modulations of the artistic text. In this sense Idris is undisputedly a master. His language, though constantly changing in the course of his career, is impressively rich, his imagery original, and above all, the different levels of contemporary Arabic are fully utilized in the service of his story.

In the following pages, which draw on a more comprehensive study of Idris' style,[6] we shall concern ourselves with one of the manifestations of the art of language in his fiction. By analyzing one of his short stories, and comparing it to two longer ones, we shall try to illustrate the employment of sound and rhythm

105

as elements of structure. In so doing, we hope to call attention to one feature which might prove significant, indeed crucial, in the study of Idris' narrative art.

III

The first story in question is entitled "Marsh al-Ghurub" ("Sunset March").[7] It first appeared in the Cairo monthly *al-Hadaf* in May 1957[8] and was later incorporated in the volume *Alaysa Kadhālika* ("Isn't That So?" 1957).[9] In point of fact, the title of the story, when it was first published, was "Lahn al-Ghurub" ("Sunset Tune"). The significance of the change of the title will be commented upon later in this paper.

Thematically, this story is in line with most of the author's early sketches, which mostly draw their subject matter from the life of the impoverished masses in Cairo and in the Egyptian countryside. In these stories, however, the description is not naturalistic, nor is it neutral in tone. The point of view is, more often than not, identical with that of the simple and down-trodden characters; and a great sympathy with their predicament is always evident, although it is sometimes mingled with a tinge of irony.

In "Sunset March" we are presented with a story of one of the wretched; and although we are not directly in touch with the inner feelings of this sole character, the seller of liquorice juice *('irqsus)*, we are definitely made to identify with his plight.

Two questions pose themselves at this juncture. The first: Is the man's unhappy lot the main theme of the short story? Indeed, at first sight it impresses its reader as nothing but a portrait of a hapless vendor of cold drink on a cold day. It has no plot in the usual sense of the term, and we hardly know anything about the personal background, problems and thoughts of the vendor. Which brings us to the second question: Is there a "story" in "Sunset March"?

We shall first try to answer the latter question, and then go on to consider the thematic essence of our short story.

IV

Admittedly, we are presented with a portrait. But it is by no means a static picture. Although most of the text presents the man in a stationary position, he is in fact constantly changing in relation to the background scene. Furthermore, there is a constant "inner movement" which amounts to a "plot".

At first we have a scene in which "it was . . . wintertime, and the sun had just set. The whole universe was reeking of that sickly atmosphere which immediately follows sunset till it gets dark. People were proceeding in silence across the bridge; their haste reflected all the gloom of a dying day and all the cold of winter."

Later on, the seller "looked around him and noticed people disappearing into the distance, slinking by as though they were being swallowed up by some hidden lair or other. He noticed the bloody wound which the sun had left in the sky as it made its way into the world of darkness. "

Still later — "It was getting dark and gloomy everywhere. The chill in the heavens now began to settle on the earth. People dwindled away. Everything assumed a greyish-blue hue and looked cold and lifeless."

And again — "It was getting darker and darker as the heavens continued to impose themselves on the earth. By now, the wound in the sky had healed and the red sky of twilight had vanished. People were being transformed from beings into spectres."

Towards the end of the story we note the image of the juice-seller turning into a spectre too, and deserting the scene. "His figure melted away into the night and disappeared. . . And there was nothing in the world, big, so big; and the darkness so plentiful."

This succession of scenes, portraying, as they do, the passing of day and the arrival of evening, do not fail to lend the setting itself a dynamic feature, and remind one of such impressionist painters as Claude Monet in his Rouen Cathedral series of paintings. The changing scenery is not a sheer "setting". It reflects and amplifies the vendor's anxiety and his growing desperation until he finally leaves the Shubra Bridge.

However, while the changing background is instrumental in lending the character a measure of life, it is the variety of noises that turns the text into a story. In other words, the noises constitute a major structural device. At least two kinds of noises are involved: Those produced by the man's cymbals, and those of his own voice. The combined operation of these two types is modulated to produce a reflection of the man's fluctuating moods. In fact, we have four stages in the inner psychology of the protagonist, all reflected "acoustically".

Stage I: The man is hoping against hope. He is well aware that to sell juice on a cold day is next to impossible, and that it is only by intensifying the clatter of his cymbals and by raising his voice that he can hope to attract some passers-by. At this stage the cymbals produce loud and strident noises, coming in spurts rather "like the call of a turkey cock." In the story these noises have yet another function: To reflect the man's fears and doubts. Every time he looked at the same setting sun "the intervals between the cymbal clashes became shorter, and the sound they made was louder and sharper."

Stage II: This starts with the words "The minutes went by quickly. Time was rushing by just like people. . ." The cymbal clashes are now shrill and hysterical. His calls include an appeal to God *(ya karim satrak* — "Your protection? generous God") and not just the words [*ya-mna'nish*] ("Delicious" or, rather: "How refreshing", the reference being, of course, to the quality of the juice), as in the first stage. This pious formula, coming straight from the man's heart, is elongated "as though he wished to make a thin rope out of it to stretch over the bridge and stop people."

Stage III: This stage also begins with words denoting the passage of time — "Time slipped by, and the number of passers-by diminished." The man has not given up hope completely. His submissive appeal to God now fully replaces the reference to the juice. The same submissiveness and despair applies to the music of the cymbals. "They sounded like the heartbeat of someone close to death, quiet for a long time and then suddenly bursting into action in some final struggle against the oblivion of death."

Stage IV: The words "A total despair now came over him" introduce this part. In fact, we are now witnessing a stage whicl. is *beyond despair*. In this final part of the story, "The cymbal clashes, which had been well-spaced, become frequent again and even harmonious. But now there was a strange timbre to the sound . . . , a kind of melody, subdued, lilting and sorrowful. The man's hands were working unconsciously, and the melody came out the same way, pianissimo, and shrouded in darkness. No one else could hear it."

But the spontaneous, indeed unconscious, effort soon gives way to a more elaborate one: "He began to apply himself wholeheartedly to the process. He was a virtuoso at cymbal clashing, and set about timing and improving the melodic line. . . It made him feel so overjoyed that he started nodding his head sedately to the beat. Soon the nods spread to the hairs in his beard which started an undulating dance of their own." Finally, he departs from the bridge to the beat of the hushed melody of the cymbals, "one step per clash, a mournful, aching sound; one per step, with a deal of sorrow in each gentle clash."

In other words, we witness a gradual but acute psychological change: From hope against hope, to alarm, to despair, and finally to *catharsis*. All these stages are conveyed chiefly by means of acoustic references. The language is studded with sounds and metaphors denoting the various qualities of sound.

It will now be clear why the author, in an afterthought, decided to change the title of the story from "Sunset Tune" to "Sunset March". In fact, the word "march" is not only designed to underline the final stage, that of the man's self indulgence in reflective music, or his rhythmic departure from the scene. It is also instrumental in foregrounding the role of acoustics and rhythm in the story. In replacing "tune" by the more technical term "march" the author is calling our attention to this aspect of his text.

As for the thematics of our story — it does not now seem proper to speak of the "social" theme in isolation. The story, as we have seen, portrays a series of psychological shifts, of anguish, fear and relief; and we would do the author an injustice if we excluded these aspects from the "theme" of his work. Furthermore, the final stage, as demonstrated above, suggests yet another thematic element: that of art as a soother and redeemer. For in the first three stages of the story, the "art" of the cymbal clashes is directed towards the passers-by, and is meant to help bring about a material relief. However, it produces few if any results. In the last stage (and in certain parts of the third stage) the music generated by the cymbals is inwardly oriented, and directed at the "soul". This music has no other function than soothing the man's anguished self by means of beauty and harmony. At least in this pursuit he proves to be a "successful" artist.

In other words, we have a triple thematic construct, which might be schematically designated as destitution — trepidation — art. It is this multi-layered thematic structure, combined with the rich acoustic texture, that gives the story its human depth and poetic richness.

V

"Sunset March" is by no means the only work by Yusuf Idris wherein acoustic and rhythmic elements feature so prominently. In many of his other stories the sensitivity towards such elements, and the manner in which they feature, amount to a major artistic hallmark. In fact, these elements seem to occupy an even more central role in Idris' later works, those written in the 1960s and 1970s.[10] His recourse to the world of voices can be further demonstrated by the sheer mention of the titles of two of his more recent collections of short stories: *Lughat al-Ay-Ay* ("The Language of Ay-Ay", 1965), and *Mashuq al-Hams* ("Crushed Whispers". 1970).[11]

To return to the use of the acoustic and rhythmic devices in the texts of the stories, I would like to refer to two more examples which might further illustrate my point. In discussing "Sunset March" we have seen that the rhythmic and acoustic components were instrumental in reflecting a succession of psychological stages. In "The Black Policeman" ("al-'Askari al-Aswad"), a story published in 1961,[12] we are presented with another example of the use of similar elements in a psychological context, though not necessarily in an identical fashion. Here the noises are not produced by a protagonist, but by an external agent. They serve to reflect and progressively enhance the feeling of tension among the characters of the story (as well as in the reader).

The protagonist of "The Black Policeman" is a young physician, Shawqi, who has been imprisoned and tortured by the secret police. Accompanied by a friend (the narrator) and a male nurse, he pays a visit to the house of a retired policeman who served for many years as a master torturer, notorious for his sadistic treatment of prisoners. The ex-policeman was afflicted by a hideous malady. On entering the policeman's shoddy residence Shawqi and his friend are extremely uneasy. Dreadful memories from the past are no less tormenting than the apprehension that precedes the renewed meeting with the bestial man. An interval lapses before they are finally allowed into the policeman's bedroom. During this period the tense and melancholic atmosphere that surrounds Shawqi and the narrator is conveyed in the text by means of a rhythmic device:

> Near the middle of the courtyard there was an overturned metal wash-basin, on which stood a chicken pecking in staccato jerks with its beak at the bits of dirt and mud clinging to the underside of the basin, in hopes of finding food. But its pecking only served to clash its beak against the washbasin which rang in reverberating regular and tedious knocks. The knocking rose, resounding in a ceaseless and obstinate ringing, only augmenting the gloom in the large, bare courtyard.[13]

Later on the policeman's wife emerges from the room, but soon disappears. Here the narrator remarks:

> She left us standing there, looking around the courtyard, rather surprised. Before long, the chicken, which had been startled and scared off by the woman, re-emerged and once again mounted the wash-basin and its beak began again to produce that gloomy, regular, resounding knocking.[14]

After a while the woman makes another appearance, but once again re-enters the bedroom. As for the three men, that narrator now tells us:

> All was blanketed in a silence which was broken only by the chicken's steady pecking on the surface of the wash-basin. Now the woman's coming and going no longer disturbed or interrupted its knocking.[15]

The chicken's rapping is mentioned again for the fourth and last time as follows:

> We had no idea why we were made to wait. There must have been some reason for it. The most embarrassing thing was the silence which engulfed us, and which expanded and spread to the point of even absorbing the chicken's rapping. We no longer noticed it.[16]

The scene in question, burdened as it is with a tense anticipation, is a crucial juncture in the story, and the employment of the rhythmic-acoustic devices which serve at once to enhance the anxiety of the narrator and his friend Shawqi, and to convey the feeling of these men. It is to be noted, in passing, that here, as in "Sunset March", we have four "beats" or "waves" of reference to the noise, although in "The Black Policeman" they do not necessarily convey distinct psychological phases.

VI

A third story worth mentioning in the context of our study is "City Dregs" [17] ("Qa‘ al-Madina"), a long short story, incorporated in *Alaysa Kadhalik* (this volume also includes "Sunset March"). Here we also find the recurring appearance of voices (again, in four or five separate "waves"), punctuating a crucial (or transitional) stage in the story.

The protagonist in "City Dregs" is a young Cairene judge, 'Abdallah, who suspects his former housemaid, Shuhrat, of having stolen his wristwatch. He therefore decides to make a surprise visit to her house. Accompanied by a friend and a doorman, he proceeds from his own affluent quarter to the slums where

Shuhrat lives. The journey, which begins as a frivolous adventure, turns into a nightmare. The fastidious young judge discovers a horrible urban scene of which he knows nothing. He is dismayed by what he sees and hears in the shabby, narrow alleys. However, far from commiserating with the fate of the dwellers of the alley, Abdallah is filled with disgust and rage. His malice towards Shuhrat is multiplied by his "ordeal". The growing rage is reflected in the text by a series of passages describing the reception of the unsavoury scenes in Abdallah's mind. The scenes are depicted by a variety of artistic means, making use of a number of different senses: sight, smell, and most remarkably, the aural sense. Naturally it is the latter which concerns us here. To return to the story: soon after the three men leave behind them the clean and quiet residential quarter where Abdallah lives, a crowded and tumultuous city begins to emerge. When their car reaches al-Azhar Street, "the bustle becomes intense. In the road all mingle; this one and that, those mounted and those on foot. One hears the screech of wheels, the wails of motor-horns, the tinkle of horses' bells, the whistles of traffic policemen, the cries of street vendors and passersby. The heat reaches its peak, the throng its thickest."[18]

But these scenes prove to be only the beginning. As the men proceed on foot into the narrow alleys, the scenery becomes progressively more depressing. At first the alleys are straight. The houses are decent and the people relatively well-dressed. At this stage the language spoken is refined *(rāqiya)*, made up of coherent words and sentences.[19]

But as they advance the scene becomes uglier, the noise less pleasant. There are four different passages, each describing a further step into the heart of wretchedness. I shall quote from each stage those sentences relating to the realm of language:

> Stage 1. "Language disintegrates; it becomes single words, calls, insults."[20]
>
> Stage 2. "Language crumbles to half words or even quarters, to locutions that only the speakers understand."[21]
>
> Stage 3. "Language becomes hisses *(sarsa'a)*, vowels and consonants arising out of greatly protuberant larynxes."[22]
>
> Stage 4. "Staccato mutterings merge into the barking of dogs and into the creaking of great doors as they are pushed open."[23]

Now the judge's march into this unfamiliar territory constitutes, as I have pointed out, the backbone of the story and this is also suggested by its title. It is in this section that Abdallah's towering egotism is brought out, and it is through what he sees and hears and smells that he is incensed. The constant references to human and other noises in "City Dregs" is yet another example of the centrality

of acoustic and rhythmic elements in the art of Yusuf Idris. The recurrence of
these elements in clusters (often consisting of some four components) demonstrates that they are definitely used as a structural device.

VII

In section III and elsewhere in this paper, we have seen how Idris produces
concatenations of astounding similes in order to portray the acoustic universe in
a literary text. Furthermore, the passages quoted from "City Dregs" demonstrate
the rich "meta-language" that he concocts to describe the speech and hubbub of
people.

There is, however, another feature which Idris uses in abundance, and which
is not usually discernible through translation. That is the onomatopoeia. The
sheer quantity of sound-imitating morphemes in his stories is dazzling. No less
impressive is their variety.

In the chapter of "City Dregs" discussed above we find, among many others,
the following "acoustic" words: 1. *hafīf* ("rustling"), 2. *za'īq* ("screaming"), 3.
hamhama ("mumble"), 4. *sarsa'a* ("hisses"), 5. *habhaba* ("barking") and many
others. Elsewhere in the stories discussed we find such words as: 6. *qazqaza*
("cracking [nuts]"), 7. [*sakhsakha*] ("titter"), 8. *tarqa'a* ("crackle").

This list constitutes but a fraction of the rich onomatopoeic inventory to be
found in Idris' stories . However, this random sample does demonstrate one more
characteristic of the author's style. Some of these words, (e.g. the first three) may
be considered to belong to a classical *fusha,* or at least to the modern *fusha.* But
most of the others do not come from the classical inventory, and can hardly be
found in dictionaries of the classical or modern *fusha.*[24] In fact they are drawn
chiefly from the spoken language of Cairo.

It will be remembered that Idris has been often taken to task for his "excessive"
use of the dialect in his stories. Such criticism seems to imply that the *fusha* is
equipped with all the necessary linguistic and lexical elements necessary for
modern fiction. However the case of the onomatopoeia proves that there are
certain linguistic items of the spoken language that are not readily replaceable by
fusha equivalents. It also indicates that the use of *'amiyya* items by Idris (and
others) is not necessarily haphazard, neither is it a private whim. At least in the
case of "acoustic" items, the author resorts to vernacular items as part of his
efforts to portray "local reality" . In so doing he is definitely enriching the
language of fiction, rather than damaging it, as certain critics seem to imply. The
fusha, which is basically a written language,[25] can hardly be expected to provide
the author with all the onomatopoeic items which the modern reader regards as
reflecting "real" voices. If he is to render the "local colour" or rather the "local
vocality", he has little choice but to fall back on the spoken variety of language,
which is infinitely richer in items pertaining to local *realia* and *vocalia.*

Footnotes
[1] A list of Idris' short-story volumes can be found in my article " Language and Theme in

the Short Stories of Yusuf Idris", *Journal of Arabic Literature*, Vol. VI(1975), pp. 89-100. In recent years Idris has published two new volumes of short stories: *Ana Sultan Qanun al-Wujud* (1980) and *Uqtulha* (1981) as well as a novella, *New York 80* (1981).

[2] Roger Allen (ed.), *In the Eye of the Beholder: Tales of Egyptian Life from the Writings of Yusuf Idris*, Minneapolis and Chicago (Bibliotheca Islamica) 1978; and: Yusuf Idris, *The Cheapest Nights and Other Stories*, translated by Wadida Wassef, London (Peter Owen) 1978. A list of other stories in translation can be found on p. 195 of Kurpershoek's book (see next footnote). In 1984 another volume of Idris' stories appeared in English translation: Yusuf Idris, *Rings of Burnished Brass*, translated by Catherine Cobham, London and Washington (Heineman and Three Continents Press). This volume includes four novellas, one of which is "The Black Policeman", discussed in section V of this article.

[3] P. M. Kurpershoek, *The Stories of Yusuf Idris: A Modern Egyptian Author*, Leiden (Brill) 1981.

[4] See, for instance, Muhammad Zaghlul Salam, *Dirasat fi al-Qissa al-'Arabiyya al-Haditha*, Alexandria 1973, p. 368.

[5] See, for instance, Taha Husayn's introduction to Idris' second volume of short stories, *Jumhuriyyat Farahat*, Cairo 1956.

[6] S. Somekh, *Lughat al-Qissa fi adab Yusuf Idris*, Acre 1984.

[7] Translated by Roger Allen, *Journal of Arabic Literature* XVI (1985): 91-4.

[8] See the bibliographical list in Sayyid Hamid al-Nassaj, *Dalil al-Qissa al-Misriyya al-Qasira*, Cairo 1972, p. 176, also Kurpershoek, p. 191.

[9] The subsequent editions of this book were published under the title *Qa' al-Madina*.

[10] *Cf.*, e.g., the clear structural function of the word "silence" *(samt)* and its derivatives in the title story of *Bayt min Lahm (1971)*. This story ("House of Flesh") was skilfully translated into English by Denys Johnson-Davies and included in his book *Egyptian Short Stories*, London and Washington (Heinemann and Three Continents Press).

[11] *Mashuq al-Hams* is, in fact, a second edition (with only one story omitted) of *al-Naddaha* ("The Clarion" or "The Voice"), which is also of a somewhat "communicative" connotation.

[12] This story ''al-'Askari al-Aswad" was originally published in the Cairene monthly *al-Katib*, June 1961, and incorporated in a volume bearing the same title which appeared in 1962.

[13] *Al-'Askari al-Aswad*, Cairo 1962, p. 43. I am grateful to Carol Bardenstein for translating the four quotations from this story.

[14] Ibid., p. 44.

[15] Ibid., p. 46.

[16] Ibid., p. 46.

[17] An English translation of this story by Pierre Cachia, can be found in Roger Allen's anthology (referred to in fn. 2 *supra*), pp. 17-77. My quotations are based on Prof. Cachia's translation (hereafter referred to as "trans.").

[18] Orig. (= *Alaysa Kadhalika*, Cairo 1957), p. 344, trans. p. 62-3.

[19] Orig. 346; trans. 64.

[20] Orig 346, trans. 64.

[21] Orig. 347, trans. 64-5.

[22] Orig. 347; trans. 65.

[23] Orig. 348; trans. 65.

[24] None of the words listed here appears in *al-Mu'jam al-Wasit*, a dictionary of *fusha*

published in 1960-1961 by the Cairo Language Academy.

[25] The oral use of *fusha* is becoming widespread, mainly under the impact of mass communication. See: Al-Sa'id Muhammad Badawi, *Mustawayat al-'Arabiyya al-Mu'asira fi Misr,* Cairo 1973; Gustav Meiseles, "Educated Spoken Arabic and the Arabic Language Continuum", *Archivum Linguisticum* 11 (N.S.), pp. 89-106.

Sasson Somekh, *Journal of Arabic Literature* XVI (1985): 95-104.

The Novels of Yusuf Idris

Hilary Kilpatrick

The most recently published novel, *Al-Baida* was written in 1955 and serialised in *Al-Jumhuriya* in 1960. The author justifies bringing it out in book form by saying that:

> 'it is a living document of an important period of life in our country a period which I believe no-one has treated.'

He ends the short preface: 'I am very proud of this part of my (sic) life and that of my country.' Publication was probably delayed because Idris could not find an Egyptian publisher to accept it, and so he took it to Beirut, as he did *Hadithat sharaf* whose contents might also have seemed unacceptable to Cairo publishers.

The two main themes are politics and a love affair. The hero, with whom the author clearly identifies himself in the preface, is an idealistic Marxist, yet although his commitment to the revolution is beyond question, politics for him are confined to production of the political magazine, relationships between the committee members of the opposition group to which he belongs and relationships with the police. He does not show any real interest in social inequality and injustice as it is exemplified at the railway repair shop, for instance; the emphasis is on an individual who sees his own problems magnified.

The problems are not trivial, however. For anyone with a highly developed sense of personal freedom the difficulty of belonging to an authoritarian party is obvious. Yahya finds himself disagreeing with Al-Barudi during his period as editor because he and others would like to exchange the traditional 'world-wide' slogans for ones which Egyptians will find relevant and understandable. Later, when Shauqi has taken over, the disagreements are on a more personal level because of Yahya's abandonment of work on the magazine; in the view of the editor this can only be the result of some private problem, because

> 'it was quite impossible for them to imagine that anyone would oppose a thing because it was a mistake, simply a mistake.'

Intellectual freedom is forbidden, and how much more powerless the individual feels when the authorities refuse to admit the possibility of disagreement on logical grounds. Yahya himself later summarises the difference of outlook between him and Al-Barudi:

> 'I began to realise that my disagreement with Al-Barudi was a fundamental one; he considered that man's consciousness of himself should be the highest value, and I considered that man himself, with his consciousness and unconscious, his rightness and wrongness, was the highest value.'

Discussion has extended beyond the individual to the people. Yet they have for Yahya, only a theoretical existence and no real political significance, and it is perhaps this approach divorced from reality which goes far to explain the failure of his own, and his group's activity. The imprisonment of almost all the members of the group and its subsequent dissolution prevents the issue being resolved.

The value of the human being, which Yahya emphasises, is undermined through the particular circumstances of the opposition groups which are faced with the enemy of the secret police. Life must be a series of

> 'meetings, resolutions, little pieces of transparent paper, roneos, minutely planned appointments with other ones as a precaution, false names, enmities, disagreements, in-fighting and heroism,'

This way of life has a corroding effect on many of his colleagues, as indeed on their opponents, yet others are ennobled and abandon their former frivolous amusements. But this is a fairly objective and balanced account of the trials of underground political activity, compared with the terrifying picture of degradation and brutality in the story *Al-'Askari al-aswad*.

What takes up most of the novel is the second theme — the love affair between Yahya and Xanthe (the 'white woman' of the title). It seems as though this part of the book was expanded in order to satisfy the readers of *Al-Jumhuriya*, but despite its repetitions it is important, because of the permanent effect which the affair has on Yahya. What attracts him to Xanthe is the challenge she represents, and the more he is obsessed by her the stronger it appears to him. Each time she repulses him the feeling of failure increases, as well as his determination to overcome her, and yet when, in the end, she yields to him at a moment of weakness, the feeling of failure is so ingrained that he hardly registers his victory, for it has ceased to have any meaning. He himself suggests a reason for his reaction to Xanthe, when he recalls his relationship with his mother, who refused to show him affection during his childhood and remarks that that experience has permeated all his later relationships with a sense of doubt and uncertainty. This may be an unsatisfactory explanation, but it is to be preferred to any which gives

Yahya's failure a symbolic significance and takes Xanthe to represent European civilisation, with which he cannot hold his own, since Laura can also be considered a symbol of Europe. Xanthe's fatal effect on Yahya extends to taking him away from work at the clinic, driving him to use tranquillisers and sleeping pills, and distracting him from developing his political ideas. In the emotional, physical and intellectual spheres she defeats him, either directly by resisting him, or indirectly by deflecting him from his aim. In addition, Yahya's work at the railway repair shop contributes to the destruction of his ideals.

His conditions of work are made extremely difficult, because unrealistic regulations about lateness and sick leave force healthy men to apply for paid sick leave when they have been prevented by bad transport from arriving on time and face the possibility of losing what to them is a large sum of money. At first he tries to solve the problem by granting sick leave to all comers, but this comes to an end when so many workers are absent that work is halted. A fresh crisis occurs with the proposal to give workers a weekly day off without pay. This is resisted by many since it means a reduction of income, and they hope to get round it by claiming sick pay, thus confronting Yahya with a problem which none of the administrators will resolve and obliging him to take sides with the 'establishment'. He loses faith in Trades Union officials, who are sly and dishonest, and even in the workers whose cooperation in the Committee of Students and Workers some years earlier he remembers with admiration.

This aspect of the book illustrates certain points well: first, the changes in Yahya's attitudes as he passes from student to responsible adult life and discovers that his ideals are inapplicable or simply misplaced, secondly the generally pessimistic conclusions that this leads him to, and thirdly the individualistic view which lies behind the whole work. It would have been possible to emphasize the wickedness of the system which drives workers to seek sick leave when they are well, and work when they are not, and from this to conclude generally that those who make rules are frequently unaware of the practical circumstances in which they must be applied. Despite Yahya's evident discontent he does not go so far; perhaps his disillusionment with the workers prevents him from identifying himself with them, or he thinks that, since he has been unable to achieve the radical changes he would like in the political group he belongs to, the task will be unthinkable in a more hostile environment.

Another element of the change in Yahya's life relates to his attitude to his relatives. They do not appear to be wealthy, and are certainly not educated, except for the young brother who is sitting his exams. Apart from his uneasy relationship with his mother Yahya feels attracted and repelled by life in the village, which for him represents the reality in comparison with which life in the city is a long dream. As he explains,

> 'we perceive (in the country) that we are crushed, concealing
> our disgrace (i. e. poverty) with tricks in order to live.'

He feels correspondingly guilty about the comfortable life he leads in Cairo, and about the alienation which he now experiences among his own family after his long absence from them. Although Idris touches on this theme only lightly he conveys well the conflicts within his hero, thereby adding a touch to the picture of the young man in the process of being defeated and dehumanised by life.

Yahya's attitude to the area of Cairo in which he lives is equally ambivalent. He has a flat in the Bulaq section of Shari' Fuad, where the noise of trams, cars, carts and buses mingles with the sounds of weddings and funerals; outside his window the neon sign flashes on and off all night, advertising the restaurant below which fills the building with the smell of fried liver. But

> 'I did not think seriously of changing (that house). Something drew me to all this, and made nothing equal my distaste for it except my love of it. For some reason I felt that in this house I was living in the midst of our people with all its faults and virtues, so much so that I was sometimes ashamed of myself for the hatred I harboured towards the owners of the shops, the cafe and the restaurant, when they greeted me lovingly, wanted to have conversations with me and demonstrated their readiness to do me service. Why shouldn't I admit that I was sometimes glad to live there and enjoyed it?'

Although the surroundings are not ideal for a man living a busy life, Yahya only thinks of changing them when he wants to meet Xanthe in a quiet atmosphere, and then he moves to Zamalik, the quarter where so many foreigners live, The change represents a further step away from the life of the ordinary mass of Egyptians, and perhaps unconsciously the writer has revealed the way in which he too has been torn by the same dilemma, for the pages where he describes life in Shari' Fuad, like those about Yahya's feelings towards his family, are some of the most lively and memorable in the book.

These conflicting emotions are the background to Yahya's nationalism, which shows itself in unexpected ways, He admits to liking the European way of life and culture, and especially its women, but his strong sense of the distinctiveness of Egyptians leads him to be suspicious of applying imported political ideas in his own country. Hence his problems with the magazine committee. He also feels uneasy with Egyptians who he thinks have become too imbued with European culture. Yet there is none of the xenophobia which appears, understandably, in the collection of stories *Al-Batal*, where so many themes are connected with the British occupation and the Suez attack, but simply the reaction, at times confused, of someone brought up too close to European culture to free himself from it, and at the same time critical of its role in his country. His loyalties, however, are straightforward; he accepts without question the help of such foreign 'comrades' as Xanthe and Laura, but for him Egypt will always come first.

Al-Baida is an interesting, if a sad book. Despite faults of construction it is important because it raises real issues, and traces the general development, often based on incidents from the writer's life, of a young Egyptian who finds himself faced with insuperable political, emotional and social problems. Yahya describes, hidden deep within himself,

> 'a feeling of unbounded confidence in myself, facing life, the feeling which colours the height of our youth and the dawn of our manhood, the feeling that nothing under the sun is impossible for us'.

He reflects:

> 'Like others I believed that. . . if I wanted a girl to love me she would have to, however great my faults and whatever the circumstances of our meeting and the way I treated her. More than this, the more difficult the circumstances were, the more the situation attracted me, and I imposed my will and being on it, to win, and to have more self-confidence, and more self-confidence in my self-confidence.
> Maybe I wanted Xanthe so much better because I believed that she was really unobtainable and distant.'

The novel describes the destruction of that self-confidence, through failures in many different areas of life.

Al-Haram is a different kind of novel in setting and subject, describing the life of an Egyptian village from an outsider's point of view. The idea of *haram* is only intermittently touched on, and there is no profound study of one character affected by a strict social system as might be expected, but there are three cases where the taboo's working can be observed. The first is that of the chief clerk's daughter, Linda, whose name rumour has linked with Sawfat, the overseer's son. When Masiha, her father, learns of the discovery of the baby, he is overwhelmed by doubts which he never entertained before, and which are all the more serious because he has trusted his wife and daughter. Now that his confidence is undermined, he is lost.

Masiha's doubts about his family are profoundly analysed, for two reasons. First, there is the sub-plot between his daughter and Ahmad Sultan for which this suspicion is an ironic preparation. By the rigid application of the social customs of the countryside Linda has been prevented from meeting possible husbands, and so she is an easy prey for Umm Ibrahim's suggestive conversation, finally being persuaded to go against her up-bringing and meet a man her family disapproves of, not only because of his inferior social status, but also, although Idris does not bring that out, because of the difference in their religions. The episode is unsatisfactory, however, because it is not explained why Linda escapes so lightly in her brush with *al-haram* when she could easily have had her

reputation ruined and lost all chance of marriage. Perhaps Idris wants to imply
that the trust her parents place in her is an effective control where society's
prohibitions would not be; she knows that her father will in the end forgive her
so long as she has not become irrevocably outcast, whereas where harsh
conventions are applied they distort the natural course of events and cause much
unnecessary suffering.

The second reason for considering Masiha's family in detail is because they
provide an interesting contrast with others in the village, especially Fikri's.
Masiha's wife, who is known by her own name, 'Afifa, shows up the ignorance
and lack of sophistication of Fikri's wife, who is referred to in the traditional way
through her relationship to her son as Umm Safwat. Although married to a man
with a prominent position in the village, Umm Safwat remains a simple peasant
at heart, happiest when listening to her maid's stories about every-day events, Her
husband's attitude to her is summed up as follows:

> 'He was a man who did not marry a woman to share his life,
> he married someone to serve him, so he chose a pretty woman
> who could cook well and knew nothing of that strange world
> which existed beyond the door of the house, evil and full of
> sin.'

Umm Safwat epitomises the woman whose life is regulated by *al-haram*; kept in
ignorance, confined to her house, with her own feeling that she should curb her
curiosity, she is in the normal course of events excluded from any dangerous
contact which might induce her to violate taboos. So long as this state of affairs
is maintained there is no problem, but with the first crack in the wall the situation
becomes unmanageable. Linda's father, who allows her relative freedom, is not
a true believer in *al-haram* he is more humane, and consequently the individuals
in the family have some opportunity to develop, but the dangers he runs in this
halfway stage are considerable.

Al-haram has put Umm Safwat into a straight-jacket, figuratively speaking; it
has caused Linda to make a rash marriage; what of 'Aziza, the third victim of the
grim code? First, she has been forced to break it in principle, by going out to work
without her husband, for although among the poor the wife works outside the
house, the accepted fact is that the husband supports the family, as 'Abdallah
knows well. But *al-haram* has not warped 'Aziza as it has her seducer. Muhammad
the son of Qamarain

> 'was about twenty, and people were talking about his mar-
> riage to the daughter of one of their relatives. He was known
> for his bad temper, so that he did not even stop at cursing
> women, but he used to go from the field to the house and the
> house to the field ignoring the cafe, jokes and chat which the
> young men of the village were familiar with.'

In other words he is terribly repressed. It must be a rare occasion when 'Aziza asks him to let her dig for potatoes, although he probably has not planned the sequel. And yet the circumstances of her life must have earned her general sympathy in the village, and in view of her special position the seduction might be a little unlikely. The events afterwards, however, are entirely convincing; the whole institution of *al-haram* is symbolised in the tight belt which 'Aziza has to wear to hide her pregnancy and can only remove when she is alone at night.

At this point Idris introduces another theme, that of the beginning of solidarity between farm workers and *tarahil*, and in order to illustrate it he shows 'Aziza gaining the sympathy of her fellow-labourers and of the farm workers. Thus the author detracts from her tragedy, and although the general drift of his attack on *al-haram* remains, the implication that in fact these values are not taken too seriously diminishes its force.

Since he distorted the ending of the central part of the *haram* plot, one wonders whether Idris might not have been wiser to call his book after the *tarahil* workers, even if they proved a commercially less attractive subject. The idea of writing about these wretched individuals is good, and Idris begins well by describing the gulf which the peasants of the *'izba* perceive between themselves and

> 'the poorest people in their (own) part of the country, whom
> poverty forces to resort to work on a distant estate, leaving
> their houses and villages in an effort to earn a daily wage,
> which does not exceed a few piastres'.

The two groups scarcely come into contact with each other, but the peasants have a definite attitude to the *tarahil* which is revealed when they learn of the discovery of 'Aziza:

> 'The only effect which the news had on the prominent peas-
> ants and farmers was. . . to arouse their concealed aversion to
> the stranger, so that conversation about them was preceded or
> followed by a stream of curses and spitting. In their view, the
> *tarhila* were human scum who descended on their estate once
> or twice a year like an unavoidable plague. How much worse
> when they discovered that the scum had produced something
> *haram* like what had happened a few days ago, and had tried
> to hide it and pin it on the farm people? The *tarhila* them-
> selves almost became something accursed and it seemed that
> everybody was decent and they alone taboo.'

That mentality is gradually broken down as 'Aziza's life draws to its end, first by the village children and then by the villagers, who begin to visit her out of curiosity which turns to pity. The change in their attitude is made clear when the peasants offer condolences at her death, and the new-found friendship between them and the *tarahil* is symbolised by the willow tree said to have healing properties, which is believed to have sprung from the twig 'Aziza held in her final agony on the canal bank.

The artificiality evident in the development of the theme of the peasants' acceptance of the *tarahil* need scarcely be pointed out; from the sombre tone of their hatred and contempt we move to the rosy hues of optimism and brotherhood, inspired by the suffering of a woman who has violated the accepted moral code. Idris's purpose becomes clearer when he gives, in the final pages, a brief history of the estate from Aziza's death till the present: its passing out of the hands of the foreign owner, Zughaiyib Pasha and eventual purchase by Al-Ahmadi Pasha, who changes the system of land tenure, renting the land out to the peasants on fixed conditions. However, the agricultural reform following the revolution enables them to buy their own plots, and in consequence the overseers and hired labour disappear, some leaving the estate, others becoming farmers. The *tarahil* pass out of memory.

Just as Idris chooses a good target in the theme of *al-haram* and then shifts his sights so that he misses it, he fails to say anything important about the *tarahil* after he has described their original situation perceptively. To raise the issue of their future and point out that they have ceased to come to the estate begs the question; it is at least possible that they became more wretched after the land reform because it deprived them of even seasonal labour without making any other provision for them, but Idris does not come to grips with this problem. He clearly dislikes inhuman class distinctions, just as he dislikes the brutal social conventions relating to women's behaviour, but in both cases the solutions he offers are so unsatisfactory that it would have been preferable if he had expressed his original idea powerfully in a short story and left the reader to draw his own conclusions.

Al-'Aib is Idris's least satisfactory novel, from the point of view of ideas, intensity of feeling and vividness of description. It also deals with a less momentous subject than the previous one, for *'aib*, which means 'shame', 'disgrace' or 'defect', has a much weaker connotation than *haram* and the society which is described is urban, and less strict than a rural one.

The 'shame' of the book is woman, according to the traditional system of values which is expressed in

> '. . . a world in which women, in men's eyes, and. . . in the eyes of the women themselves, are an incarnate shame, wearing dresses and using cosmetics to make themselves beautiful, their every desire or demand bearing within itself the eternal stigma of disgrace. They were created a shame and will remain to their dying day a shame.'

For these creatures working outside the house is the greatest disgrace, and shut in, their thoughts turn always to what is their raison d'etre — sexual relationships. The woman who does not hesitate to plunge into subjects of conversation which embarrass the girls listening to her is obsessed, as Bahija was until she began to work and meet men as a matter of course. But Bahija discovers that once a girl is free to go out to work her attitudes change, she ceases to think of men in exclusively sexual terms and begins to see them as people with careers, learning to evaluate them on the basis of their present position and future prospects. The logical conclusion of this development is that she should think in terms of her own promotion, aiming to occupy a post where men will compete to propose to her.

After demonstrating the attitude of women enmeshed in the 'aib system and those liberated from it, Idris turns to the other side of the picture, the masculine view of women's employment. However, after the first masterly sketch of the fluttering in the dovecote as the word goes round, he ceases to follow it up. Sana must suffer petty irritations like being given the worst place in the room, but in the canteen her colleagues condole with those whose offices are still inviolate, enjoying the presence of the girls even when they are convinced that they cannot last the pace for more than a few days. Her subsequent problems are caused by the illegal traffic in licenses or the pursuit of Al-Jundi, and have nothing to do with al-'aib of which the men seem not to have heard; they have no objection in principle to girls working, although some of them, for example the chief clerk, a conservative and paternalistic figure, might be expected to oppose the idea.

For Al-Jundi, the type of anti-social anarchist, al-'aib is in any case a meaningless concept, except in so far as it attracts him. Not surprisingly he terrifies Sana even after her complaint to their superiors has silenced him, since with his obstinate character he cannot be restrained for long. Yet when he resumes his attentions Sana does not find him so repulsive because she has changed, as she recognises; instead of closing her ears to his flattery she looks straight at him and embarrasses him. He has been clumsily changed from an unbelievably evil anti-social Don Juan to a sincere if misguided suitor, presumably in order that Sana's moral collapse should appear more plausible. The reason why the author is driven to these lengths is that he has fallen under the influence of another idea which he cannot happily combine with the 'aib theme.

This idea is that of corruption, which originates in the derisory salaries paid to civil servants and their necessity of supplementing them as easily as possible. They justify the dishonesty they are forced to practise by saying: 'Nice morality is one thing, earning a living is something else. The chief clerk, expounding this view, does not consider whether his family might prefer not to be supported by illgotten gains, although Sana's lightly suggested alternative, to take the children away from school and find them jobs, is unworkable in a country of chronic under-employment. Paradoxically the agreement between them not to interfere with one another is sealed by the *Fatiha*, which strikes Sana as a classic example of a double standard of morality, especially since she does not pray and has not recited the *Fatiha* for years. The other girls are able to supply stories of their own about the double standard men maintain in relation to their work and their family life, and Sana concludes:

'Men have a dossier for each principle. Honour at home is
different from honour at work, what is forbidden at night is
permitted during the day, virtue does not prevent vice; they
are all found together in a state of peaceful co-existence.'

For the girls, on the other hand, a person is either moral or immoral as a whole,
and Idris accepts this view, showing how his heroine collapses completely once
she has accepted a bribe; he does not believe that a whole system of ethics is as
much a product of the environment as one value is, and though the girls re-think
their relation to al-'aib they cannot free themselves from the network of ideas to
which it belongs. They still think of themselves primarily as women, even on
occasions where this is not expected, In the scene when Al-Jundi tries to involve
Sana in a deal and so in the whole business of selling the licences, one of her
reactions to his proposition is to feel insulted, because 'she was a girl, a female,
and it was a man who had thought (that she would agree)'. The preceding pages
have shown that Sana does not encounter professional problems because she is
a woman; why then does she feel insulted as a woman, on this occasion, even if
the issue is clouded by the fact that the man who insults her is Al-Jundi? The
situation is particularly hard to explain since it is likely that what prevents her
from co-operating with her colleagues is a desire to remain morally superior to
them rather than a real principle. This emotion would be more easily undermined
than a firmly-held conviction, and its nature would explain her unexpected
yielding to Ibadat's persuasion after she has refused to pay Usama's fees with
tainted money. But this conclusion is no more than speculation, since the author
has not presented Sana's thought coherently.

The issues of corruption and of responsibility to family and state are here
treated perfunctorily; Safwat's justification of his conduct to Sana shows that he
does not visualise the state as the community of his fellowcitizens, but it reads like
a remark from a sociological textbook. Likewise Sana's gradual collapse under
the pressures at the office and the sense of isolation at home, which in itself is
plausible, is briefly stated, and the author does not attempt to describe her
emotional and ethical development in any detail. The theme of corruption has not
received more than a superficial treatment. As far as the 'aib theme is concerned,
Idris has unintentionally revealed an interesting attitude; he disapproves of the
idea of women being a 'shame', walled up in their houses, but he believes that
there are fundamental differences between them and men with regard to the moral
code. If his theory is correct, then because of their integrated approach they
should be labelled not an 'aib but a khatar (danger) for whom the consequences
of making false income tax returns, for example, scarcely bear thinking of.

There are certain fixed points in the universe of Yusuf Idris, foremost among
them the quality of humanity; 'the humanity of man alone, of which thoughts may
be considered one of the elements, is the essence of man' and anything which
attempts to emphasise one element at the expense of the others is to be con-
demned, for the human being is more important than any question. In Al-Baida

it is mainly the political threat to this quality which is attacked; in *Al-Haram* class discrimination and harsh conventions are the target, and in *Al-'Aib* similar social laws and corruption. Some of Idris's best stories have been on the same theme, for example *Al-'Askari al-aswad* and the more amusing *Alif al-ahrar* (The alif in the word 'ahrar').

'Humanity' is chiefly connected with the development of the individual's potentialities unchecked by society. Idris is suspicious of those who lay down codes of conduct; the wise men and the prophets who do so are without the passions of ordinary people, and they ignore the entire personality with its faults as well as its good qualities. Instead of those unfeeling judges people need advocates to defend them with all their faults. But his characters receive no helpful advice, instead standing, lonely figures, trying to resolve their own problems outside the framework of an ethical system.

Holding the views he does about society, Idris is naturally interested in the area of behaviour where its laws are strictest and the group most bound by its judgements. His concern with sexual morality and with women is genuine, yet despite passages where he writes with great insight he is still a prisoner of the attitudes with which he grew up - not in considering women as an *'aib*, but in regarding them as having entirely different mental processes from men.

It is easy to see how this anarchic attitude to a moral system should develop in a society still rigidly bound by tradition, especially when its propounder is endowed with as much sympathy and understanding as Idris. Yet its expression has gradually been stifled as the country has witnessed an ever-increasing interference of the state in all aspects of life, and so he has come to adopt a facile romanticism, as a comparison of *Al-'aib* with *Al-Haram* demonstrates. He can no longer voice his criticism of injustice in society; perceiving it, he must either keep silent or present it in softened tones. It is almost inevitable that the fate of the *tarahil* is left in the balance and the existence of corruption in the civil service scarcely criticized, for those who protest too strongly face the same fate as Shauqi in *Al-'Askari al-aswad*.

Hilary Kilpatrick, *The Modern Egyptian Novel: a Study in Social Criticism*, London: Ithaca Press, 1974, pp. 113-26.

Guilt and Ego in Yusuf Idris's Novels

Ali Jad

In the case of Yusuf Idris, universality of interest (which is typical of this phase of the history of the Egyptian novel) takes the form of his concern with some aspects of the psychology of human behaviour, notably the conduct of individuals during crises of conscience and group prejudice and self-esteem.

Idris's method is perhaps essentially characterized by the near-ubiquity of the authorial voice (of the omniscient author or 'I' narrator). This is a generalizing, philosophizing voice: the author consistently moves from the particular to the general, making generalized statements about the world and human nature. His books are full of such phrases as 'Little things may change the lives of people', 'I felt the kind of ecstasy that discharges happiness in our hearts and makes us find it in everything we see', 'Happiness makes poets out of us', 'We are living in one of these moments in which two people dissolve in each other', 'All people . . .', 'Man . . .', 'Some people . . .' that . . .', 'People have to . . .'. Perhaps it is because of his interest in making such direct comments upon life and human nature that the author insists on the continuous presence of his own voice. Not for him the late Jamesian, almost total, authorial withdrawal, the tendency to let a story 'tell itself' through unceasing dramatization.

Another general characteristic of his method is his interest in analysis: he is immensely concerned with the intimate presentation of his characters' states of feeling, with many shades and nuances. But he usually does this through direct description and analysis: his presentation of his characters' feelings is usually mediated and intermingled with the generalizing authorial voice:

> 'Abd al-Muttalib did not run; instead he found himself burst-ing into loud laughter . . . for he realized somehow that what lay in front of him was not an afreet . . . but a forsaken new-born bastard . . . At any rate, he did not go on laughing for long, for he was soon pulled up by a sudden sense of responsi-bility . . . For some people can hardly come across a misdeed [committed by an unknown culprit] without attaching the blame to themselves. . . . Thus he stood there planning in his head how he would defend himself against [the accusations

127

of] people, of the Agricultural Officer, and even, should the
worst come to the worst, against formal charges in the courts.

There are occasional passages of private drama in which the authorial voice
disappears completely. Such passages represent a pure dramatization of the
character's consciousness. But they are rare: normally, the author's voice is too
present for us to cherish, effectively, the illusion that what we read is a given
character's dramatized consciousness, even when the description has such a
degree of immediacy and intimacy that the boundaries between direct description
and dramatic presentation are no longer discernible, as for instance in the passage
quoted above. *Al-Haram* (1959) deals largely with aspects of group psychology
such as group prejudice and group self-image and as such it furnishes a good
example of the author's interest in studying and commenting upon human nature.
The novel is about the difficult position in which migrant land-tillers find
themselves as strangers in a village, to which they are imported by contractors
from work-starved regions in Egypt, where there are better chances of work but
where they are exploited by contractors and landowners. They are utterly humble,
even when compared with the poor, exploited fellaheen. The migrants are
despised, mocked and badly treated by everyone in the village. Even the
shopkeeper curses their fathers while taking their farthings; the villagers cannot
even think of them as human beings without some difficulty.

The novel offers us an admirable picture of the agitations caused in the village
by the discovery of the body of an illegitimate new-born baby near the irrigation
canal. The scandalized villagers are torn between their complacency and strong
prejudices, that make them insist that the mother *must* belong to the camp of
migrant farm-labourers in their village, and a sneaking self-doubt that makes
them alive to the possibility that she could be one of their womenfolk. When,
eventually, the mother is found in the camp of the migrants, the village is
confirmed in its prejudice against them. (Nevertheless, when they see the
suffering of the feverish, hysterically conscience-stricken mother which finally
leads her to commit suicide, all their severity of judgement towards, and scorn for,
the migrants disappear: "The barrier between the two communities was removed
altogether and for ever". I doubt if this reflects the reality in such situations: it
seems to have to do with the author's vision and his message of all-inclusive
human sympathy.)

A great deal of the value of the book derives, I believe, from the author's ironic
approach to the commotion caused in the village by the discovery of the baby's
body. The author shows us that despite their agitations at first and their self-
congratulation when the mother is found, the scandalized village is not exactly
spotlessly clean: the irony is driven home through direct authorial commentary
and direct narrative as well as through dramatic presentation:

Whenever the word 'adulteress' was mentioned a thrill would
go through his body: not that . . . he [the Agricultural Officer]

had not known women before he got married, or had not had
extra marital relationships after he got married: ... but it
seemed as if those women who committed adultery or fornication with him were neither adulteresses or fornicators; it seemed
as if only those women who committed such acts with other
men deserved such appellations!

Moreover, a fair amount of fornication and adultery takes place in the village, or
rather, the author makes it appear as if this is what actually happens in the village.
Much of such goings-on remains private; but about some of it there is public or
semi-public knowledge. The local postman discovers by accident that his wife
makes him [in a roundabout manner] carry her letters to her lovers. The flirtatious
and flighty wife of the local Imam and ingenuous Sufi has had an affair with the
village's young bachelor Don Juan, Ahmad Sultan, and facilitates his approach
to local girls and married women. The same Ahmad Sultan reveals to the foolish
and spoilt only son of the Agricultural Officer:

    the other face of life in the estate, the hidden face ...
    which contained unbelievable relationships between sons and
    their step-mothers, respectable persons and flagrant persons.

Thus, it is this hypocrisy-ridden community that judges the wretched mother:
they cannot conceive of her as anything other than whorish and heartless; but we
soon discover the inexorable circumstances that have led first to the conception
and later to the death of her baby.

Al-Baida, the author says in the introduction, was written in the summer of
1955 and then partly serialized in the Cairo daily, *Al-Jumhuriyyah* in 1960, after
which it appeared in book form in Beirut in 1970. It deals with the obsession of
the narrator Yahya with a Greek girl Santi (Xanthe?) whom he wants to possess,
body and soul, for no better reason than to augment his own ego. At first he thinks
that it will be easy for him to have a quick love affair with her and nothing further;
then he discovers that she is married and is in love with her husband. What is
more, he discovers that she does not love *him*. But the more difficult he finds it
to possess her, the more obsessed with her he becomes. Yahya is a doctor and a
radical journalist; he works in a surgery attached to a railway workshop and also
for a radical paper. Glimpses of his practical activities alternate with the
treatment of his obsession with Santi, putting us back into the stream of everyday
social and political life, as a change, after periods of concentration on the detailed
analysis of one man's private feelings. His obsession with Santi does not end until
she starts to visit him less and less frequently (because she has found someone
else to satisfy her vanity? We do not really know) and until long after the editorial
board demand that he should not see her privately.

Al-'Aib, 1962, deals with some great pressures and shocks that lead to the
moral disintegration of the heroine. Sana' is one of five girls who are newly

appointed in a governmental department from which women have hitherto been excluded. The novel concentrates on Sana''s experience in the office in which she is installed. She finds herself alone with four male colleagues who are amused and even a little scandalized to find their world encroached upon by a young woman. Their reaction does not stem merely from their male prejudice: they also have things to hide (corruption). They fear that the arrival of an outsider, let alone a female outsider, will disturb their convenient arrangements. The novel deals with Sana''s tribulations as a novice civil servant; but more importantly it presents the effect of exposure to a 'corrupt' atmosphere upon a previously protected and rather innocent girl: 'she seemed idealistic and as pure as a piece of white cloth', 'a girl who has never come across [such] people [as Al-Jundi, her colleague in the office] who would tell a flagrant lie'. She is first bothered by the unwelcome attentions of this Al-Jundi, a thick-skinned, twanging husband of two; she scolds him and reports him to her boss, but in vain. Finally, she decides to ignore him altogether and this works. But her problems do not end here. She runs into financial difficulties at home and she talks about these to a girl from another office in the department who sometimes comes to chat with her in her office. Al-Jundi overhears her and decides to use her difficulties as a vulnerable spot through which he can carry out his designs upon her.

The newcomer, Sana', soon senses, rather vaguely, that there is a secret world which lies within the visible one of the department, a secret fraternity cooperating for some mysterious ends. Before long, the fraternity decide that they will have sooner or later to let her in on their secret; ultimately Al-Jundi finds a chance to bring pressure to bear upon her. One day, one of the most important 'customers' of the office comes on business and negotiations start between him and Al-Jundi. The latter starts talking loudly, deliberately and cunningly involving Sana' as 'one of us', the bribe-taking fraternity in the department. Sana', who of course has never had anything to do with the matter, is astounded; she bursts into uncontrollable tears:

> She felt humiliated not only because she was present on such an occasion . . . or because Al-Jundi had tried to involve her however indirectly; but . . . because he must have felt, when he made his plans, nearly certain that she would agree . . . How humiliating it was for her honour that a *man* should think of her in this way.

In the end, she tells Al-Jundi what she really thinks of him, and leaves the room threatening to expose him. Her immediate boss in the office argues the situation with her: they have to do what they do in order to supplement their salaries and to live up to their responsibilities as fathers and husbands. She is not convinced; integrity is integrity, she tells him. But in the end, she tells him that they can do what they like provided that they leave her alone. This, we shall see, reveals another vulnerable spot in her moral armour.

In the meantime, the financial difficulties at her home come to a climax: examinations are at hand and her brother will not be allowed to sit for them unless the family pay up the last instalment of his school fees. But they cannot pay up. Sana' tries in vain to discuss the matter with her colleagues and her utter loneliness starts to have a damaging effect upon her moral character. The designs of those around her (this time specifically those of 'Abadah Bey, the office's most important 'customer' and a veteran corrupter of the consciences of civil servants) hasten her moral collapse. One day he comes upon her while she is alone in the office, the others being out for the day for various reasons: 'Abadah wants her to do some business for him which, in the absence of her colleagues, only she can do. She does not tell him frankly that she will not be party to questionable transactions; instead she merely tries to wriggle out through various pretexts which he dismisses easily. He also opens one of the drawers of her desk and puts in a hefty bundle of banknotes which tempt her inexorably. She does not come to a definite decision about the money but does for him what he has come for. All the time, 'Abadah Bey, who is a shrewd student of human character, has been subjecting her to relentless observation and analysis:

> He expected her [after what happened the last time he met her when he and Al-Jundi humiliated her by trying to involve her in their transactions] to meet him . . . with disgust, clear or hidden . . . That she did not, interested him . . . Moreover, the objections she made against his present business and the obstacles she raised were not in fact so much against him and his business as against her own self . . . She wanted some circumstances beyond her control, to settle the question for her, to stand between her and the execution of his business. Very well then, what would happen if he removed these external circumstances and left her moral will, naked, unpro-tected? . . . Well, what happened was exactly what he himself had expected. She was morally paralysed . . . Now, he needed to push her a step forward before she decided to take one backward, suddenly and decisively.

It is here that 'Abadah Bey puts the money inside the drawer of her desk; he leaves soon after. After some hesitation and a momentary suspicion that she might be facing a plot planned by her colleagues to compromise her, she takes the money. At home, she is still uneasy about it; but this in fact merely indicates the last convulsion of her defeated conscience:

> [At home] she tried to listen to one voice . . . to come from inside her and tell her to return the ill-gotten money . . . but in vain. Instead she had an overwhelming feeling that the ques-tion had been settled and that what mattered was not the

money but the steps she had taken before and after taking the money: steps which could not be 'un-taken' now whatever she might do.

Ironically, Al-Jundi has been on the point of reforming, thanks to her uncompromising attitude, and her harsh words: a near reversal of roles had been in the offing but her own collapse has come too soon for that.

The question of right and wrong, the intricacies of moral sensibility, the nature of morality and our conventions and values, and moral attitudes with all their contradictions, these are things that seem to interest the author and are usually central in his fiction. In the first place all his leading characters have alert questioning consciences. They err but they are not humbugs: they do not deceive themselves or rationalize their deeds. In fact one may say that there is an element of neurosis in their severity towards themselves: we see how, despite the inexorable circumstances that have led, in *Al-Haram*, to the conception and birth of her illegitimate baby, and to its death later on, the mother's sense of guilt kills her. Her integrity and her severity on herself are further emphasized by making them stand in sharp relief against the villagers' complacency, hypocrisy and self-righteousness:

> she struggled with the man [who raped her] but in vain; in fact she even did not know why she found it difficult to resist him when he put his arms around her . . . and this was why, in the end, she moaned and groaned in the manner of someone that was wronged but who did not entirely exculpate herself of all the responsibility for what happened to her.

The central character in *Al-Baida'* tells us that he was a sensitive child and that his mother made him so much afraid of making mistakes that he always made them in fact. In *Al-'Aib*, the leading character's lack of moral resilience makes it difficult for her perhaps to endure the knowledge of evil and the exposure to its influence; it plays a role in her moral disintegration. So does her (or the author's?) attempt to deal with the matter on her own in a social vacuum:

> The terrible moment during which she suffered from the sense that she was excluded, an outcast, made *her* turn her back on people as they ceased to have any influence upon her thought and behaviour and no longer did she care to please them. Thus almost overnight she started to feel that she could not and need not care except for herself.

Here we see a confirmation of a fact we could have inferred from her decision to let her colleagues do as they pleased, provided that they do not involve *her* in their transactions. There are elements in her ethics of self-righteousness and excessive concern with social respectability and with what people may think of her; perhaps this is one reason why she eventually falls victim to the pressures of her situation and the designs upon her of those around her. Now she is no longer sure of her moral convictions or of her own integrity:

> Was she expressing what she really believed? Did she merely want to humiliate Al-Jundi because of his attitude to her? Or was she in fact saying what she *wished to be her real belief*? (Emphasis mine.)

Later we read:

> Was what was happening to her brother [she thought] the price of her own blemishlessness, a price which *she* did not pay, but which the guiltless lad did (and was crushed in the process) . . . Had she made him suffer . . . to remain respect-able . . . in her own eyes and in the eyes of others?

Her taking of the bribe brings in its wake her entire moral disintegration:"'Never mind', . . . was to be her favourite response in future . . . to any attempt made to censure her, by others or by her own conscience".

Ali Jad, *Form and Technique in the Egyptian Novel 1912-1971*, London: Ithaca Press, 1983, pp. 286-74.

The Novel *The Taboo* as a New Phase

'Abd al-Hamid 'Abd al-'Azim al-Qitt

For me The *Taboo* represents a new phase in the author's literary output. By that I do not imply a move away from the framework of the traditional novel form, nor can it be said to represent anything new with regard to the form of the Egyptian novel; the form in fact is utterly traditional. What is new is the subject. This novel shows, in my opinion, that the author has managed to escape the shackles that have bound his more successful contemporaries; to be specific, Ihsan 'Abd al-Quddus in his novel, *There's a Man in Our House* (1953). It can truthfully be said that *The Taboo* represents a unique structure among its author's novels; the plot is completely different from that of any of his other novels.

The events of the novel start at the climax, then move inexorably forward till they reach the beginning all over again. They then complete their journey, unravelling the principal plot first and then the subsidiary plots as well. One might well ask why the author should begin with the climax of the plot; what is the result of such an inversion of the chronology of events? The novelist will normally do this if he wants to place a particular emphasis on the events themselves and an even greater emphasis on their significance. In that case, he will invert the usual order of beginning and end so that the final result of the entire tale will be known at the beginning, something that forces the reader to transfer his attention from the issue of what happens to why and how it does so. In the novel things start when 'Abd al-Mutallib the guard stumbles on a dead newborn baby in an irrigation ditch. As a result of this discovery we follow the course of events as Fikri Efendi doggedly pursues his search for the murderer of the baby, only to end in failure. He washes his hands of the whole affair and so informs the responsible authorities. The case is closed and the foundling buried.

This part of the novel is full of action and life. It covers a single day, but, even though it is a short time period, it takes up almost a quarter of the entire novel. Yusuf Idris then puts a few days aside while he moves on to the point in time when Fikri Efendi comes across the murderess quite by chance. With that, he switches back to a brief survey of 'Azizah's past. We learn about her life both before and after she was married until the point when her husband fell ill and had a craving for potatoes; how she went out to look for some and "succumbed" in spite of herself. At this point Idris brings us back to the course of events. We see 'Azizah

135

terribly ill and finally dying; her body is returned to her own town for burial. The story does not end here however, but proceeds to tell us the way things have developed in the lives of the estate inspectorate and the effect of the 1952 Revolution and the Agricultural Reform Law on the people who live there. The author waits almost two years to record the effects of this new development on Egyptian peasants and to resolve the subplot contained with his novel. We will have occasion to consider this ending later.

The principal course of events moves at a leisurely pace; the only things impeding its forward movement are occasional interpolations by the author of material essential to the portrayal of what is going on in the inspectorate; to introduce us to both the "Gharabwah" [migrant workers] and the year-round inhabitants of the estate. This procedure is entirely in line with the structure he has chosen. Thus, when the Ma'mur [Police Officer] points the finger of blame at the Gharabwah, accusing them of responsibility for the existence of this foundling child, the author has to say something to introduce the reader to them. He proceeds to describe their miserable lives of poverty and the aversion that the inhabitants of the estate feel towards them, as though they were not fellow human beings at all. To the estate dwellers these migrant workers have their own particular smell, clothing, and appearance, so much so that you cannot distinguish men from women.

Idris pauses more than once to describe the estate inhabitants to us, their life and relationships with each other; in particular, their illicit sexual relationships. This he does because of its connection with the discovery of the foundling's corpse and with Fikri Efendi's concern with finding the foundling's mother. We watch him doing a survey of all the Gharbwah in case he can recognise the culprit woman among them; we also see him pausing to do a mental check of all the estate women too in case he can recall any signs of pregnancy among them that he did not spot at the time. Idris also uses this method to introduce the figure of Ahmad Sultan, but he immediately pushes him to one side because Fikri Efendi is not interested in discovering the identity of the father but only of the mother. He is looking for the person who fits the mother's role, not the father's. Thus he is prepared to believe in such a taboo among men, but the thing he finds so difficult to swallow is that it is there among women too. Man's role in the taboo is purely coincidental, whereas woman's is crucial. It's the mother he is looking for, and no one will escape his search.

In depicting secondary characters in this way and reviewing their illicit sexual relationships, Idris seems to be establishing some kind of parallel or comparison between on the one hand 'Azizah's tragedy, the public scandal she suffers, and the price she has to pay for a mistake that was in no way under her control, and, on the other, life on the estate. Here there are any number of illicit relationships between men and women, but the society is prepared to tolerate them: these involve Nubuwwah, Umm Ibrahim, and above all Ahmad Sultan through whose narrative we learn of several of his escapades with women on the estate. The primary instigation may be to prove his virility and manliness in front of Safwat,

Fikri Efendi's son, or to confirm the very idea we are discussing here, or to establish yet another comparison — this one between the surface life of the estate and what goes on beneath that surface. Outward appearances suggest that everything is above board and without blemish, whereas realities tell us that there is a good deal of fornication going on. The author reveals to us this other aspect of life on the estate. . . .He is particularly keen for us to know that, even though Masihah Efendi has cut off his daughter, Linda, his letters to her imply that he forgives her for marrying Ahmad Sultan, a Muslim, while she herself is a Christian. Idris seems to imply here that, in provincial societies that are relatively well-off, women can enjoy a certain amount of illicit sex and that their activities will be viewed with understanding and even connivance. This finds some confirmation in the story of Zakiyyah, the wife of Mahbub the mailman, and her lover. Her husband absolutely refuses to divorce her even though he is well aware that she has a lover and is deceiving him. The Ma'mur takes a flippant attitude to the story of Zakiyyah and her lover and uses it to spice up his evening chatter.

However, one cannot overlook the fact that Idris spends a great deal of time exposing this taboo element in his novel, particularly in view of the fact that some of the women involved do not give way to temptation for sheer pleasure but, taking Nubuwwah as an example, out of the basic needs of poverty. . . .The exhaustive detail that goes into the description of the relationship between Linda and Safwat, and then between her and Ahmad Sultan — details that are, after all, a tangential part of the main story — add to the impression the reader has that all these ancillary facts weigh the novel down, particularly in view of its relative shortness.

The second and crucial strand in the plot concerns the relationship of the estate inhabitants with the migrant workers. At first this involves a sense of superiority on the former's part over the latter; after all, migrant workers are poor and have no real possessions. The estate views them with contempt and stays out of their way. . . .All this changes when the foundling is discovered; the events send the entire estate community into turmoil. . . .When the body comes to light and it is discovered that 'Azizah is its mother, they all rage against the migrant workers. But the mood rapidly changes when they learn that 'Azizah is married and begin to realize that the calamity is not 'Azizah's alone but involves the entire community. Soon after, the estate children are allowed to play with the migrant children. Among their elders things are more bashful and hesitant at first, but gradually the estate inhabitants come to visit 'Azizah and offer her their assistance in her time of trial. Nubuwwah kills a rabbit for her to eat, hoping that she will recover from her illness.

In the end the inhabitants of the estate and the Gharabwah come together; it is as though 'Azizah's tragedy has dissolved all the artificial barriers between them and cemented their relations with each other. Idris shows great sophistication in his treatment of the relationship between these Egyptian peasant groups, making clear quite how well he himself knows the life of these migrant peoples in our Egyptian countryside and the miserable existence they live. . . .

As we noted above, the disappearance of the culprit woman is Fikri Efendi's problem, almost his alone. As the Ma'mur reviews his doubts concerning the various women in the community with a scandalous past, the reader senses that the Ma'mur expects the secret to be revealed fairly soon. But things are not that simple. Nubuwwah, around whom a number of rumors are flying, is clearly in the prime of health as she walks past the Ma'mur. This happens as the Ma'mur is marshalling all his cognitive energies to identify the culprit. At this point, tongues that have been wagging in accusation suddenly fall silent; the vague glimmer of hope, that Nubuwwah may be the culprit, having vanished, the problem reappears in all its original complication. Even so, people are still hopeful that the culprit may be found among the migrant workers. Fikri Efendi does a survey of all the women and girls in the field, and we follow behind him as he returns in failure. When the baby is buried, the problem becomes even more complicated and seems insoluble. . . .

The author's desire to leave things obscure is confirmed by the fact that he does not bring 'Azizah into the picture at all until Fikri Efendi comes across her. He has of course made sure to show the effect of the foundling's discovery on relationships among the inhabitants of the estate and on the feelings of both men and women, but 'Azizah has remained outside that framework. Even when the identity of the foundling's mother is known, the problem is only partially solved. The mother is married, and so there can be no excuse for killing her own child. A new question now arises: why did she kill the baby and throw it in the ditch? The partial answers provided are obviously intended to make the reader want to continue until all the answers are known. Those answers are provided about half way through the novel, when a brief summary of 'Azizah's past history is given along with the reasons that led her to kill her child. But the author does not stop there; after all he is not writing a detective novel. He proceeds to track the events in his novel to its conclusion and to show the relationships that bind the characters to each other. . . .

The character of Fikri Efendi seems to me little different from that of a detective. He really wants to find out who the culprit is, something that can be explained by his inquisitive nature as depicted for us by the author. Coupled to all this is the fact that he represents authority on the estate, something that makes his role close to that of a police detective; as a result he can only relax when the secret is finally disclosed and he finds out why the foundling was killed. . . .

Some people think that The Taboo should finish with 'Azizah being taken away for burial in her own village; it would then be open-ended and would make 'Azizah's tragedy a personification of continuity. However Idris is constrained to deal with all his sideplots such as the story of Linda and Ahmad Sultan. He has to proceed with the description of the life of Masihah Efendi and other inhabitants of the estate, indeed of the estate as a whole — its inhabitants and owners — in the wake of the 1952 revolution. . . .

          'Abd al-Hamid 'Abd al-'Azim al-Qitt, Yusuf Idris wa-al-
     fann al-qasasi, Cairo: Dar al-Ma'arif, 1980, pp. 14-25.

Idris's Novel: *The Sin*

Ghali Shukri

The novel, *The Sin*, deals with the question of sin as a product of urban society. The young girl, Sana', starts work in a government department. It is not long before she discovers that she has joined a world that is completely different from her own. Her colleagues, she notices, extort enormous sums of money from department clients for doing special favors for them. Needless to say, her colleagues do their best to get her to join their little group, but she steadfastly refuses to do so. Even when her own brother is not allowed by his school to take an examination because he has not paid the fees, she still resists the temptation. Muhammad al-Jundi goes to great lengths to cast aspersions on Sana's reputation. Since she is a beautiful woman, he is anxious to get his hands on her, although he realizes that she has to join the bribery group as well. Eventually however, Sana' comes to realize that what she is doing is like trying to fumigate a brothel. The whole scenario is comic; there is nothing heroic about it. She gives in at one and the same time to the hundred pounds that have been placed in her drawer and to the advances of Muhammad al-Jundi. The psychological tragedy that affects her personally is reflected on the societal level as well.

It is too hasty a judgment to suggest that the intellectual focus of this novel has spoiled it as a work of art. Every great artist lays out plans for the intellectual content of his works; by which I imply that he organizes the general framework before considering details of construction. In *The Sin* the intellectual aspect seems directed towards the Idrisian equation which states that human beings are a product of their unsatisfactory societal environment. Idris manages with considerable success to follow every single psychological qualm that Sana' feels and every aspect of her external behavior. He shows admirable precision by selecting the minutest details that provide every scene with its own raison d'être. Then comes the basic contradiction to be found in Idris's works: all this detail fails to provide an integrated vision of what society should be. Instead we are left with a set of abstractions that flounder around in absolute generalities. Good, evil, heredity, environment, these factors may all have represented a reasonably close approximation to the factors that have an impact on the development of society at its various stages. But by now science has advanced to the point where we can confirm that man, existence, and society are extremely complicated entities; any

139

other arbitrary method of classification makes no sense. We may indeed say that society is the primary source of sin and continue by noting that such a statement is no longer sufficient for a real appreciation of the human essence. On the most general level that may all be fair enough. However, contemporary narrative should not deal in clichés but create something absolutely miraculous, namely a sharp delineation of the dense and complex particulars of man, existence, and society. When Yusuf Idris follows the actions of Sana' in such microscopic detail without providing his readers with such insight, it is because he has chosen to use a different means of analysing the real meaning of mankind, one that is simple and absolute. This ideational simplicity is reflected on the level of expression too. How easy it is for an artist to portray the struggle between good and evil and finish up by showing that evil is the fault of factors external to the will of mankind. Those factors become a clothes-peg on which we can hang all our sins.

Yusuf Idris never falls into the trap of fake optimism as some politically motivated writers have been tempted to do. His view of good and evil is neither mechanical nor one-sided. He considers them from a number of angles and in a variety of circumstances. With him experience is something rich and innovative. However, the expressive mode he uses propels both himself and his work into an abyss full of mathematical equations. To be sure, the experience of any woman who enters a man's working environment for the first time in the history of the agency is certainly going to be authentic and a true reflection of our society, quite apart from documenting an important phase in our societal history. While giving sentimental expression to his portrait of this phase Yusuf Idris seems content merely to note that the old way remains powerful and capable of eradicating the new. That is true enough. However, the real crisis does not lie in this process of eradication, and thus has nothing to do with the hundreds of bitter circumstances that beset civil servants in general and Sana' in particular. Civil servants represent neither absolute good nor absolute evil, even though Idris sometimes describes people that way. Differentiating the two is extremely complex. Thus, when one citadel in someone's personality collapses (as when Sana' decides to accept the bribe), it does not imply that all the other citadels fall at the same time; just that on one occasion her sense of honor lapses. Where individuals and society as a whole are concerned, the collectivity of values is of labyrinthine complexity; so much so that it is impossible to gather them all together on a single white sheet of paper. If someone disavows one of them in a moment of weakness, he does so with them all; by adhering to one, he does so to all of them. It is this perception that gives rise to the impression that Yusuf Idris wrote *The Sin* with a predetermined intellectual matrix in mind, something that leaves no room for elements of the random or unconscious. What we get instead is more a detailed study of society, a search for new tools and methods with which to express the latest of society's dicta. In *The Sin* there is a single crisis, but it falls strangely flat because the author has chosen to enclose things in a fence on two separate sides, those of good and evil. Man is made to rely on good, whereas circumstances resort to evil. In the ensuing struggle the two exchange positions a number of times. Man's struggle with his own circumstances is undoubtedly the true subject of art, but such circumstances cannot be traced back to fate, heredity, or environment. In our era problems have multiplied in an unprecedented way; features of the crisis of conscience that have manifested themselves on the brow of our generation are far more profound than surface appearances might suggest (such as the author's entry into an organization that is admitting female employees for the first time)....

The novel suggests that the crisis faced by Sana' has absolutely nothing to do with sex; men and women are both concerned far more with the quest for a living wage. The crisis of conscience consists in an attempt to preserve a set of values that conflict directly with reality. But this is not the case. In fact, the work itself suggests — and this is striking — that Sana's fall from grace as a woman is a consequence of her decision to accept the bribe. The logic already established by the author forces him to slide into the statement that this moral downfall has to encompass all other values as well. As the Christian woman says: "If you commit one sin, you commit them all." If this is to be the logic, then the human soul is so excessively naive that at the start of the novel Sana' has to enter the organization as a pure, unsullied angel; it is the need for food to eat that compels her to accept a bribe. With that, she instantaneously turns into the devil incarnate.

Thus, even though some people have commented on the intellectual rigor of the novel's structural organization, the dramatic pivot is flawed. This emerges clearly in the intensity with which the author introduces Sana's problem with her brother, only to be followed by her utter unadaptability when the storm breaks. Later we are completely surprised when she finally gives way without any forewarning. The event totally fails to provide a plausible justification for the change, most especially because the process is not confined to the acceptance of the bribe but constitutes a major transformation point in Sana's life. Idris allows her to collapse unconcernedly in front of Muhammad al-Jundi with the words, "It's none of your business." There is no further explanation for this major moral downfall. Expressed differently, the first transformation finds no justification in terms of details, and it serves as the trigger for a whole series of other changes that cannot be justified artistically. The dramatic pivot of the novel — Sana's crisis of conscience — actually incorporates within it a number of factors that contradict the notion of the final downfall. Idris has deliberately enveloped her in an iron cage of detail that leads inexorably to a particular end, but he has overlooked a large number of circumstances and values that manage to envelop Sana' in an even larger circle than the narrow one he has designed for her. In the context of that situation — the larger circle that comprises Sana's crisis — she could certainly operate with a great deal more freedom than she does and thus plot a course that might be completely different from the one portrayed by the author.

But it is the use of this carefully constructed intellectual equation that pulls the girl apart between the twin poles of good and evil as she struggles valiantly again the forces of sin in society. When Sana's downfall occurs, it seems like a gesture of hanging dirty washing on the clothes-line made up of those very forces. It is precisely these elements of generalization, abstraction, the resort to the absolute, and a purely mechanical vision, that lead one to conclude that this novel could happen in any place and time—were it not for some purely local Egyptian touches. It could even take place outside the bounds of time and place, were it not for the few historical events that the author has incorporated into the plot. In this case, the words "take place" do not imply that there is any correspondence between information provided within the novel and photographic reality. Unfortunately it means that the artistic experience is stripped of its most essential element, that utterly particular thing that separates one experience from another.

Ghali Shukri, "Al-'Ayb," in *Hiwar* 2 (1963): 115-17.

The Plays of Yusuf Idris

By M.M. Badawi

Yusuf Idris, who gave up his career as a physician to devote himself to writing and journalism, is probably the leading short-story writer in the Arab world, but he has from time to time been drawn to the theatre, for which he wrote a number of realistic plays before *al-Farafir*, plays revealing his strong social and political commitment: *Malik al-Qutn (The Cotton King*, 1954), an angry denunciation of the exploitation of the poor peasant, who is touchingly attached to his soil, by the greedy, rich landlord and of the gulf separating the haves from the have-nots. This was followed by *Jumhuriyyat Farahat (Farahat's Republic*, written in 1954, but performed in 1956), a more mature work, based on one of his short stories: an elderly, simple policeman sits at his desk in the appalling conditions of the police station, facing a number of miserable people, arrested for different offences, and dreams up the plot of a film which he relates to the educated young man, who he thinks has been arrested for his political views. The fantasy is about a poor, honest man, who wins a fortune and creates an ideal republic of which the prosperity, social justice and humaneness contrast sharply with the incidents that keep interrupting the policeman's tale, and even with his own behaviour. *Al-Lahza al-Harija (The Critical Moment*, 1957) was Idris's first major drama, inspired by the 1956 Suez war. It differs radically from the bulk of ephemeral plays speedily turned out to serve as propaganda, glorifying the struggle of Egyptian patriots against imperialist aggression. In his introduction, Idris says that he wrote his play 'to be acted and not to be read', and that he had hesitated before publishing it. Yet it is not likely that *The Critical Moment* will yield its total significance during a single visit to the theatre.

The play describes the reactions of an average middle-class Egyptian family to the war and through them Idris makes his comment on Egyptian society, as well as on humanity at large. Nassar, who comes from a poor and deprived back-ground, by dint of hard work and self-denial rose from his humble beginnings to build a small carpentry business, which he runs with the help of his son by a previous marriage, Mus'ad. He lives in his own house in Port Said, with his wife and five children, of whom the eldest, Mus'ad, is married and lives with his wife in the family residence. The others are Sa'd, an undergraduate, studying engi-neering, Kawthar, a young woman still unmarried, a boy of ten and a much

143

younger girl, Sawsan, the baby of the family, on whom her father dotes. The events of the play, which consists of three acts, all take place in Nassar's house. The family, despite the usual squabbles that characterize all families, is realistically portrayed as a strongly united, happy one, but their life is disturbed by the threat of war, as a result of the nationalization of the Suez Canal. Sa'd secretly joins the National Guard, but his mother discovers his secret and, unhappy at the possibility of losing her son should war break out, she desperately tries to dissuade him from going to his military training. When the father finds out what is happening he is resolved to stop him, unable to understand why, despite his self-sacrifice and the care he has lavished on him to secure for him a bright future as an engineer, Sa'd should want to risk his own life in the defence of a country which offered his father no help whatsoever when he was poor and which he does not feel belongs to him - Nassar's loyalty stretching no further than his own immediate family. In vain does Sa'd try to make his father understand that his primary duty is towards his bigger family, his country, Egypt. Furthermore, the father is convinced that the British government is merely sabre-rattling and that there will be no war. Matters come to a head when war actually breaks out and Sa'd is called up. The father locks him up in his room and takes no notice of his beating on the door wanting to be let out and his screaming and shouting abuse. The house is stormed by British troops, who have been given orders to shoot the National Guard. Nassar is found in the house, ironically enough engaged in praying, in gratitude for the safety of his sons. He is shot by a British soldier for failing to respond to his orders. The soldier, however, is upset by the sight of the little girl crying over her wounded father, as the girl reminds him of his own daughter at home. Meanwhile, Sa'd, whose critical moment has arrived, finds himself failing the test: he is frightened of being found by the British soldiers, takes off his uniform, and hides under the bed. After the soldiers' departure he is let out of his room by his little sister, who pushes the door open, as the faulty lock had not really properly caught. He comes out to find his father dying, and frankly admits his cowardice to him, since he says he must have known all along about the door and in any case he could have blown the lock open with his gun. The father, in his turn, assumes responsibility for having been too protective towards his son. This brutal self-confrontation seems to have had some effect upon Sa'd's behaviour, for when the British soldier, his balance of mind disturbed by his killing of an innocent man, returns to the house to look for the girl who, in his confused state, he now believes to be his own daughter, Sa'd kills him. He then goes off to join the National Resistance.

Despite its somewhat melodramatic ending, and relative lack of concentration, *The Critical Moment* is a serious drama with plausible characters grappling with life-like problems, interacting with one another and revealing their real nature when placed in an extreme situation. The difference in outlook between father and son is meant to carry a political significance: the father, who had faced a life of deprivation under the inhumane government of the *ancien régime,* was incapable of understanding that the country belonged to anyone except to those few who enjoyed all the privileges; but the son, brought up by a caring father, and having enjoyed a good education, and living under a new egalitarian system, realized that the country belonged to him and that it was his duty to defend it. Yet in several places we notice that what we are witnessing is also the perennial generation gap: the young struggling to break free from the hold of the overprotective parents. Saʿd admits that in joining the National Guard he is motivated not solely by patriotism, but also by his desire to prove himself. Saʿd's cowardice, underlying his self-deception, and his failure of nerve at the critical moment is convincingly portrayed by the dramatist, who skilfully prepares for it and hints at several possible explanations, social, political and psychological. He even provides a parallel to it in the behaviour of the British soldier who - unlike Saʿd, who intellectually has no doubt about the justice of his struggle - is made to fight in a war he clearly does not believe in and whose feeling of guilt, a result of forcing himself to kill an unarmed old man, unhinges his mind. Idris's sympathy is broad enough to embrace an enemy soldier, saving him from a simplistic, xenophobic or jingoistic position; on the contrary, Idris was severely attacked and even his patriotism was questioned because he chose to present his protagonist as a coward during Egypt's struggle against imperialism. Saʿd, of course, is in no way falsely idealized. Apart from his cowardice, he is a very ordinary young man with ordinary weaknesses (e.g. his flirting with the girl next door) and a penchant for striking attitudes. His emergence as a patriotic fighter occurs only after a painful process of baptism by fire. An interesting feature of this play is that while Idris uses the colloquial for the dialogue of his Egyptian characters, as indeed he does in all his other plays, he makes the two English characters converse in literary Arabic. It cannot be said that this is a successful way of distinguishing between the two linguistic planes of reality, in order to maintain the dramatic illusion.

Idris's next play, *al-Farafir (The Farfurs/The Flipflaps,* 1964) is generally regarded as 'an important monument in the history of modern Egyptian drama'. During the intervening seven years since the publication of *The Critical Moment,* in the course of which he wrote no plays (though he produced much important prose fiction), Idris says he had been thinking hard about the need to write specifically Egyptian drama, which has its roots in the indigenous folkloric theatrical tradition. More has been written about *al-Farafir* than about any other dramatic work during this period, and that is largely because Idris led the world to believe that it represents a practical application of his revolutionary theory of Egyptian drama, expounded in a series of articles entitled 'Towards an Egyptian Theatre' in a leading literary periodical, *al-Katib.* In brief, his argument is that all Egyptian drama to date, even the most successful, had been written according to the western model and it was time a form of drama was devised to express the authentic Egyptian spirit. His search for autonomous dramatic form, motivated also by his conviction that only genuinely local art can attain universality, had led him to the more primitive indigenous folk art of dramatic entertainment, such as the shadow theatre, the Karagoz and more particularly the village *samir,* a popular type of social get-together at which villagers amuse themselves by

singing, dancing and impersonation. The *samir,* he argued, should be the starting
point for the Egyptian dramatist, who should develop and refine it and make it a
suitable vehicle for his sophisticated work. The important principle to be
observed is of breaking down the barrier between actors and audience, so that
drama may become a truly collective and creative shared experience, instead of
making the audience passive spectators of an illusion of reality. He makes a
number of points in the detailed prefatory notes on the staging of *al-Farafir,* the
most important being the following: that he wrote his play on the basis of
audience participation, so that actors should form part of the audience and vice
versa; that the play should be performed in 'theatre in the round', so that the
audience as far as possible should form a circle round the actors; that actors
should not lose themselves completely in their parts. Idris also provides suggestions on what kind of person should play the part of Farfur, the main character in
his play (the word, the singular of Farafir, was thought up by the author, and
means 'someone light, flimsy and fluttering' and has been translated as flipflap).
From these suggestions it emerges that what Idris had in mind is someone who
represents the Egyptian sense of humour, a wag, who combines charm with a
sharp tongue; a natural wit, who pokes fun at everything and everybody, friend
and foe alike, including himself; a licensed fool who through laughter seeks to
reform mankind. A man with abundant energy, both mental and physical, an
acrobat who could turn somersaults, a music-hall comedian capable of improvi-
sation and of silencing a rude spectator with a withering reply, he should at the
same time be a man of vision who impatiently, though lovingly, berates us for
failing to live up to his moral ideal. It is interesting to see how Idris's description
of his ideal actor contains ingredients from the *commedia dell'arte* as well as
traditional Arabic humorous literature: the Harlequin as well as the witty
protagonists of the *maqamat* and Juha, together with the popular Egyptian
comedians, 'Ali al-Kassar and Najib al-Rihani.

The play itself opens with the author addressing the audience, preparing them
for the kind of drama they are about to experience. He stands on a bare stage,
behind a lectern, tall, distinguished-looking, wearing a starched white shirt and
dinner jacket, but later, when he moves forward, he is seen to be wearing at the
same time very brief shorts, exposing his long thin legs, and shoes without socks.
He introduces Farfur (Flipflap) in much the same manner as the Presenter in Ibn
Daniyal's shadow play introduces his main character, Tayf al-Khayal; but before
he finishes the mock formal introduction he is rudely interrupted by the music
announcing an entrance and Flipflap very noisily comes on the stage, dressed in
a clown's suit, his face covered with white powder and wearing an old tarboush.
The stage direction describes him as coming, again in the manner of the character
in the shadow play, 'swirling like a tornado, circling round the stage', and hitting
out at random with a stick made of cardboard or thin cracked card, making a noise,
but causing no harm. Farfur, who has been aptly described as 'a combination of
the Figaro factotum and the perennial clown', refuses to go and insists on starting
the action, laughing at the author's ridiculous costume, which the latter defends

by saying that it is meant to show an author's originality. He commands the author to produce a Master for him to serve as well as a Mistress, so that he can get on with the show. After much fumbling and fooling around, the Master is found - a man who is fast asleep in the front row of the auditorium - and the Author, who is anxious to go off to complete the writing of an urgent instalment for a radio serial, promises to send him a Mistress. The Master asks Farfur to choose an occupation for him; the latter suggests several jobs, such as an intellectual, an artist, a lawyer, a doctor, an accountant, a footballer, a broadcaster, a traffic policeman, a thief, a police informer, an engineer; all of which the Master turns down, after making fun of most of them, finally settling for a grave-digger. When ordered to begin digging by his Master, Farfur objects and the Author is summoned to tell Farfur that he must do exactly as he is told. At first Farfur accepts his lot, but as the Master's orders grow increasingly arbitrary, he begins to ask fundamental questions as to why he was made a Farfur and his Master, a Master. It is decided to call the Author and put the question to him: the Author enters, still wearing short trousers, but now half his original size; he states that this is simply 'a fact, like the sun, the moon and hell fire' and that his play 'doesn't contain any "whys"; it contains only "yesses"'. He threatens to punish Farfur if he shows disobedience, by signalling with his hand to two enormous thugs with grotesque masks who promptly appear on the stage. Farfur, now thoroughly frightened, gives in and suggests to his Master that he should get to work; but the latter shows no interest, because he wants to get married, and instructs Farfur to find him a bride. Farfur manages to find him a woman, sitting in the front stalls, allegedly from among the audience, who is prepared to be his wife, but soon the lovely mistress sent by the Author arrives, dressed as a belly-dancer, and the two women, both anxious to marry the Master, get embroiled in a row which is settled when the Master decides to marry both of them at once. The author also sends a bride for Farfur: a tall, thin, ugly man, dressed as a woman in black, who forces herself on him. Both Master and Farfur get married and start begetting children. The wives need money for their housekeeping. Farfur is told by his Master to find a corpse to bury, to kill someone, if need be, otherwise the Master will have to kill Farfur himself to provide work for him. A man in the audience conveniently happens to be looking for someone to end his life for him. The Man stands with his head bent, waiting to be killed, Farfur is ordered by his Master to kill him, he refuses and appeals to the Author, whose voice is heard off stage, threatening to send his ruffians after him and the two thugs in the form of ghosts appear near the door. Farfur still cannot bring himself to murder the Man, so his Master himself kills him and gets Farfur to bury the corpse. Farfur, horrified at his Master's crime and his growing lust for blood, decides he has had enough of serving him. He rushes off the stage into the auditorium, making his way out through the audience, paying no heed to his Master's calling him back, and worrying about the second act of the play.

The events in Act II take place some time later: the Master, angry and miserable because of Farfur's desertion, is wondering where he can find him. Farfur is seen entering from the back of the auditorium, a rag-and-bone man pushing a handcart down the centre aisle - on which are surrealistic models, representing Europe, America and bits of guns, aircraft and gallows - and calling out for anything old for sale: old iron, old glory, a hydrogen bomb, a philosophy, an author or an audience. He and his Master are delighted to see each other; they exchange news about each other's children: the Master's children have all been given names like Alexander, Napoleon, Mussolini, and Hitler, and relieved their father of his work by themselves burying millions of corpses, while Farfur's children were named after famous dark-skinned characters and slaves in history. They decide to resume their life together but not on the old basis: first, on an equal footing, both as servants; then they try switching the roles of Master and Servant; and then both as masters in an instantly created republic; then an empire of freedom in which each enjoys absolute freedom to do as he pleases. When all these attempted solutions fail, they resolve to turn back to the Author, who they are now told is back although they had assumed that he had gone for ever. This time the author is delivered in the form of a bundle, looking like a newborn baby, which they untie only to find smaller and smaller bundles inside, until what remains is too small to be seen. Finally, at the suggestion of the burly Theatre Curtain Attendant, anxious to get away to be with his wife, who is having a baby that evening, they commit suicide as a way out of the problem, since death obliterates all distinctions and renders all men equal. But to his horror Farfur discovers that instead of their becoming two equal atoms with neither Master nor Servant, he has been turned into an electron, spinning for ever round the proton, his Master. Farfur's last words to the audience, as he pathetically gasps for breath, weeping and spinning round and round, are: 'Good people, Flipflaps: Save your brother! My voice is going, Find us a solution! A solution, someone. A solution, otherwise I'll stay like this. There must be a solution; there must be a way out. Your brother is finished. A solution, I beg you. Not for my sake but for your own. I'm just acting. [His voice fades] It's you who are going round and round'.

Despite its prolixity, repetitiveness and digressions, faults common to much of Idris's work, *al-Farafir* is a deeply disturbing and original play, which operates not only on the political and social levels, but also has a metaphysical dimension. The large issues it raises are not confined to those connected with the relation between man and man, namely authority and freedom and the hierarchical structure of society, the tendency of power to generate evil; the gradual shrinking into nothingness of the author of the play suggests a world deserted by God, with man left to his own devices - hence his pathetic attempts to make sense of his existence. The final terrifying image of Farfur spinning dizzyingly round his Master like an electron round the proton implies that the division of beings into master and slave is an absolute and unalterable principle of cosmic application. Yet far from being a solemn work, the play is full of humour: largely through Farfur, his licensed Fool, the author never tires of ridiculing not only political tyranny and social injustice, but also all forms of hypocrisy and cant, and current fashions in thought and art, from existentialism to the Theatre of the Absurd.

As for Idris's claim that he has produced an Egyptian form of theatre, it must be admitted that, despite the various links which the play has with the popular theatrical traditions and folk art, several critics have been fooled by Idris's assertions. There is no real audience participation in *al-Farafir;* there are only actors or actresses strategically placed among the audience, much in the manner popularized by Pirandello. The vogue of the theatre in the round had been very much part of the preoccupation of the European theatre since the fifties, of which Idris and other Egyptian dramatists were aware. Idris's dissatisfaction with realistic drama can best be seen within the context of the experimental European theatre. The questioning of fundamental assumptions in drama has helped Idris and others to reconsider their own drama and seek ways of relating it to local culture. Idris's deliberate attempt to destroy dramatic illusion, either by the Author/Presenter/Narrator addressing the audience directly or by one of the other characters stepping out of his role to draw the attention of the audience to some point or other, has obvious Brechtian ancestry and will be found in the work of many of Idris's contemporaries. Finally, despite Idris's poking fun at the Theatre of the Absurd in more than one place, he has certainly made use of its technique in *al-Farafir.*

Idris's rejection of the form of realistic drama which started with *al-Farafir* continued to mark his later plays. In *al-Mahzala al-Ardiyya (The Farce of the World,* 1966), reality and dream are mixed together in a work clearly designed to be symbolical, though the exact significance of the symbolism is difficult to ascertain. Occasionally one can detect echoes of *al-Farafir:* in some of the satirical remarks reminiscent of Farfur and in the topsy-turvy world of the trial scene; but gone is the obsessive interest in creating an Egyptian dramatic form. In the prefatory note to the play, Idris suggests that 'because of its general atmosphere and in view of the way it has been written, the play should be presented as an unrealistic dream, so that characters should move about and talk in a manner that has little relation to reality'. The result is a work of considerable obscurity, in which it is difficult to decide which action takes place in the protagonist's mind and which is intended to happen in the outside world. The curtain rises, revealing a second, white curtain with the words: 'There is no poverty in the world, there is only poor judgement', signed: 'an Old Egyptian Peasant'. The setting is a public health clinic of distorted appearance, with crudely painted pictures and health advertisements on the wall, warning against the dangers of drug addiction; the doctor, a tiny man, is sitting at an enormous desk; his male nurse, called Sifr (Zero), is a tall thin hunch-back. The clinic is crowded with patients, men and women of different ages and degrees of elegance who seem to sit there silent and motionless during most of the action. The sound effects heard now and then are the cacophany of noise inside Cairo Railway Station. The plot, or what can be disentangled of it, is as follows: a Doctor, whose wife talked at the breakfast table about the need to make some financial arrangement to provide for the children's future, goes to his clinic, obviously deeply disturbed by his wife's remarks. He is asked to certify an allegedly mentally ill patient, called Muhammad III, by his brother, whose name is Muhammad I. Just as the patient is being taken by his brother to be put in an asylum, accompanied by a policeman, a second brother, called Muhammad II rushes in to stop them going and to warn the Doctor that the patient is not really mad, but that his brother is plotting to put him away so that he can seize his share of the land they inherited from their father, having already swindled him (Muhammad II) of his inheritance. At gunpoint, he forces them to do as he wishes. The Doctor, who had some doubts about the patient's insanity during the medical examination, is prepared to accept the story, but Muhammad I is persuasive in his self-defence and in attributing Muhammad II's behaviour to his recent mental breakdown. The patient himself, a highly educated man and a brilliant ex-scientist, whose life was ruined as a result of his imprisonment on a false charge of being a Communist, is not averse to the idea of being put away in a mental hospital, as an escape from a monstrous world which, as an idealist, he can no longer cope with. The Doctor, who is made to witness the domestic argument between the three brothers, has to decide about the patient's sanity. The only proof he can think of is to recall the patient's alleged wife, who has testified to his madness. When he is told firmly by all present, including his nurse, that no woman has been there, the Doctor begins to doubt his own sanity. At this point Act I ends, and had the play stopped here it would have been an amusing and rather witty work, dealing with a theme made familiar by al-Hakim's drama: the relativity of truth and indeed of madness itself. However, in two further acts Idris brings in a farrago of characters, symbolical and otherwise, from the world of the living and the dead, and abstract discussions of countless themes, social, political and moral, resulting in confusion and loss of dramatic tension. At the end, convinced that if human nature continues to live in the jungle it has been inhabiting, brothers will go on fighting one another over inheritances and possessions, the Doctor decides to put himself in a straitjacket, asks his nurse to tie it for him and instructs the policeman to take him to the asylum. The point Idris seems to be making, albeit in a tortuous and roundabout way, is that possession inevitably leads to evil, even though, in the eyes of the perpetrator of this evil, his actions always seem justified. The vision expressed in this play is very pessimistic indeed, since the only way the Doctor could think of to avoid the evil attendant upon possessions is to run away from sane human society to the safety of a lunatic asylum.

Even more gloomy is the atmosphere of *al-Mukhattatin (The Striped Ones*, 1969); besides 'striped' the title also means 'planned' or 'programmed', an obvious, deliberate *double entendre*. It is an 'absurdist' political allegory, which lashes out savagely at the totalitarian one-party state, and reminds us of George Orwell's *1984*, from which it seems to derive the character of 'Big Brother'. *The Striped Ones is* one of the most outspoken political satires written during the Nasser era, and it is amazing that its publication was not banned by the censor. The play consists of three acts; Act 1, set in a Samuel Beckett-like bleak wasteland with a high object to the right of the stage, looking like either an old tree stump or (significantly) the remains of a ruined mosque minaret. A character called 'Mere Talk', shabbily dressed, with long uncombed hair, wearing one shoe and one slipper on his feet, and a match box stuck to his beard, wearily climbs up the raised object, and muezzin-like, proceeds to give a mock call to the dawn prayer — although the time is not dawn, but just before nightfall and the people he is trying to rouse from their slumber are those of 'this miserable land', presumably the audience. He is joined by other characters, a motley crew of suspicious-looking individuals with strange, comical names, indicating certain not laudable attributes, clearly members of a secret organization. They assemble and wait for the arrival of their leader, called simply 'Brother', who descends from the sky in a helicopter. He is clearly an authoritarian bully and inflicts upon them undignified, if not downright brutal punishment, and expects blind obedience from them. They in their turn are scared of him and flatter him in ridiculously exaggerated terms. He informs them that today is the most crucial day in their life, as they are planning to take over power and go public. They are only waiting for the person who will complete their number, a well-known film actress, who turns up dressed in a tight-fitting garment with black and white stripes; they all change into similarly striped clothes and make for the theatre. Act II takes place in the theatre, where they occupy the front stalls and watch a play entitled 'The Foundation of the Greatest Happiness'. During the performance of this play within a play, in which many absurd incidents take place, the Actress attacks the show, accusing the Foundation of fraud and corruption. She goes on to the stage, and eventually, relying upon her physical charms, she and her accomplices manage to take over the management of the Foundation, with Brother ousting the Chairman of the Board of Directors. Act III takes place 'one hundred months later'; slides or a film are shown, revealing the entire globe painted in huge black and white stripes, and everything and everybody similarly striped: aeroplanes, buses, houses, shop fronts, people, even birds and fish! A voice on the loud-speaker blares out a message of self-congratulation and gratitude to Brother on the anniversary of the day the entire world was striped: chaos was replaced by order and design and universal happiness prevailed. The film ends with a huge picture of Brother, wearing a coat and tie and breast-pocket handkerchief- all striped in black and white, seen dangling from the ceiling and remaining there for a while alone, and lit up. This is followed by the appearance of Brother and members of the World Board of Directors, the original conspirators, but now all holding important positions of authority and showing obvious marks of affluence. Brother is in a pensive mood: apparently he has been worried for the last year by doubts about the truth of his vision of black and white stripes and by the fact that people's conversion has not made them any happier. He now sees that the world is really full of colour and is convinced that people should therefore be allowed to choose any colour they want. When he expresses his views to his colleagues, who, now that they enjoy power and privilege, are no longer inclined to obey him, they refuse to listen to him, accusing him of reactionism, betrayal and reneging on his past revolutionary principles. When he goes out to a cafe, dressed in red, to preach his new-found philosophy to the people, he is suspected of being a government secret agent and they first pretend that they are happy, then, not wanting any further trouble, they beat him up. He is taken back to the

Foundation headquarters, whence he is made by his colleagues to broadcast to.the people an official message prepared for him on a tape, and is physically prevented from telling them what he now truly believes. The play ends by showing him as a victim of his own past principles and practice, in despair, resigned to his position as a mere figurehead, kept for the benefit of the corrupt and power-hungry few whom he has himself appointed to positions of power.

The Striped Ones is essentially a political play, in which Idris is primarily interested in *Homo politicus;* man is reduced merely to his political role, thereby becoming a caricature. There are no flesh-and-blood individuals, only types or abstractions, representing political positions. The little humour it has is of the black variety, and the function of some absurd and improbable events, such as the appearance of the medieval poet al-Ma'arri, is not always easy to explain. Nor is it easy to see the point of the device of the play within the play, although an ingenious attempt has been made to show that it is meant to suggest the sham nature of the Foundation of the Greatest Happiness.

The last of Idris's plays to be considered here, *al-Jins al-Thalith (The Supermen,* 1971) is a work of pure fantasy, in which he seems to move away from the narrow and stifling world of politics. It is a love story of a rather spiritual kind, with elements from the world of the supernatural as well as science fiction: an irresistible mysterious female voice, surrealistic beings, strange hybrid crea-tures: a dog/sheep, man/trees and woman/trees. Although as drama it is not nearly as impressive as *al-Farafir, it* provides a welcome change from the dark vision of Idris's political dramas. Its happy ending restores hope, even though it is within the context of science fiction and fairy tale. *The Supermen* represents Idris's dream of a superior order of human being who can will himself to do great things, even including flying; who does not destroy himself, but is capable of love, sympathy and harmonious coexistence with his fellow beings.

The play begins and ends in the laboratory of a young biologist, significantly named Adam, who is engaged in scientific research, assisted by Nara, his young female technician. While he is working on an experiment with DNA, trying to discover a life serum as an antidote to his 'death serum', he hears an irresistible female voice, which sends him on his fantastic adventures in the land of strange, hybrid creatures. There he meets an elderly Scientist, who tells him about the sole survivor of a breed of morally superior human beings, a young woman whom he wishes Adam to marry, for the sake of the future of mankind. At the end of the play Adam, now convinced that he has missed the chance of marrying this woman, is upset at the failure of his last experiement, but is shocked to find that Nara, who has given up all hope of Adam ever discovering that she is that sole survivor, has injected herself with the 'death serum', thereby virtually commit-ting suicide. By a scientific miracle his 'life serum' proves successful on her and she is brought back to life and they are united in love, announcing that the time has come to breed a new race of men, the superman.

M.M. Badawi, *Modern Arabic Drama in Egypt,* Cambridge: Cambridge University Press, 1987, pp. 153-64.

Yusuf Idris and the Drama of Ideas

Faruq 'Abd al-Wahhab

Preface

Yusuf Idris had already written a whole series of superb short stories when he started to write for the theatre. He seems to have had in mind a particular impression or concept of drama and to have stuck to it most of the time, only occasionally branching out — whether consciously or not. What I am trying to express here may become clearer when we take a closer look at some of Idris's dramatic works.

"The Cotton Baron"

In this play Idris focuses on a specific class relationship, the one between landowners and peasants who work on the owner's land; these two types are seen in the characters of Qamhawi the farmer and al-Sinbati the owner. Idris also tries to convey his ideas on other levels through the relationships between 'Awad, Qamhawi's young son, and Sa'd, al-Sinbati's son, and also between Muhammad, Qamhawi's elder son, and Su'ad, al-Sinbati's daughter.

The general theme is clear enough: a cotton baron's exploitation of peasants and a condemnation of such behavior. This is, needless to say, a thoroughly excellent and laudable concept, one that brings with it a specific invitation to side with the peasants against their exploiters. But is this humanistic idea and the call that comes with it sufficient to support an enduring and worthy work of art? That is the question we will try to address as we analyze the play itself.

As the curtain opens, we are rapidly placed into the appropriate atmosphere, along with clues as to the personality of al-Sinbati the owner. This is achieved by means of a short conversation between him and his wife which underlines many things, not least of which are al-Sinbati's crooked character and his complete domination by his wife. It also serves to establish their social status: what she wants out of her husband is a luxury item, an essential accessory for social cachet, namely a gold necklace. At the same time, Idris presents us with another image, the relationship between 'Awad, the poor peasant's son, and Sa'd, the owner's son. They play a game together in which Sa'd insists that he will always be the train itself while 'Awad will be the caboose. 'Awad is obviosly cleverer and more sensible that Sa'd, but it doesn't make any difference.

154   CRITICAL PERSPECTIVES

When Qamhawi comes on stage, the predominant features of his character are quickly drawn:

> "Enter Qamhawi wearing long trousers that hang well be-
> low his knees and a vest. He has a greying moustache and a
> generous growth of beard. He always walks bent over. On his
> head he wears a dirty turban. He always mutters when he
> speaks. When al-Sinbati sees him enter, he is still wearing his
> son's gallabiyya over his own; he is busy checking and writ-
> ing in his ledger-book. Qamhawi walks right past him without
> saying a single word, still muttering the end of his prayers. He
> keeps bending over, picking up the wads of cotton on the
> ground, brushing them off, and then putting them in his hand."

The annual argument now starts between al-Sinbati and Qamhawi over the amount of cotton he has produced. After a lot of complicated calculations it emerges that, because of cotton losses, Qamhawi should only get 560 piasters for six months' hard work. Needless to say, Qamhawi doesn't agree. . . .When the argument comes to an end, Qamhawi leaves. The scene moves to another aspect of the class relationship, that between Su'ad, the owner's daughter, and Muhammad, the poor peasant's son. . . .This is followed by a scene in which Muhammad's mother upbraids her son for imagining that he can form a relationship with Su'ad and even dream of marrying her. While Muhammad assumes that gallantry is all it will take, his mother is fully aware of the obstacles that class differences will place in their way. At the conclusion of this short scene, al-Sinbati comes in once again, followed by Qamhawi who brings along with him al-Hajj al-Shawadifi to go over his accounts with al-Sinbati once more. Here Idris provides us with a short glimpse of social hypocrisy: when it seems likely that al-Shawadifi will take Qamhawi's side, an unsubtle hint from al-Sinbati — that he will expose al-Shawadifi's exploitation of other people as well — quickly brings him back into line; the two of them then gang together against the poor peasant.

All the while, the class conflicts are reflected in the behavior of the two boys, 'Awad and Sa'd. The latter still insists on being the train all the time, but 'Awad wants to have a turn, if only once in a while. Sa'd always refuses. . . .The arguing comes to an end when al-Sinbati himself interferes, swears at 'Awad, and tells Sa'd that he must never play with peasant boys. Being children however, they are soon back to playing the same game.

However, the main issue — Qamhawi's account — cannot be solved this easily. Qamhawi cannot believe that six months of effort can be worth so little. With the arrival of a cotton merchant, another discussion starts, this one about cotton prices. . . .It emerges that al-Sinbati has swindled Qamhawi over the price of his cotton. Even so, everything is eventually settled — after an infinite number of ramifications — by Qamhawi accepting the offered amount. Al-Sinbati goes on to remind him what happens every year. He won't be paid in cash anyway; it will all be added to his account for the following year. In short, he will receive nothing for all his work.

In the last few minutes of the play, a fire starts right out of the blue in the cotton warehouse. Qamhawi rushes away to help put it out. When al-Hajj al-Shawadifi prods him in the side and suggests that he let it burn, saying "What are you so het up about? It's not your concern. Just let it burn!" Qamhawi yells back: "How can I let it burn? You wouldn't be saying that if you were the one who'd grown it! That's my sweat and blood going up in flames! It's part of me. How I am supposed to let it burn?!"

As noted above, the point of this play is to show the way peasants are exploited and how inhumane the distinctions of class can be. It is an excellent conceptual basis for the play, but it remains just that because it has been presented too directly. Yusuf Idris has allowed his topic to get the better of his art. What ties everything together here is the idea alone, and not the artistic necessity that every word in the dialogue, every single gesture, must have a specific organic function; the sequencing of events must flow from the situation itself and adhere to the work's internal logic, rather than that of life in all its abundance.

By using an abstract concept as his organizing principle, Idris has been forced to use the mechanical logic of a simple anecdote in order to develop his plot-line. His insistence on the use of a photographical naturalism makes this anecdote seem insignificant and flat. The struggle that we are supposed to imagine taking place is not a continuous, lively process, but rather something entirely superficial; it does not spring from a particular situation or start from one specific point. The end of the play relies on pure chance, like the "Deus ex machina" device as often used by Euripides whenever the plot becomes extremely complex. However, in Euripides's case there is no problem since Greek plays were mostly performed within the context of sacred rituals and thus the notion of gods was always there in the minds of the Athenian audience.

Idris's total adherence to the idea of realism in the way he portrays the events in his play means that the canvas he is working on is cluttered with unessential details; all they manage to do is to scramble the emotional unity that the play should be able to stimulate. Even the relationships between the peasant's two children and the owner's son and daughter seem detached from the general context of the play; they emerge simply as examples of societal relationships, with no firm links to the overall context. This aspect is amplified by the fact that the play only has one act. The focus of events on a single, concentrated area is weakened; like the short story, a one-act play must use the smallest possible number of details and tangents so that the emotive weight of the drama will have the same powerful impact on the audience.

"Farhat's Republic"

In "Farhat's Republic," Idris manages to avoid this adherence to a narrow and specific idea with its excessively direct approach. In this second play he sticks to a combination of both idea and art. In fact, the very fact that it is so difficult to detect the principal theme of "Farhat's Republic" in a direct way may be one of the most significant reasons for this play's integrity. I have to admit that, in my personal opinion, it is the best play he has written thus far.

Yusuf Idris resorts to an almost photographic kind of realism in this play too, but he also manages to create another layer consisting of Farhat's dream (or film). The ironic tension that this level creates with Farhat's actual reality succeeds in producing an artistic composition that amplifies the wealth of human experience shown in the play itself and deepens the emotional impact that the work has on the audience. This same irony also helps to establish a kind of dramatic balance that is so lacking in "The Cotton Baron" and in some other works of Idris as well.

In trying to summarize the central theme of "Farhat's Republic," we are confronted with a number of possibilities. It isn't merely a picture of what can happen in a police station where a variety of societal evils and diseases come together; nor is it a picture of an ideal city dreamed up by an old station-sergeant nearing retirement; nor a call for integrity; nor an illustration of the adage that contentment is a priceless treasure. Rather it takes the form of a lively visualized picture consisting of various segments that eventually blend into an integral whole. This entity is not based on the principle of similarity, since that alone cannot fashion a dramatic work, but on the process of combining a series of acknowledged incompatibilities into a single shell. Nor should the result be considered a product of this process of combination since what eventually emerges is a completely fresh creation whose constitutents cannot revert to their original form without running the risk of destroying the entire work of art.

The first of these constituents is the reality that surrounds Sergeant Farhat and has done so for over thirty years. It emerges clearly from Idris's description of the scene and also from the events that transpire in the station itself:

> "The walls are painted black to halfway up. It's about nine o'clock at night; the light is feeble. People look overwhelmed by it all; their expressions are grim, evil. As the curtain rises, a group of people under arrest are standing in front of the duty sergeant and obscure him completely from the audience's view. You only get a glimpse of his face when they all stand in a row. The whole atmosphere is pervaded by a feeling of alarm and oppressive authority."

In the very first moments of the play Idris uses Farhat's dealing with the police-station's "customers" to establish a general atmosphere of callousness and inhumanity. . . .But then comes the opportunity to chat with Muhammad, a young political detainee or prisoner. In the process of writing his report — during which he assumes that this young man, Muhammad, is an educated person with a specific request to make at the station — Farhat begins to create this dream world which is the complete opposite of the world in the police-station and the grim, miserable world it represents. . . .This world comes together bit by bit; every time he proceeds with his story, something from the world of reality — an event, a problem, an inconvenience — something happens in the station to distract his attention. Farhat's dream rests on a remarkable coincidence:

> "One day an incredibly rich guy is leaving a hotel when a bag
> of diamonds drops out of his pocket; today it'd be worth about a
> hundred and seventy or eighty thousand pounds! He's not even
> aware that he's dropped it! So who finds it? A young guy down
> on his luck just like you and me! But he's out of a job. . . ."

Farhat insists that the young man in his dream should be down on his luck so that he can empathize with him; his desire that the young man also be jobless reflects his secret longing to be rid of the exhausting job he himself has to carry out in the police station. The picture he paints of the young man, honest and upright, is almost too good to be true; he turns down the Indian's offer of a rich reward because he has no desire to sell his honor for "a handful of gold." In keeping with Farhat's belief in the power of chance, he turns the Indian's reward to the young man into a lottery ticket with a huge prize attached. The ticket is a winning one; that puts an end to his hidden interest in the young man's story, although it does provide him with self-fulfilment, if only in a dream or a film. . . .

Thus is the irony between reality and the dream achieved. Its effect is all the more powerful because the dream is continually being interrupted by events that create a cruelly sarcastic counterpoint to the events in Farhat's dream world. For example, just at the point when Farhat is describing the young man's frugality in using money at a time when it is in plentiful supply, a bus conductor and worker come into the station arguing furiously and proceed to explain to Farhat, the police sergeant, that the row that has almost led to the conductor's being killed...is all due to the fact that the conductor claims he has no small change.

As noted above, this juxtaposition of the events of Farhat's dream with those of the real world are the principal source of irony, but it is greatly enriched by a second, namely the gap between the world that Farhat describes and the way he treats the customers and people under arrest in the station, something that seems utterly unaffected by what happens in the dream. There is also a third irony, that between Muhammad's actual status as a political detainee and Farhat's assumptions about him. Once the truth of Muhammad's position is disclosed, Farhat's dream comes crashing to the ground, the hard ground of a callous reality. . . .

The ending succeeds in bringing all these strands together. The life of the upright and honorable young man in Farhat's dream, Sergeant Farhat's overworked existence in the police-station, even perhaps the career of Muhammad, the political prisoner, up to that point, all these facets are resolved. While it is true that this play also contains some unnecessary details and betrays a certain amount of repetition and prolongation (especially when reality is being portrayed), we manage to overlook these faults as we are swept up in the enjoyment of our tour through the two contradictory worlds of Sergeant Farhat.

Faruq 'Abd al-Wahhab, "Yusuf Idris wa-masrah al-fikrah,"
Al-Majallah 31st July, 1966: 165-68.

Yusuf Idris and the Art of Drama

Louis 'Awad

I read Yusuf Idris's play, *The Crucial Moment,* two years ago when it was still in manuscript. The author had not yet decided what to call it. To be more precise, at that point the author was calling it *The Door,* but when it was published, it appeared under the title, *The Crucial Moment.* That is the title being used for the production at the National Theater.

Yusuf Idris has changed the course of the action more than once as well as the title, and for a variety of reasons. Some of the alterations have worked, but, even with all these changes, we can still look at the work as a whole and suggest that there is still room for more. The reason is that Yusuf Idris has chosen to treat a topic that is at once subtle, profound, and ticklish. It is a quintessentially dramatic theme, but one that is beyond the capabilities of average playwrights; it may well be beyond that of Yusuf Idris himself. And, because that is the case, the author should have realized that he should finish with it before the entire structure was put in final form.

Yusuf Idris deserves to be saluted for embarking on such a theme, namely fear. This is not fear in its simplest sense, but fear as a complex; not the fear cowards feel, nor that of heroes, but instead something even more complicated; something like the courage of cowards. As we examine the course of events in the play, it will become clear why Yusuf Idris merits our salutations.

Sa'd, the hero of the play — if indeed it has one at all — is a typical young man going to university; to be precise, he's an engineering student. He's been brought up in a family that can be described without exaggeration as being like thousands of others within the lower middle-class. The pillar of the family is al-Hajj Nassar, who owns a small but successful business. Beginning his life in abject poverty, he has managed by dint of sheer effort, economic sense, endurance in the face of humiliation, and courageous resistance to hunger, destitution and misery over a period of some thirty years to go from being a wretched laborer to a successful small businessman. He is the proverbial local success-story. Al-Hajj Nassar is married to Haniyya. He has an elder son named Mis'ad, a younger son named Sa'd, and a daughter named Kawthar. Al-Hajj Nassar's innate practical sense has

159

made him realize that he has to make a choice between his two sons; that way one of them and perhaps the entire family can escape the clutches of poverty. He has chosen the eldest, Mis'ad, to be the victim and has deprived him of an education. He has made him part of the business and trained him to be a worker who will strive and struggle so that the family income will grow. He has married Mis'ad off to a girl named Firdaws from the same class in order to put him in his natural environment. It is the younger son, Sa'd, who is selected to complete his education and be graduated as a big-shot engineer on whom the family can pin all its hopes and aspirations...

This then is the family whose inner life we get to see very closely. Everything proceeds quite naturally. The family bothers about the daily problems that no family is ever without. Kawthar, the daughter of the family, is always arguing with Firdaws, the wife of the working son, Mis'ad, about living in her father-in-law's house. Rightly or wrongly, Firdaws gets the impression she is being treated like a servant, even though neither al-Hajj Nassar nor his wife are unkind to her; indeed, they are particularly kind to her. But Kawthar gives her a tongue-lashing morning and night. There is something else that is even more irksome. She realizes that her husband, Mis'ad, is working very hard, not to build a family home for the two of them, but rather to pay for his brother to finish his education. She notices that he seems quite content with this constant work-load and justifies it with considerable enthusiasm and magnanimity; in fact, he justifies all effort aimed at the general good in the same way. He finds the very greatest pleasure in helping someone else along and envisages his own success as lying in that of his own brother. Firdaws on the other hand uses the bitter logic of life itself: she is thinking of their children who are being deprived by their father of opportunities in life because of his younger brother. She realizes that in the end all this effort of Mis'ad will only lead to his children remaining those of a poor laborer while Sa'd's children will be those of a big-shot engineer. In spite of all her husband's efforts, she still feels a guest in someone else's house rather than the mistress of her own; or, even more so, a servant who spends her time sweeping and washing for other people. It is hardly surprising therefore that there is continual quarreling between Firdaws and Kawthar, or that Kawthar snubs her nose at everyone. Firdaws demands that her husband move out of his father's house and set up house on his own where his efforts will be for the two of them and their children alone. She threatens to leave her husband and return to her father's house because he never listens to what she is saying and subjects her to all kinds of hardship that she cannot endure.

This then would seem to constitute a big enough problem for the family, but before long we discover that there's another issue that is much more profound. Sa'd, like many other young men of the time, has felt himself constrained to participate in the nationalist struggle to throw the British out of Egypt. Along with a group of his colleagues in the National Guard or a youth organization somewhat like it, he is secretly in training to carry weapons. All this is supposed to be in preparation for the major confrontation between us and the British. I say "training secretly" because he realizes that neither his father nor mother understand the kind of "abstractions" that young people involve themselves in, things like "nationalist struggle" and "resisting imperialism." In fact, when his mother finds out quite by chance, she starts wailing and moaning as though some disaster has just struck the household. She worries about what the British and their bullets may do to her son. When the father gets to hear about it, at first he tries to make light of it so as to calm his wife down. He suggests that training is just a game young men play, just like flirting with the neighborhood girls. There's all the difference in the world, he claims, between training and the actual dangers of fighting which hardly seem imminent in any conceivable circumstances.

But the father's attitude becomes much clearer when the Canal War [1956] and the Suez conflict begin. Day and night, al-Hajj Nassar watches as his son, Sa'd, actually makes ready to go where the conflict will take place. At that point he becomes more anxious, and his concerns are expressed in a variety of ways. Sometimes he tries to persuade his son gently to abandon his idea; at others he yells bitterly at him. His point of view is completely clear: he has worked for thirty years to build some capital and is proposing to defend it for all he's worth. But that capital does not consist of the business he's built up through the sweat of his brow. It is quite simply his son, Sa'd, for whom both he and his other son, Mis'ad, have sweated and suffered. Everything in the house is devoted to the cause of Sa'd; he is the focus of all the family's hopes. It is inconceivable for al-Hajj Nassar to watch as his whole life's efforts are exposed to danger and the possibility of loss. There are others who can defend the homeland. As far as al-Hajj Nassar is concerned, it is this small family, struggling to keep its head above water, that represents the homeland, and no more. Al-Hajj Nassar's homeland is his life, children, and grandchildren. Everything beyond that is sheer hot air.

But if only the family's problems could be confined to this weeping mother and stubborn father. As becomes clear in the play, Sa'd's real problem is far greater than any of this. Sa'd harbors his major problem within himself. His head may be filled with wonderful ideas about the nation and the struggle on its behalf; his heart may glow with a longing for dedication and self-sacrifice for the cause, together with all those lofty ideals which young people believe in. But we soon discover that, in spite of Sa'd's enthusiasms and all the fine words that emerge from his mouth, his will to act is in fact strapped. We rapidly learn that this portentous hero whose ringing tones would lead you to believe that you were in the presence of Achilles, Hector, or Aeneas, is actually a craven coward. In fact, his cowardice is a complex phenomenon because he doesn't realize that he is a coward. When he does come to that realization, his cowardice brings about a series of disasters for his family. We do not witness his downfall, but he takes a new direction which is totally alien to his real nature.

Here is how we learn he is a coward. On the night he is supposed to go out and fight, he is supposed to join up with his friends on the train. He is to do it stealthily while his family are still asleep so that there will be no tears and pleadings. His brother, Mis'ad, someone who acts instinctively, backs him up, suggesting that he slip out quietly before dawn so that he won't wake up the rest of the family. He is willing to give Sa'd this advice because, even though he may be naive and understand relatively little about the abstract ideas that his educated younger brother Sa'd keeps discussing, he still has an instinctive sense that Sa'd is correct; that blood is part of the wages of freedom and that fighting the English is a sacred calling. He senses all these things in his heart without any real understanding of the concepts of freedom, independence and national duty. He feels proud of his younger brother, Sa'd, because he will go to the battlefront with his colleagues as a hero; as far as he is concerned, it doesn't matter whether his brother falls in battle as a martyr to the cause or returns home safe and sound with a garland of triumph on his head.

We realize that Sa'd is a coward when he is leaving the house for the battlefront and manages to make enough noise to wake up his father and mother. In fact, the entire house wakes up and, as expected, everyone tries to stop him leaving. We realize Sa'd is lying when he defends his actions by saying that he couldn't leave without saying farewell to the people closest to his heart. When al-Hajj Nassar and al-Hajja Haniyya try to persuade him not to go, the big loud-mouth within Sa'd boasts that he's a great hero. The more angry words and pleadings he hears, the more big talk he produces. He seems to be listening to none of the arguments and pleas of his family. When his father's patience is finally exhausted, he tricks his son (or thinks he does). He gradually leads his son back to his bedroom and then locks the door on him, all this in a tone of triumph. The young son, Sa'd, is now a prisoner in his father's bedroom; he yells and screams but is unable to get out. The departure time for the train going to the front passes, and all the young heroes go except for Sa'd. Even the uncouth Mis'ad has a row with his father, goes to the scene of the battle for a few hours, and returns home wounded. The girls in the family also go out to provide first-aid and other help to the fighters. Sa'd, the platoon commander, stays locked in the room, sometimes pacing up and down, and at others banging on the door, his yells and curses clearly audible.

It is the little daughter of the family, Sawsan, who opens the door for Sa'd without his father knowing about it. She manages to open it with no trouble, with one turn of the handle. Sa'd emerges in a fury, his hair all disheveled. It is then that the bitter truth is revealed: the locked door wasn't locked at all; the lock was broken. An even more bitter truth emerges: when Mis'ad comes home wounded, he rounds on his brother, Sa'd, and accuses him of cowardice. We now learn that Sa'd knew full well that the lock was broken and that one turn was enough to let himself out. Deep down inside, Sa'd did not want to fight; he was scared. Either he really forgot the lock was broken, or else pretended to do so as a way of justifying staying inside the room and keeping his cowardice a secret from other people. Sa'd still retains his arrogant air; he insists that he didn't know the lock on the door was broken. All the while his uncomplicated brother is well aware of the fact that he's a phoney, a coward, and a wretch because he knew the truth about the door as did everyone else in the house. We have to presume that al-Hajj Nassar was the only one who did not know, otherwise he would not have "locked" Sa'd inside to stop him from leaving (although it has to be admitted that Idris fails to mention clearly why al-Hajj Nassar does not know about the door). In any case, the whole thing is despicable. There a well-known saying to the effect that the carpenter's door is always off its hinges; it's also logical to assume that the carpenter himself is the last person to know about his own door.

Sa'd's arrogance and his continuing claims not to have known about the door definitely leave the audience with a bad impression. It shows that he is more than just a coward; he is a coward in his morality and sense of honor even before we take the ideals of conflict into consideration. If his cowardice were confined to the latter sphere and he showed some sense of honor, then he would not have continued to be so arrogant and deceitful. . . .

Even worse than all this is the fact that, before little Sawsan opens the door and lets Sa'd out, a major disaster besets the family. A British patrol in the process of eliminating pockets of resistance raids the house. One of the soldiers shoots al-Hajj Nassar while he is performing his prayers. Sa'd hears everything from inside the room, but doesn't move. He listens as "George" yells out, as he searches for freedom fighters, as his father is shot, as little Sawsan goes over to talk to her stricken grandfather, not realizing that he is dying — totally unaware in fact of what death means. Sa'd, the fully trained warrior who can blast open the lock with one shot and come out to save his father from his murderers, he hears all of this. How is Sa'd supposed to come out and confront George in the next room when he can't even look at him on a train ride!

However the play ends with a very strange scene indeed. The audience sees Sa'd emerge from his room. He looks at his dead father and undergoes a complete transformation. His courage reappears, almost as though he has been born again. We also watch the bereaved wife, who just a few minutes earlier had been filling the air with groans of fear for her son, as she brushes aside her anxieties and as also born anew. She now urges her son to go, fight the British, and seek merciless vengeance. Sa'd does indeed leave the house, brandishing his gun and accompanied by the joyful shouts of this wretched woman, almost as though she were exulting on her wedding-day. Sa'd gathers up his courage, fires at George, and kills him. For him this represents the beginning of a new life; he is now completely ready to launch into the conflict wholeheartedly, confident in his manliness like a roaring lion.

That is the way this play, full of strengths and weaknesses, comes to an end. We are left at one and the same time admiring the playwright and yet wondering about his work...

We commend this work of his because he has produced a study of fear that is genuinely profound. The struggle on behalf of one's homeland is almost a sacred topic, and it is by no means easy to tackle such a weighty theme. Very few other authors have dared to portray the way in which heroes tend to lose their fortitude when the crucial moment arrives and they find themselves confronted by death, especially when the context involves the cause of God and freedom. Yusuf Idris has scored a major success by showing that this particular wilting hero is among the first to yell out slogans. It is people who labor in silence and even in total ignorance who are expending the most energy for the cause. Such people are no good at making loud, vacuous speeches. Idris clearly intends to use this authentic picture to point out the difference between, on the one hand, the commitment of intellectuals which takes the form of expansive phrases, lofty ideas, and good intentions, all of which usually collapse completely in the face of brutal reality — with its bullets, blood, corpses, and wounded, and on the other, the commitment of most other people who commit themselves to doing what is right as a result of something akin to animal instinct and whose understanding never achieves the level of abstract ideas.

Idris has managed to present this issue clearly and even to portray these different stereotypes reasonably well. He has also succeeded in showing how certain segments in society restrict their concept of nationalism to a very small circle, that of the family. For al-Hajj Nassar, it's his family that is the nation; for Haniyya it's her husband and children. Anything happening outside this circle doesn't concern them. . . .Idris has also managed to make a convincing change in the attitude of the mother at the end of the play. He shows us how this woman who at first is afraid her son may catch cold — let alone face British bullets, turns into a bloodthirsty woman when her husband falls dead. She becomes the pillar of the household and demands vengeance for her martyred husband. She uses all her energy to make her son go out, face the British, shoot them, and drink their blood, if possible. She whoops in delight as he leaves, as though he were on the way to his wedding rather than going out to confront death. This transformation in the character of Haniyya is natural and realistic; it conforms with the elements of this stereotypical person whom we in Egypt can easily recognize. . . .

However, while Idris has been successful in these aspects of his play, he has failed in his portrait of the hero, Sa'd. The play itself does not have a solid dramatic basis, most especially in the actions of the third and last act when events pile up on one another in a totally unconvincing way. The depiction of Sa'd in this play is unsuccessful because the hero is supposed to show certain heroic traits (put another way, to be an idealized human being) so that we can sympathize with his degeneration and collapse. If we look for the underpinnings of Sa'd's heroic nature, we find nothing in either his words or deeds to draw him close to us. All we learn is that he is a fervent nationalist who is longing to struggle and sacrifice himself for the sake of his homeland. He expresses these sentiments through big talk and nothing else. . . . Some people may say that this is precisely Sa'd's problem and the root cause of his weakness, the essence of his personal tragedy. True enough, but simply shouting out slogans does not establish a sufficient basis for a character over two whole acts of a play with only three acts altogether. A search for any other qualities in his makeup proves utterly fruitless; indeed we find no other details or characteristics of any kind whatsoever. All we learn is that, like other young men of his age, he lets his hair down in front of the neighborhood girls. When the play is over, if you ask yourself what you have learned about the character Sa'd, all you can say is that he's a university student enthused by the idea of nationalism. The character is extremely one-dimensional, and that is a major flaw in the play.

An even greater fault in the way Idris portrays the character of Sa'd is that, from his relationships with other people, whether it be his family or his colleagues, we deduce that he is an extrovert rather than an introvert. He is in charge of his colleagues in the platoon. People who are in charge of others are normally extroverts, they know how to give orders, how to organize, and how to gather other people around them. His boorish way of treating his family and especially his mother, and the fact that neither his behavior nor his conversation show the slightest sign of thought, reflection, or inner feeling, prove that he is essentially an extrovert. We can easily understand that a person who is totally introverted or even a pensive intellectual whose resolve collapses at the crucial moment may turn out to be a coward. We can appreciate all that because we know there is a considerable gap between thought and deed, or between the ideal course of action and actual reality, a gap that cannot easily be traversed by anyone who is introverted or excessively idealistic. When we see such a character wilt at the crucial moment, we sense the tragedy of the utopian idealist and feel pained by his ineptitude and downfall.

But what excuse can there be for a total extrovert who has absolutely no propensity for thought, contemplation, or self-examination, if he cowers in fear when the hour of conflict comes? I would go further and suggest that the extrovert character's only real function is to do rather than to think. Any failure on such a character's part to plunge right into the battle when the crucial moment arrives can only arouse a feeling of repulsion in us, and certainly not any feelings of sorrow. . . .

Another problem is that Yusuf Idris makes Sa'd overcome his sense of weakness at the end of the play and go out of the house to fight. The mistake here is as great in the case of Sa'd as it is successful in the case of his mother, Haniyya. She is an uneducated woman. Such people can be moved to acts of vengeance by personal rather than public motivations. But it is completely improbable that this young man, Sa'd, who is not only educated but utterly convinced by all the arguments in favor of self-sacrifice, should undergo such a transformation because of his father's murder. This is even more so because his cowardice goes to such repulsive lengths that he cringes at the thought of coming to his father's rescue when he's attacked by George, even though he's standing fully armed just a few feet away. If at some earlier point Idris had managed to show how much Sa'd loved his father, something that transcended the normal love that sons have for their father, then we might have been convinced of the possibility of Sa'd's rapid transformation in this way. As portrayed for us by Idris, Sa'd's feelings towards his father never transcend the strictly normal. . . .

All these are significant faults in this play and in the portrayal of its characters. They betray a haste and lack of genuine understanding of the artistic dimension of drama. I have not mentioned all the faults here, but only the most significant ones. . . .

That said however, I have to come back to my earlier statement to the effect that *The Crucial Moment is* an important landmark in the history of our modern drama. I have criticized it harshly here on purpose, precisely because I believe that it is an important landmark. In my opinion it brings us close to the spirit of tragedy as generally understood with reference to its origins and earliest sources; it is based on the notion of the hero's weakness or the weakness of man who deserves to be depicted as such. The play contains within it enough elements of inner turmoil to raise it to the level of a tragedy of the highest order. Yusuf Idris should have made his hero Sa'd fail when confronted with this difficult test and proceed to his natural end. He would then have discovered the appalling nature of his own position and, in utter dismay at its implications, come to hate that lower self of his that had brought all this shame upon him and disasters on other people. From such self-hatred there would be just one way out, and that would be to make amends by destroying this foul self with a bullet from the very gun that had failed to fight the British or save his own father. If Idris had done something along those lines, the tragedy of this hero with great aims but flawed personality would have worked. His death would then be a victory, a victory over himself and his inherent weakness. On that basis we would seek to forgive him. That is the only way that the eternal circle on which tragedy is based can be resolved: crime or sin and punishment, followed by forgiveness.

But Yusuf Idris wanted to do something else: rather than have his hero be victorious over himself, he wanted him to do so against the British. Sa'd's going out to fight is not a victory over himself, but over others. The reason is very simple: the person who has killed al-Hajj Nassar is not the British, but Sa'd himself who stays behind the door fully armed so as to avoid his major responsibility to protect his unarmed father. . . . Idris has chosen to do something outside the bounds of the logic of tragedy; to resurrect the hero without either death or suffering as precedents. This points very clearly to something I have complained about many times before, namely that the Egyptian mentality is still governed by concept of the epic with its external struggles and heroic victories, all this under the influence of the cultural heritage of the past. *The Crucial Moment* is a tragedy in every sense of the word, but Idris has turned it into an epic, or rather what begins as a tragedy ends as an epic. This is a confusion of genres, as the saying goes. This is not just Idris's fault alone. Had he taken the tragedy to its proper tragic conclusion, there would have been plenty of people to accuse him of a lack of national spirit or even morals. Some people might even have demanded that his work be taken to court and banned because it chooses to portray an Egyptian in such a state of weakness and collapse when faced with the enemy. . . .

But Idris has done enough by pointing to the primary factor in any tragedy, the concept of the fall of the hero or mankind. There is a little of Sa'd in all of us, and by pointing to it in this play Idris has taken a major step forward in introducing the art of tragedy into our modern literary tradition. The play manages to cover half the territory between epic and tragedy. In the future, when we come to realize that the only way out of the hero's fall is through penance and learn how to grieve at the hero's fall when he does his penance, then and only then will we have a great theatre tradition. Let us hope that Idris himself will be one of the major pillars of that tradition.

Louis 'Awad, *Al-Katib* (April 1961): 85-96.

Yusuf Idris's Play *Al-Farafir*

Nadia Ra'uf Faraj

Drama of Provocation

For Yusuf Idris drama needs a societal stamp: it is merely "one of the elements of the social collectivity of which he is a part." As a result, the writer's task is "to reflect a social class as a whole." This does not imply that the act of composition or standing on stage is a complete reflection of life itself. The writer will select certain aspects of societal reality and present them on stage with a particular import. Idris does not wish his plays to be mere entertainment; his desire is that the audience should discover life as it really is and recognize themselves in what they see on stage. This view of the writer's role is extremely close to that of Bernard Shaw. Shaw was anxious to attack and indeed demolish all the erroneous conceptions that the audience had regarding drama; it was to be a merciless exposer of hidden realities and a forceful iconoclast. Idris wants to strip his society bare on stage so that people can see themselves, but he actually goes beyond the limits set by Bernard Shaw and comes close to another Western point of view, that of Antonin Artaud and his "theater of cruelty." Like Artaud, Idris believes that theater has to be unkind to man, to show his evil side. Theater has to force man to face the hideousness of his own situation and the belief that "the very heavens may fall on our heads." In his theorizing Artaud expresses the belief that "theater can be useful because it forces people to see themselves as they really are; the veil falls away, and everything is revealed: the deception, futility, weakness, hypocrisy, and baseness."

Idris wants his audience to confront such revelations so that they will all be gripped by an overwhelming desire for change. Yes, I mean "all of them." Idris as a socialist dramatist does not intend to criticize individuals or to take aim at them alone, but rather at society as a whole. For him, the particularity of drama is a general one, and in that way his plays differ from those of Brecht that speak to the intellectual side of man. Idris by contrast is always addressing the collective emotion of his audience. While his plays may produce a version of life, they also shape it and change its aspect. To his audience the play may be a strong incentive to bring about personal change while at the same time suggesting an equally strong societal need for transformation in their way of life. The final goal of drama is irrevocably bound up with the theater of cruelty and also with Brechtian drama. . . .Brecht also aims to reveal and expose reality to the audiences at which he projects his plays. Like Idris, he does not regard the theater as merely for entertainment purposes. As a Marxist, Brecht believes that drama has a role to play within society. He sees actors as teachers, explaining things to the audience who have sat in the theater in order to witness the arguments and explanations. He expects them all to take decisions and comport themselves in such a way as to bring about change in the world, society, and themselves. All this allows us to designate Yusuf Idris's drama — and that of Artaud and Brecht — with the heading "drama of provocation." Let us explore the dimensions of this designation further:

Many critics believe that Yusuf Idris's plays are Brechtian in form and essence. He utterly rejects this idea and insists that his drama is intrinsically Egyptian and that Brecht's influence on him was considerably less than that of the literary heritage that endeavored to arouse the audience. It is difficult for us to assess the extent of Brecht's influence on Idris. At first glance, many aspects would seem to be derived from Brecht's drama, but they could equally well be derived from Idris himself or from his own literary heritage. As noted earlier, the one-act comic play (such as the *karagöz*) deliberately poked fun at people and aroused the audience so that they would change their way of life. Furthermore there are some aspects of Idris's drama which run completely contrary to Brecht's definitions.

Taking a closer look at Idris's "drama of provocation," we find that this Egyptian playwright does not believe the actor should become so totally involved in his role that he forgets the audience, nor should he completely abandon his acting role either. As Idris sees it, the actor should have "one eye in heaven, the other in hell." This provocative drama is aimed essentially at the audience as a whole, not at any individuals. The actor is thus compelled to follow the audience reaction carefully so that he can alter his acting style to suit the situation. Since the audience changes every night, the actor must always be aware of their psychological state and make instantaneous adjustment. If he feels he is losing them, he has to color and tune his acting in such a way that he can regain their attention. In this type of drama the actor much always be completely aware of himself as an actor and ask himself: What it is that I want to express and what do I want to achieve?

The similarity between Idris and Brecht actually lies only in the question of concentration or emphasis. Brecht demands that his actor "present or show people an action; he must show himself to them in the course of showing them the event." In this way the actor is decisively dissociated from his role; he may not make any pretense of being the character involved or show the audience his feelings or sense of involvement in the part. This differs from Idris's expectations from his actors: he insists that the actor be at one with the action, while at the same time being able to come out of his role in order to watch and assess his audience, and then immerse himself in the part once again. For Idris, the term drama is a synonym for acting; in fact, the closest significance may be something like "collaboration" or joint collaboration in the drama by actors and audience alike.

The actor needs the audience to feel his role; expressed differently, he extracts his own awareness of the role from the audience. The actor will only succeed when he manages to get the audience to collaborate in the performance of the role, something that can be illustrated by the opening lines of *Al-Farafir*. . . .

The audience should feel at one with the actors — a feature that Artaud also defends. In Idris's view they should fuse with the performer. Brecht turns his audience into observers at whom he directs challenges rather than becoming part of the acting and dramatic action. However Brecht is in complete accord with Idris in requiring that the audience be completely aware of what is happening on the stage and of their responsibility to adopt a positive attitude towards what they see. Here however Idris and Brecht approach their eventual goals by two separate pathways. The Brechtian audience is "distanced" from the drama through music and noise, not to mention the dissociation of the actor from his role. . . .While Brecht makes use of such devices as music and noise to achieve "distancing," Idris uses the very same features as an additional entity to help the audience unwind, to link the play with the folkloric heritage, and to reflect daily life. In the popular quarters of Egypt it is still the custom to greet someone returning from a journey — the Hajj or time in prison, for example — with noise, shouting, and music. In *Al-Farafir* it is precisely these kinds of musical instrument and noise that greet Farfur when he first enters. . . .

There is a further element in "drama of provocation," namely the gestures and movements the actors make. In Brechtian drama it is said that the principal role of gestures and movements is not to portray or present an action, but rather the opposite: to terminate it. For Artaud movements, noise, and gestures have as important a role in the play as language itself. In his use of gestures and movements Idris's model is Artaud; every action of Farfur is accompanied by movements and gestures.

We might also point out that Japanese theater may have had some influence on Idris. Kabuki actors imitate dolls, all the while remaining very realistic. The Japanese actor also addresses the audience, exactly as happens in Idris's play (at the very beginning, for example).

The one way in which Idris differs from Western and Eastern traditions of drama is in the use of masks. He firmly believes that the audience will probably dislike the use of masks, and insists that it is better to follow the Egyptian folkloric tradition which permits the use of make-up — powder or flour. The same principle applies to costumes; the actors are encouraged to seek inspiration from the *karagöz* or any other Arabic literary tradition.

For Idris then, the "drama of provocation" is merely one of the fruits of his being an artist who wishes to express himself. He wants to awake and arouse his fellow human beings to the realities of life today. He is an artist who has never operated in isolation; his background includes Western and Eastern literary traditions of a wide variety, but the majority of them are clearly culled from the local folkloric heritage.

Tragicomedy, Lampoon, Sarcasm and Humor

Yusuf Idris has chosen tragicomedy as a genre for his drama. *Al-Farafir* is a tragedy concocted from humorous (comic) material. The reader laughs at the individual sections, but the play as a whole is a reflection of the tragedy of mankind. *Al-Farafir* presents a vision of the world as a place where man has to confront forces that he cannot surmount because they are life itself and control the world. . . .Mankind is enveloped in despair, and his sense of pessimism is profound. But, as Eric Bentley notes, despair is for the most part hope, and there can be no real hope except from the perspective of real despair. That is why the characters in *Al-Farafir* experience boundless hope in spite of all the despair..

The basic aim of *Al-Farafir* is to make the audience realize the realities of their situation, or attitude, or circumstances. These realities have to be genuine in order for anyone to be able to recognize himself on the stage. So it is full of alarm and misery. At the beginning of the first act, Farfur and his Master are searching for the most appropriate job for the Master. They investigate a whole series of jobs and professions. It is Farfur who undertakes the task. As he does so, the audience sees the veil ripped away from their own existence, as Farfur looks into the environment of intellectuals, artists, lawyers, judges, doctors, import and export agents, civil servants, and so on. Some of this criticism of jobs and groups may hit the spot with regard to practitioners anywhere in the world, but a certain amount of the satire is purely local [such as the segments on intellectuals, artists, singers, lawyers]. . . .

But this segment of dialogue is not merely an exposee of professions, but goes beyond that to include political and social attitudes. Amid all this angst-filled laughter the members of the audience come to recognize themselves, their attitudes, and their current circumstances. It is also the play's goal to arouse the audience's anger and even recalcitrance. However, as is the case with any social drama (including those of Brecht), the laughter needs to be channeled through jokes and humor. That is precisely what Idris does: his tragic dialogue is steeped in humor. To make sure that his audience will not be distanced from the fierce criticisms that he is leveling, the author uses a particularly savage kind of comedy. As Ronald Knox notes in an article on humor and sarcasm, the effect of satire is often to provoke hatred and cause real hurt; it can cause an audience to separate themselves from what they are watching. The value and good taste of humor can only be estimated when the listener is prepared to tolerate jokes at his own expense along with everyone else in the audience. In *Al-Farafir* Idris makes use of both satire and humor to attract his audience's attention, to maintain contact with them, and to communicate his message.

Northrup Frye notes that satire is based on two things: firstly, jokes or humor that rely on the imagination, a sense of the grotesque, or jest; the second is the object of attack. In *Al-Farafir* we find that, even though the play discusses real issues, it nevertheless plunges into a world were there is no concern whatsoever with either time or place; in fact, Yusuf Idris points out that the second act can be performed before the first. The play has no place for the traditional plot consisting of a story with a beginning, middle, and end. We are taken to a planet like the earth where absurdity and unbridled imagination are the norm. We find two weird and absurd characters arguing about social, political, and philosophical topics, and other ideas that preoccupy the mind of modern man. All this is a gross satire on human vice and folly. Man is stripped bare on the stage; boasting and pretense become fair game. Satire always has a moral message to it. With Idris it also fulfills another important function, in that he hopes to make use of the heavily satirical drama that confronts the audience with a picture of themselves and their world to arouse their anger so that they will have a powerful urge to bring about improvement and change. . . .

The point of Farfur's role is to show the stupid way that man behaves. He attacks young people for wanting to grow up, and then attacks adults for behaving like children when it comes to choosing younger members of the opposite sex (although these are societal phenomena that don't apply to Egypt). Farfur's method involves sarcasm; the ridicule is expressed through inverting the way things are. Thus, adults don't have moustaches, but children do. Old men choose very young women and vice versa. As Frye notes, humor has to rely on convention, and the scenario in Idris's play is a good illustration of the fact. It is a given in his way of making the audience laugh that one should see an elderly man trying to cling to his long-lost youth in the personage of a young girl; he is attempting to don a mask which will allow him to pretend that he can do things that are no longer in his power. When the audience sees this elderly man trying to behave like a youngster, all they can do is to burst into laughter. This forms a link with humor as defined by Pirandello who believed that every humorous situation involved a secondary supporting element. We laugh at elderly men and women when they pretend to be younger than they really are because they seem weird or even grotesque, but at the same time the situation also involves enough distress to bring us up short and make us take note. Farfur does this when he says "Yes, it's funny! See how I'm laughing!" (as he pulls his mouth wide open to reveal his teeth, but without a smile to be seen). Yes, it is all funny enough, but how much greater is the pain the audience feels when they penetrate beyond the humorous dialogue to the realities behind it. By rubbing the audience's nose in the dirt satire endeavors to make them fully aware of the reality they have been unaware of till that point. The eventual goal of satire is to arouse, to provoke the listener; to prod him into changing the situation he observes. . . .

Language

No one is more skillful that Yusuf Idris when it comes to the use of language in drama. He has come to realize that the principal problem facing Arabic in Egypt at present is the combination (or opposition) of the standard written language and the colloquial dialect. He has chosen his path with great care, acknowledging both the written and oral folkloric tradition as being literature in every respect, and as a result he has doggedly pursued the colloquial. For him language is above all a mode of expression, and so he insists that it must faithfully reflect what he feels and wishes to communicate to people and that everyone must be able to understand it. It follows that the dramatist cannot use the language of high literature because it creates a distance from the uneducated populace. Nor is there any point in using a colloquialized form of the standard written language which has colloquial words scattered through it. Idris prefers an artistic colloquial language because it is closest both to his own artistic intentions and to his audience. While language must emerge from the people and thus appear spontaneous, it should not be instinctive. When colloquial is used in a literary environment, the dramatist must give it a poetic flavor while avoiding the artificialities of a "third language" which Tawfiq al-Hakim advocated in his play, "The Deal."

Idris believes that the colloquial dialect today has reached a higher cultural level than ever before. If one compares the language today with the plays of Najib al-Rihani written thirty years ago, one finds that Egyptians have used education, magazines, radio and television to polish their language. Thus, when we read *Al-Farafir*, it is easy to find items from the vocabulary of standard Arabic that have found their way into the colloquial. When the author in the play says: "Make sure there's no talking, not a single word!" the word for "make sure" is from the standard written language...Analysing Idris's use of language further, we find that the monologues and dialogue are completely authentic and succeed in cancelling the distance between audience and characters. Most sentences begin with the first-person pronoun, a feature of the Cairene dialect that is expressed differently in standard Arabic. . . . The features of repetition and pulse that we detect in individual paragraphs within the play can be extended to a larger frame of reference. The way in which particular themes are reintroduced throughout the play gives the work a musical resonance. Among such themes are the relationship between man and women: woman desires man and forces him into marriage, thus imposing on him the responsibility for looking after her and the children. Throughout the play women appear on the stage to remind their husbands of their need for food and money. Another recurring motif is Farfur's questions about his situation or his position as Farfur. . . .

Another way in which Idris makes use of sarcasm and humor is the insertion of European phrases into the Arabic text, intending thereby to poke fun at people who use such expressions and at Western heritage in general. The author in the play describes his clothes as being "original." The Master searches for a job that will be "moderne." When his hysterical bride sees her rival, she shrieks" "Je suis nerveuse!" and, a little later, "Laissez-moi!"

In *Al-Farafir* dialogue and monologue do not merely convey the feelings, ideas, hopes, and bitterness of the characters. They go beyond that to breathe new life into concepts or phrases linked to sound, meaning, derivation, or even irony. With Idris the language of drama is bound to all of these. He has succeeded in turning the colloquial language — thought by many to be worthless — into an acknowledged literary medium of expression, a dramatic language that is both exciting and provocative.

        Nadia Ra'uf Faraj, *Yusuf Idris wa-al-masrah al-Misri al-hadith*, Cairo: n.p., 1976, pp. 115-38.

Bibliography

1. A Listing of Yusuf Idris's Works

A. *Short Story Collections*
Arkhas layali [The Cheapest Nights], Cairo: Dar Ruz al-Yusuf, 1954.
Jumhuriyyat Farhat [Farhat's Republic], Cairo: Dar Ruz al-Yusuf, 1956.
Al-Batal [The Hero], Cairo: Dar al-Fikr, 1957.
A laysa kadhalika [Isn't That So?], Cairo: Markaz Kutub al-Sharq al-Awsat, 1957.
Hadithat sharaf [An Affair of Honor], Beirut: Dar al-Adab, 1958.
Akhir al-dunya [The End of the World], Cairo: Dar Ruz al-Yusuf, 1961.
Al-'Askari al-aswad [The Black Policeman], Cairo: Dar al-Ma'rifah, 1962.
Lughat al-ay-ay [The Language of Screams], Cairo: Cairo: Mu'assassat Ruz al-Yusuf, 1965.
Al-Naddahah [The Siren], Cairo: Dar al-Hilal, 1969.
Bayt min lahm [House of Flesh], Cairo: 'Alam al-Kutub, 1971.
Uqtulha [I'll Kill Her], Cairo: Maktabat Misr, n.d.
Ana sultan qanun al-wujud [I'm The Lord of the Law of Existence], Cairo: Dar Misr li-al-tiba'ah, n.d.
Al-'Atb 'ala al-nazar [Vision at Fault], Cairo: Mu'assassat al-Ahram, 1987.

B. *Novels*
Qissat Hubb [Love Story], Cairo: Dar Ruz al-Yusuf, 1956 [in *Jumhuriyyat Farhat*].
Al-Haram [The Taboo], Cairo: Al-Sharikah al-'Arabiyyah li-al-tiba'ah, 1959.
Al-'Ayb [The Sin], Cairo: Mu'assassat Ruz al-Yusuf, 1962.
Rijal wa-Thiran [Men and Bulls], Cairo: Al-Mu'assassah al-Misriyyah al-'ammah li-al-ta'lif, 1964.
Al-Bayda' [White Woman], Beirut: Dar al-Tali'ah, 1970.
Nyu-Yurk 80 [New York '80], Cairo: Dar Misr li-al-tiba'ah, n.d.
Malik al-Qutn & Jumhuriyyat Farhat [Cotton Baron & Farhat's Republic], Cairo: Al-Mu'assassah al-qawmiyyah li-al-nashr, 1957.
Al-Lahzah al-harijah [Moment of Anxiety], Cairo: Al-Sharikah al-'Arabiyyah li-al-tiba'ah, 1958.
Al-Farafir & Al-Mahzalah al-ardiyyah [Farfours & The Terrestrial Comedy],

Cairo: Al-Ahram, 1966.
Al-Mukhattatin [Men in Stripes], in *Al-Masrah*, May 1969: 81-96.
Al-Jins al-thalith [The Third Sex], Cairo: 'Alam al-kutub, 1971.
Al-Bahlawan [The Clown], Cairo: Dar Misr li-al-tiba'ah, n.d.

D. Essays

Bi-sarahah ghayr mutlaqah [Not Quite Frankly], Cairo: Dar al-Hilal, 1968.
Iktishaf qarrah [Discovery of a Continent], Cairo: Dar al-Hilal, 1972.
Al-Iradah [Will], Cairo: Dar Gharib, 1977.
Shahid 'asrihi [Witness of His Era], Cairo: Dar Misr li-al-tiba'ah, n.d.

2. Translations in English

Short Stories

"The Aorta," trans. Trevor Le Gassick, in *Mundus Artium* X no. (1977), 83-86.
"The Carrier of Chairs" trans. Catherine Cobham, in *Contemporary Literature in Translation* 19 (Summer-Fall 1974), 13-15.
"The Chair Carrier" in *Arabic Short Stories* trans. Denys Johnson-Davies, London: Quartet Books, 1983, 1-5.
The Cheapest Nights trans. Wadida Wassef, Arab Authors Series 12. London: Heinemann, 1978.
["The Cheapest Nights," "You Are Everything to Me," "The Errand," "Hard Up," " The Queue," "The Funeral Ceremony," "All on a Summer's Day," "The Caller in the Night," "The Dregs of the City," "Did You Have to Turn on the Light, Li-li?" "Death from Old Age," "Bringing in the Bride," "The Shame," "Because the Day of Judgement Never Comes," "The Freak"]
"The Cheapest Night's Entertainment," "Peace with Honour" in *Arabic Writing Today: The Short Story* ed. Mahmoud Manzalaoui, Cairo: American Research Center in Egypt, 1968, 227-255.
"Delusion," "The Sheikh Sheikha," in *Flights of Fantasy* ed. Ceza Kassem & Malek Hashem, Cairo: Elias Modern Publishing House, 1985, 27-32 & 65-76.
"The Diploma," "To Asyut" in *Arab Stories East and West* trans. R.W. Ebied & M.J.L. Young, Leeds: Leeds Oriental Society, 1977, 46-54.
"Farahat's Republic" in *Modern Arabic Short Stories* trans. Denys Johnson-Davies, Arab Authors Series 3, London: Heinemann, 1974, 118.
"The Half-Revolutionaries," trans. Catherine Cobham, *Journal of Arabic Literature* XXII (1991), 38-46.
"House of Flesh" in *Egyptian Short Stories* trans. Denys Johnson-Davies, Arab Authors Series 8. London: Heinemann, 1978, 1-7.
"Innocence" trans. & analysis by Dalya Cohen, *Journal of Arabic Literature* XIX/l (1988), 68-78.
In the Eye of the Beholder ed. Roger Allen, Chicago & Minneapolis: Bibliotheca Islamica, 1978.
["A Stare," "The Wallet," "City Dregs," "Playing House," "The Omitted Letter,"

"The Aorta," "The Concave Mattress," "The Greatest Sin of All," "The Little Bird on the Telephone Wire," "The Chair Carrier," "The Chapter on the Cow," "Lily, Did you have to put the light on?" "In Cellophane Wrapping," "A House of Flesh"]

"The Journey" trans. Roger Allen, *Journal of Arabic Literature* III (1972), 127-131.

The Leader of Men trans. Saad Elkhadem, Fredericton, New Brunswick; York Press, 1988.

"The Point" trans. Dalya Cohen, *Journal of Arabic Literature* XXII (1991), 47-52.

Rings of Burnished Brass trans. Catherine Cobham, Arab Authors Series 21. London: Heinemann, 1984.

["The Stranger," "The Black Policeman," "The Siren," "Rings of Burnished Brass"]

"Snobbism," trans. Roger Allen & Adnan Haydar, *Journal of Arabic Literature* XVIII (1987), 88-101.

"Sunset March" trans. Roger Allen, *Nimrod* 24 no. 2 (Spring-Summer 1981), 39-42; reprinted: *Journal of Arabic Literature* XVI (1985), 91-94.

Novels
The Sinners [Al-Haram] trans. Kristin Peterson-Ishaq, Washington: Three Continents Press, 1984.

Plays
Flipflap and his Master [Al-Farafir] trans. Trevor Le Gassick, in *Arabic Writing Today: The Drama* ed. Mahmoud Manzalaoui, Cairo: American Research Center in Egypt, 1977, 335-453.

The Farfours trans. Farouk Abdel Wahab in *Modern Egyptian Drama* Minneapolis & Chicago: Bibliotheca Islamica, 1974, 351-493.

3. A Selection of Studies in English of Yusuf Idris's Works

Allen, Roger, "The Artistry of Yusuf Idris," *World Literature Today* Winter 1981: 43-7.

Beyerl, Jan, *The Style of the Modern Arabic Short Story*, Prague, 1971.

Brand, Hanita, "Al-Farafir by Yusuf Idris: The Medium is the Message," *Journal of Arabic Literature* Vol. XXI no . 1 (Mar. 1990), 57-71.

Cohen, Dalya, " 'The Journey' by Yusuf Idris: Psycho-analysis and interpretation," *Journal of Arabic Literature* XV (1984), 135-138.

Hafez, Sabry, "Yusuf Idris: The Man and His Work," *Azure* I (1977), 60-62.

Jad, 'Ali, *Form and technique in the Egyptian Novel 1912-1971*, London: Ithaca Press, 1983.

Kilpatrick, H., *The Modern Egyptian Novel*, London: Ithaca Press, 1974, 113-126.

Kurpershoek, P.M. *The Short Stories of Yusuf Idris*, Leiden: E.J. Brill, 1981.

Mikhail, Mona, "Broken Idols, the Death of Religion in Two Stories by Idris and Mahfuz," *Journal of Arabic Literature* V (1974), 147-157.

_____. "Egyptian Tales of the Fantastic: Theme and Technique in the Stories of Yusuf Idris," *Journal of the American Research Center in Egypt* Vol. XXVII (1990), 191-98.

Moussa-Mahmoud, Fatma, *The Arabic Novel in Egypt* (1914-1970), Cairo: General Egyptian Book Organisation, 1973, 43-46.

Somekh, S., "Language and Theme in the Short Stories of Yusuf Idris," *Journal of Arabic Literature* VI (1975), 89-100.

Contributors

FARUQ 'ABD AL-WAHHAB, a prominent Egyptian drama critic, now teaches Arabic language and literature at the University of Chicago.

ABU AL-MA'ATI ABU AL-NAJA, Egyptian novelist, short-story writer and critic, now lives and works in the Gulf area.

ROGER ALLEN teaches Arabic Language and Literature at the University of Pennsylvania in Philadelphia.

LEWIS 'AWAD (d. 1991) was one of the leading Egyptian literary critics of his generation and participated vigorously in the intellectual life of his country.

M.M. BADAWI has for many years been Fellow of St. Antony's College and Reader in Modern Arabic Literature at Oxford University.

CATHERINE COBHAM teaches Arabic language and literature at the University of St. Andrews in Scotland.

NADIA RA'UF FARAJ, Egyptian critic, has written a book on Yusuf Idris's plays.

SABRY HAFEZ, Egyptian literary critic, teaches Arabic literature at the School of Oriental and African Studies, University of London.

ALI JAD is Dean of the College of Arts at King Saud University in Riyad, Saudi Arabia.

HILARY KILPATRICK, a specialist on Arabic prose writing in both the classical and modern periods, has taught in both Holland and Switzerland.

P.M. KURPERSHOEK, the author of a work on Idris's short stories, is a member of the Dutch diplomatic service.

FEDWA MALTI-DOUGLAS teaches Arabic and comparative literature at Indiana University.

MONA MIKHAIL teaches Arabic language and literature at New York University.

'ABD AL-HAMID 'ABD AL-'AZIM AL-QITT, Egyptian literary critic, is the author of a book on Idris's narrative technique.

NUR SHERIF has taught English language and literature at both the University of Alexandria in Egypt and the Beirut Arab University in Lebanon.

GHALI SHUKRI, Egyptian critic, has written a large number of works on contemporary Arabic litterateurs and movements.

SASSON SOMEKH teaches Arabic literature at Tel Aviv University.

Biographical Note on Editor

Roger Allen is Professor of Arabic Language and Literature at the University of Pennsylvania in Philadelphia. He is the author of a number of studies on Arabic narrative, including *A Period of Time* (1974; 2nd ed., 1992) and *The Arabic Novel* (1982; 2nd ed., 1994). He has also published a large anthology of modern criticism, *Modern Arabic Literature* (1985), and is the translator of many works of contemporary Arabic fiction, including Najib Mahfuz's *Mirrors* (1977) and *Autumn Quail* (1985), Jabra Ibrahim Jabra's *The Ship* (1985, with Adnan Haydar), 'Abd al-rahman Munif's *Ending*, and collections of short stories of Najib Mahfuz of *Al-'Arabiyya* (Journal of the American Association of Teachers of Arabic), *World Literature Today* and the *Journal of Arabic Literature*.